Multilateral Development Finance 2020

OECD
BETTER POLICIES FOR BETTER LIVES

Please cite this publication as:
OECD (2020), *Multilateral Development Finance 2020*, OECD Publishing, Paris, *https://doi.org/10.1787/e61fdf00-en*.

ISBN 978-92-64-89765-6 (print)
ISBN 978-92-64-89026-8 (pdf)

Photo credits: Cover © file404/Shutterstock.com.

Corrigenda to publications may be found on line at: *www.oecd.org/about/publishing/corrigenda.htm*.

Foreword

Seventy-five years after its inception, the multilateral development system offers the image of a system under stress and is challenged as never before.

At the threshold of the "decade of action" (2020-2030), the multilateral development system has hardly ever been so solicited, with a highly ambitious global development agenda, and a simultaneous need to cope with the impact of global challenges – such as climate change and the COVID-19 pandemic – that could undo years of hard-won development progress.

At the same time, the multilateral development system has rarely been so criticised. In recent years mounting tensions in the global political landscape have led to a resurgence of nationalism and a new wave of criticism against the international rules-based order that constitutes the backbone of the multilateral development system.

Since its foundation in the aftermath of the Second World War, the mandate of the multilateral development system has continuously expanded to respond to new and emerging development challenges. While this attests to the continued relevance of multilateral organisations in the global development landscape, it has also led to a progressive fragmentation of the system, with the creation of myriad new multilateral channels over time, raising growing concerns of systemic inefficiency and lack of accountability. Indeed, the creation of new institutions has outpaced the suppression of potentially obsolete ones.

The COVID-19 pandemic has once again put the multilateral development system in the spotlight. The multilateral response has been unprecedented in scale and speed, far outpacing the responses of bilateral development partners. Yet, it has also revealed some limitations in the system, such as the lack of co-ordination among multilateral stakeholders.

The magnitude of the challenges lying ahead requires a multilateral system performing at its full potential: this year's edition of the Multilateral Development Finance Report makes the case that "building back better" also means improving the existing multilateral aid architecture. The renewed attention and expectations placed on the multilateral development system call for fresh insights into its collective coherence and value proposition, as well as into potential areas for improvement that could increase its development impact. For this reason, the report starts with an overview of the multilateral development system (Chapter 1), including its evolution to date, and presents some of the "building blocks" required to erect a multilateral system fit for the development challenges of the 21st century.

The OECD's Development Assistance Committee (DAC), whose members remain the largest shareholders and funders of the multilateral development system, holds a responsibility to steer the multilateral development system towards greater effectiveness and efficiency and to ensure that it is equipped to support the global development agenda. Chapter 2 of the report explores DAC members' funding to the multilateral development system and outlines the systemic implications of their individual funding decisions. It breaks down DAC members' portfolio strategies and discusses how these can affect the exposure of multilateral organisations to specific donors, and their vulnerability to political influence and the threat of funding cuts.

The challenging times ahead call for leveraging the comparative advantages of the multilateral development system and ensuring it maximises the resources made available by donors. Chapter 3 sheds light on the development activities financed by multilateral organisations and identifies areas where multilateral entities are expected to increase their contribution. It also analyses whether, and how, multilateral organisations build on their respective areas of strengths to add value to, and complement, other types of development co-operation.

The *Multilateral Development Finance 2020* report features a new format: it is leaner than previous reports, and is supplemented by (i) a new series of policy briefs on multilateral development finance; and (ii) online statistics on the multilateral contributions of official providers, available on the Development Co-operation Profiles 2020. The first policy brief, which deals with DAC members' earmarked contributions through the multilateral development system, is published as a companion paper to this report.

Acknowledgements

The Multilateral Development Finance Report 2020 was prepared by the Financing for Sustainable Development (FSD) division of the OECD Development Co-operation Directorate (DCD). It is part of the directorate's work on multilateral development co-operation. The report was prepared by a team comprised of Jieun Kim, Franziska Fischer, Edoardo Bollatti, Arnaud Pincet and Abdoulaye Fabregas, under the overall supervision of Olivier Cattaneo (Head of Unit, Policy analysis and strategy) and Haje Schütte (Head of Division, Financing for sustainable development).

This report has benefitted from the contributions of many colleagues and the authors would like to particularly thank the following DCD colleagues: Valentina Orrù (Global Partnerships and Policies division), who provided the results of the 2018 Global Partnership for Effective Development Co-operation (GPEDC) monitoring round; Emily Bosch (Reviews, Results, Evaluations and Development Innovation Division), who co-authored the accompanying policy brief on DAC members' earmarked funding; and Aimée Nichols, Alice Golenko and Marisa Berbegal (Financing for Sustainable Development division), who provided statistical advice on the OECD Creditor Reporting System.

Emily Bosch, John Egan, Anita King, Claudio Cerabino, Mags Gaynor, Ashley Palmer, Valentina Orrù, Mitch Levine, Suzanne Steensen, Jolanda Profos, Aimée Nichols, Marisa Berbegal, Cécile Sangaré and Matthew Bowie helped significantly to improve the paper and the authors are grateful for their peer review and substantive comments.

Akihiko Nishio (World Bank Group), Henriette Keijzers (United Nations Development Programme), Silke Weinlich (German Development Institute), Scott Morris (Center for Global Development), Miriam Philippe (BMZ), Monika Vadeboncoeur (Permanent Delegation of Canada to the OECD), Thomas Piesch (Permanent Delegation of Germany to the OECD), and Christoph Graf (Permanent Delegation of Switzerland to the OECD) are kindly acknowledged for their useful feedback. The authors would also like to thank Bernhard Reinsberg, from the University of Glasgow, and Vera Eichenauer, from the Swiss Federal Institute of Technology in Zurich (ETH Zurich), for sharing their multi-bi dataset.

Stacey Bradbury and Sara Casadevall Belles facilitated the editing and publication of this paper, and Henri-Bernard Solignac-Lecomte provided strategic communication advice.

The authors are grateful for the graphic support and advice received from Stephanie Coic and Cameron Bartlett on the visuals, as well as for the editorial support received from Fiona Hinchcliffe.

Editorial

The multilateral development system has been defined by key moments in history since its start in 1944, and the COVID-19 crisis marks a crossroads. The pandemic has brought into stark relief our interconnectedness and interdependence. It has also proven the need for greater solidarity and co-operation to solve challenges that are increasingly global in nature. Yet, in a context of growing needs and strained resources, the multilateral system is under mounting pressure to demonstrate impact.

Against the backdrop of a global crisis threatening health, food, social and economic security in every country, the multilateral system has been essential in addressing COVID-related shocks in the world's most vulnerable contexts, supported by its members. In the weeks following the declaration of the pandemic, multilateral organisations made available nearly USD 250 billion to developing countries. This helped address the direct impacts of the public health emergency through the delivery of emergency supplies, funding of medical staff and equipment, and providing training. In addition, multilateral organisations are also supporting governments and the private sector to address the indirect economic and social consequences.

However, the pandemic has also shone light on the limitations of the multilateral development system. The reforms put forward in this report aim to support investments in multilateral organisations that are fit for today and for the future, ensuring that they remain a space to advance and build consensus around collective priorities.

The members of the OECD Development Assistance Committee (DAC) – who remain the largest funders of the multilateral system – have a unique responsibility and opportunity to strengthen their strategic support to, and engagement with, multilateral organisations. The emergence of new multilateral stakeholders and funders creates both opportunities and risks for multilateral development finance. Private sector and non-governmental organisations rank as the sixth biggest contributor to the United Nations, and one single private philanthropic foundation is the second- largest funder of the World Health Organisation (WHO) after the United States. Overall, the share of non-DAC funding to the United Nations system increased from 22% to 29% between 2008 and 2017. While the diversification of multilateral organisations' funding has many positive aspects, DAC members also have a role in safeguarding the independence and flexibility required to deliver on their mandates.

The good news is that, in recent years, multilateral development finance from official providers has been increasing. Between 2000 and 2018, contributions to the multilateral development system more than doubled from USD 33 billion to USD 71.9 billion, and the share of official development assistance (ODA) channelled through the multilateral system continues to grow. However, multilateral impact and effectiveness go beyond finance flows, and organisations are forced to demonstrate concrete progress. This involves clarifying the unique value of each organisation, leveraging comparative advantages. It also requires learning the lessons from the multilateral response to the COVID-19 crisis.

Balancing these goals is a complex task, and one that will require careful decisions from stakeholders to ensure that multilateral development finance can contribute its best to the COVID-19 recovery. The years ahead are crucial. We need to prove how investing in multilateral development finance is worth every penny. Ultimately, our ability to support the multilateral development system will have a huge impact on our chances to achieve the 2030 Agenda, preserving the health of our planet and people.

Jorge Moreira da Silva,

Director,

Development Co-operation Directorate

Table of contents

FIGURES

TABLES

Abbreviations and acronyms

AAAA	Addis Ababa Action Agenda
ADB	Asian Development Bank
ADF	African Development Fund
AfDB	African Development Bank
AF	Adaptation Fund
AIIB	Asian Infrastructure Investment Bank
AsDF	Asian Development Fund
BADEA	Arab Bank for Economic Development in Africa
BDEAC	Development Bank of the Central African States
BOAD	West African Development Bank
BRICS	Brazil, Russia, India, China and South Africa
CAF	Development Bank of Latin America (Corporación Andina de Fomento)
CARICOM	Caribbean Community
CCD	United Nations Convention to Combat Desertification
CDB	Caribbean Development Bank
CEB	Council of Europe Development Bank
CERF	Central Emergency Response Fund
CIF	Climate Investment Funds
CIV	Collective investment vehicle
CRS	Creditor Reporting System
CSO	Civil society organisation
DAC	Development Assistance Committee (OECD)
DCD	Development Co-operation Directorate (OECD)
DRM	Domestic resource mobilisation
EBRD	European Bank for Reconstruction and Development
ECA	United Nations Economic Commission for Africa
ECLAC	United Nations Economic Commission for Latin America and the Caribbean

EIB	European Investment Bank
EU	European Union
FAO	Food and Agriculture Organization
FDI	Foreign direct investment
FIF	Financial intermediary fund
FSD	Financing for sustainable development
GAVI	Vaccine Alliance (Global Alliance for Vaccines and Immunisation)
GCF	Green Climate Fund
GDP	Gross domestic product
GEF	Global Environment Facility
GFATM	Global Fund to fight AIDS, Tuberculosis and Malaria
GGGI	Global Green Growth Institute
GNI	Gross national income
GPEDC	Global Partnership for Effective Development Co-operation
GPG	Global public good
HIC	High-income country
HIPC	Heavily indebted poor country
IADB	Inter-American Development Bank
IBRD	International Bank for Reconstruction and Development
ICSID	International Centre for the Settlement of Investment-related Disputes
IDA	International Development Association
IFAD	International Fund for Agricultural Development
IFC	International Finance Corporation
IFFIm	International Finance Facility for Immunisation
IFI	International finance institution
ILO	International Labour Organisation
IMF	International Monetary Fund
IOM	International Organization for Migration
IsDB	Islamic Development Bank
ITU	International Telecommunication Union
LDC	Least developed country
LIC	Low-income country
LLDC	Landlocked developing country
LMIC	Lower middle-income country
MDB	Multilateral development bank

MIGA	Multilateral Investment Guarantee Agency
MOPAN	Multilateral Organisation Performance Assessment Network
NDB	New Development Bank
NDF	Nordic Development Fund
NGO	Non-government organisation
ODA	Official development assistance
ODF	Official development finance
OECD	Organisation for Economic Co-operation and Development
OECS	Organisation of Eastern Caribbean States
OHCHR	Office of the United Nations Commissioner for Human Rights
OOF	Other official flows
PAHO	Pan American Health Organization
PBF	United Nations Peacebuilding Fund
PPP	Public-private partnership
RDB	Regional development bank
SDG	Sustainable Development Goal
SIDS	Small island developing state
SPC	Pacific Community
SPREP	Secretariat of the Pacific Regional Environment Programme
TOSSD	Total official support for sustainable development
UMIC	Upper middle-income country
UN	United Nations
UNAIDS	Joint United Nations Programme on HIV/AIDS
UNCDF	United Nations Capital Development Fund
UNCTAD	United Nations Conference on Trade and Development
UNDCO	United Nations Development Coordination Office
UNDESA	United Nations Department of Economic and Social Affairs
UNDP	United Nations Development Programme
UNECE	United Nations Economic Commission for Europe
UNEP	United Nations Environment Programme
UNESCAP	United Nations Economic and Social Commission for Asia and the Pacific
UNESCO	United Nations Educational, Scientific and Cultural Organisation
UNFCCC	United Nations Framework Convention on Climate Change
UNFPA	United Nations Population Fund
UNHCR	United Nations Refugee Agency

UNICEF	United Nations Children's Fund
UNIDO	United Nations Industrial Development Organization
UNISDR	United Nations Office for Disaster Risk Reduction
UNOCHA	United Nations Office for the Coordination of Humanitarian Affairs
UNODC	United Nations Office on Drugs and Crime
UNRISD	United Nations Research Institute for Social Development
UNRWA	United Nations Relief and Works Agency for Palestine Refugees in the Near East
UNSDG	United Nations Sustainable Development Group
UNSSC	United Nations System Staff College
UNU	United Nations University
UNWTO	United Nations World Tourism Organisation
USD	United States Dollar
VFVT	United Nations Voluntary Fund for Victims of Torture
WBG	World Bank Group
WEF	World Economic Forum
WFP	World Food Programme
WHO	World Health Organisation
WIPO	World Intellectual Property Organization

Executive summary

Five years on from the launch of the 2030 Agenda, the multilateral development system is under stress, perhaps as never before. The COVID-19 crisis has brought renewed attention to the crucial role multilateral organisations have to play in addressing the triple crisis looming in developing countries: health, economic and humanitarian. The global scale of the virus has highlighted the interdependence of nations and people around the world, demonstrating that the need for international co-operation and solidarity is greater than ever. Yet, the crisis has also exposed some limitations of the multilateral development system that need to be tackled to ensure multilateral organisations can best contribute to the recovery.

This report provides an overview of the multilateral system against the backdrop of the COVID-19 crisis. It presents the key trends in recent funding to the system and explores how multilateral organisations' funding bases can affect their independence and the sustainability of their programmes. It also sheds light on the development activities financed by multilateral organisations in recent years, asks how they add value relative to other sources of development finance and assesses the effectiveness of their funding.

Are we moving towards "à la carte" multilateralism?

In 2018, total funding to multilateral organisations reached a new all-time high, at USD 71.9 billion, up by 3% in real terms compared to 2017. However, this growth, which is primarily driven by a rise in earmarked contributions, spurs concerns over the declining quality of multilateral funding.

The analysis in the report suggests that the system is evolving towards "à la carte" multilateralism: the declining share of core contributions reflects the growing tendency of donors to forsake consensus-based approaches in favour of ad hoc initiatives funded by a limited number of donors. As highlighted by recent research, this "à la carte" approach to multilateralism could ultimately see decision making and accountability transferred from the governing boards of multilateral organisations to a few large donors that can influence the priorities of multilateral organisations through their earmarked contributions.

Development Assistance Committee (DAC) members remain the major shareholders and funders of the multilateral development system, and therefore have a responsibility to steer the system towards collective priorities and greater effectiveness. The report calls on DAC members to make strategic and effective use of their multilateral contributions to ensure that the multilateral development system receives funding in sufficient quantity and quality to fully contribute to the 2030 Agenda and the COVID-19 recovery.

The report also reveals that some entities within the multilateral development system have a high degree of funding vulnerability. DAC members are thus called on to ensure their financial contributions build in sufficient predictability and flexibility. This would ensure the sustainability of programmes, and allow organisations to maintain impartiality and flexibility in delivering the priorities set by their governing boards.

Multilateral organisations fill a unique niche in the "decade of action"

The multilateral system has remained a stable source of development finance over time: despite a slight drop in 2018, multilateral outflows have increased steadily since 2011. Middle-income countries are among the biggest beneficiaries of recent increases in multilateral outflows.

Development effectiveness remains at the core of the multilateral value proposition. The 2018 monitoring round of the Global Partnership for Effective Development Co-operation indicated that the multilateral system performed more strongly than bilateral providers in most areas of effective development co-operation, including alignment with partner countries' strategic priorities. On the other hand, multilateral organisations' results for funding predictability were more mixed than those of bilateral partners.

Multilateral organisations' financing patterns confirm their added value vis-à-vis bilateral development partners. For example, the analysis shows that the multilateral development system retains economies of scale advantages over bilateral aid. Multilateral organisations also exhibit a stronger degree of specialisation than bilateral development partners, make greater use of government channels and devote a greater share of resources to fragile contexts. Surprisingly, multilateral organisations devote a smaller share of their funds to multisector or cross-country activities than bilateral providers, reflecting a dichotomy between their global goals and their country-based engagement models.

Three key reform areas could help the multilateral development system stay effective

In the past, global crises have often spurred innovation in the multilateral development landscape. In the spirit of "building back better", multilateral stakeholders can use the current crisis as an opportunity to build a more effective and coherent system – one that is better equipped to address the global development challenges of the 21st century.

This report highlights three key reform areas with the potential to maximise the impact of multilateral development finance:

- The scale of multilateral finance: ensuring that the multilateral system can help address development challenges of a new magnitude (e.g. extreme climate events or pandemics).
- Efficiency: ensuring value for money in a context of constrained resources.
- Accountability: restoring trust in the multilateral development system.

Six building blocks will help achieve progress in these areas: a) greater transparency over financing and results; b) increased systemic coherence; c) improved co-ordination, both among donors and multilateral organisations; d) increased financial capacity of multilateral organisations; e) better selectivity of multilateral operations, and f) increased capacity of multilateral organisations to adapt to evolving circumstances.

These building blocks, which span all stages of the multilateral development finance process and apply to all stakeholders, outline a possible research and policy analysis agenda for the OECD DAC to contribute to the reform of the multilateral development system.

Overview

Panorama of the multilateral development system

The multilateral development system has evolved into a complex environment since its inception in the aftermath of World War II (Figure 1**).** The continued expansion of the multilateral system in terms of scope, mandate and financing volume attests to its sustained relevance from its creation in the 1940s until today. It also demonstrates the widespread recognition of multilateral organisations as effective channels of development finance.

On the other hand, the continued proliferation of new multilateral entities and channels has turned the multilateral system into an increasingly crowded and fragmented space. In a global geopolitical context marked by the resurgence of nationalism and rising international tensions, multilateral organisations have become the target of recurrent criticism regarding their alleged lack of transparency, accountability and effectiveness. Part of this distrust may stem from a growing sense of complexity and opacity conveyed by the multilateral system, often perceived as an incoherent assemblage of entities with competing, and sometimes overlapping, mandates.

Figure 1. Multilateral development finance has grown into a complex ecosystem

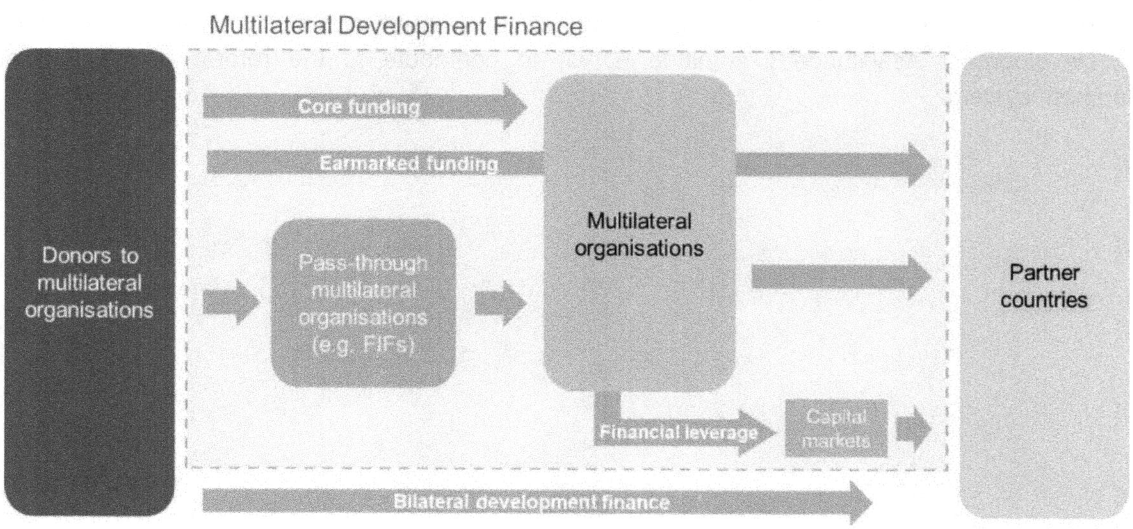

Note: FIFs: financial intermediary funds
Source: Authors' design adapted from (Eichenauer and Reinsberg, 2017[1]), "What determines earmarked funding to international development organizations? Evidence from the new multi-bi aid data", https://doi.org/10.1007/s11558-017-9267-2

The 2030 Agenda revitalised the demand for multilateral approaches to support global development goals. The recognition of the integrated and interlinked nature of the Sustainable Development Goals (SDGs) helped to put multilateral approaches on centre stage: multilateral actors were given a pivotal role and an expanded mandate with the adoption of the Addis Ababa Action Agenda (AAAA), as development stakeholders acknowledged the need to leverage the strengths of the multilateral system to support the SDGs (Gulrajani, 2016[2]; Rudolph, 2017[3]).

The COVID-19 crisis has once again swung the spotlight onto the multilateral development system by revealing the high degree of interdependence among countries. There is broad consensus that the multilateral development system has a crucial role to play in addressing the triple crisis looming in developing countries (health, economic and humanitarian). Multilateral organisations have contributed to the immediate response to the crisis with unprecedented scale and speed. Yet, the crisis has also exposed some limitations in the multilateral development system, underlining that multilateral organisations must keep adapting to the magnitude of new global challenges.

In the current context, inertia is the biggest threat to the multilateral development system. In the past, global crises have often led to multilateral innovation or the implementation of long-deferred reforms. In the spirit of "building back better", multilateral stakeholders could turn the COVID-19 crisis into an opportunity to build a more effective multilateral development system – one that is better equipped to address the global development challenges of the 21st century.

Building on recent research, this report highlights three key reform areas to maximise the impact of multilateral development finance: (i) the scale of multilateral finance, to ensure that the multilateral system can help address development challenges of a new magnitude (e.g. extreme climate events or pandemics); (ii) efficiency, to demonstrate value for money in a context of constrained resources; and (iii) accountability, to restore trust in the system.

The report also identifies six building blocks required to achieve progress in these areas: (i) greater transparency on financing and results; (ii) increased systemic coherence; (iii) improved co-ordination, both among donors and multilateral organisations; (iv) increased financial capacity for multilateral organisations; (v) better selectivity of multilateral operations; and (vi) increased capacity of multilateral organisations to adapt to evolving circumstances. These building blocks, summarised in Figure 2, apply to all stakeholders and span all stages of the multilateral development finance process: from donors' funding to the multilateral system, covered in Chapter 2 of the report, to the development activities financed by multilateral organisations (Chapter 3). Together they outline a possible research and policy analysis agenda for the OECD Development Assistance Committee (DAC) to contribute to the reform of the multilateral development system.

Figure 2. Key reform areas and building blocks to adapt multilateral development finance to 21st century challenges

Key reform areas

Scale of impact	Efficiency	Accountability

Building blocks

Transparency	Systemic coherence	Co-ordination	Financial capacity	Selectivity	Capacity of adaptation
- Identify key blind spots in multilateral development finance - Improve the availability of comprehensive and comparable data on multilateral inflows and outflows - Enhance multilateral organisations' communication on results and impact	- Clarify the division of labour among multilateral entities - Identify and leverage potential synergies among multilateral organisations - Sunset or merge multilateral entities with overlapping or obsolete mandates	- Improve co-ordination among donors based on a common set of evidence - Promote increased co-ordination and collaboration among multilateral organisations	- Ensure that multilateral organisations are adequately capitalised and funded (quantitatively and qualitatively) to address new global challenges - Increase the financial leverage of multilateral organisations and their capacity to mobilise private finance	- Improve the prioritisation of multilateral activities to optimise the use of scarce resources	- Ensure that the constitution and funding of multilateral organisations provides them with sufficient flexibility to adapt to the rapidly evolving global environment

Source: Authors' design.

Funding to the multilateral development system (inflows)

Despite growing tensions in the multilateral space, financial contributions to the multilateral development system continue to grow. In 2018, total funding to the multilateral organisations reached a new all-time high, at USD 71.9 billion (representing 38% of gross official development assistance or ODA). This represents a 3% increase in real terms over 2017 and a 32.4% increase over the period 2011-2018 (Figure 3). However, this growth is primarily driven by a rise in earmarked contributions, prompting concerns over the progressive "bilateralisation" and declining quality of multilateral funding. Between 2011 and 2018, for example, the share of earmarked funding in DAC members' total ODA rose from 11% to 15%, while the share of direct bilateral funding fell from 62% to 58%.

Figure 3. Multilateral contributions are growing while the share of bilateral aid is declining

DAC bilateral and multilateral ODA flows (USD million) | DAC bilateral flows, multilateral core contributions and earmarked contributions (share of total ODA)

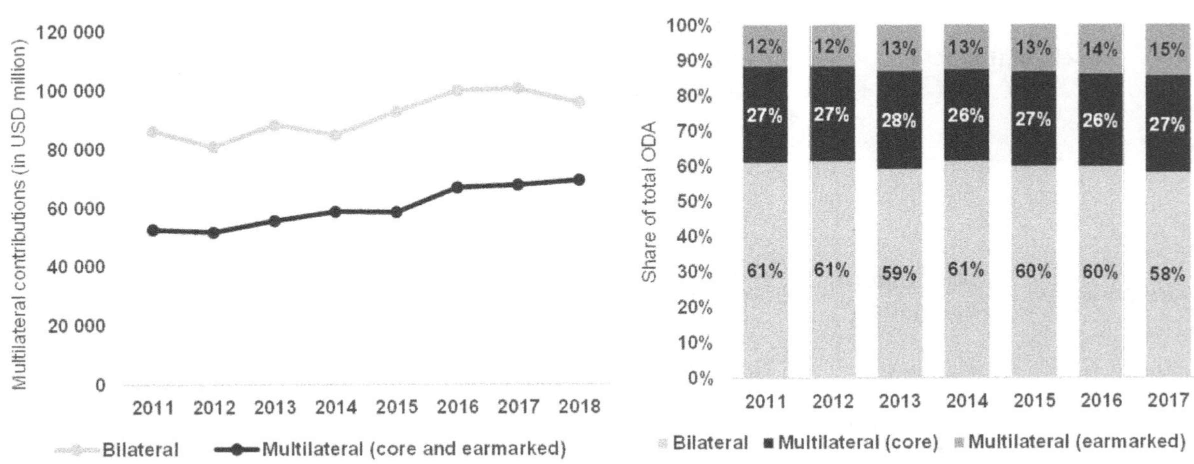

Note: Disbursements, 2018 prices. Core contributions are funds added to multilateral organisations' general budgets, while earmarked contributions are tied to projects for specific regions, countries, themes or sectors.
Source: Authors' calculations based on (OECD, 2020[4]), "Creditor Report System", https://stats.oecd.org/Index.aspx?DataSetCode=crs1.

StatLink https://doi.org/10.1787/888934177100

Legacy multilateral organisations, such as the United Nations (UN) and the World Bank Group, face increased competition for resources. The UN and the World Bank Group remain the two pillars of the multilateral development system: together they account for more than three-quarters of the funding provided to multilateral organisations. However, the emergence of new multilateral development banks and the growth of vertical funds are slowly reconfiguring the multilateral finance landscape, as evidenced by the large number of replenishments observed in 2019 (Kharas, 2019[5]).

Non-DAC actors account for a growing share of the contributions to the multilateral development system. Although DAC countries remain the majority shareholders and funders of the multilateral development system, other official providers and non-state actors play an increasingly important role. The share of total multilateral contributions from non-DAC members to the UN system increased from 22% in 2008 to 29% in 2017. This trend, which reflects shifts in the global economy, is particularly visible in some sectors, such as health, where philanthropic foundations and other private actors represent a sizeable source of multilateral funding.

The DAC has an important stake and responsibility in the multilateral development system. DAC members still retain a central role in multilateral development finance and need to make strategic and effective use of their multilateral contributions. For this reason, the report analyses the strategic implications that DAC members' funding volume and quality can have for the overall performance and governance of the multilateral development system.

The analysis suggests that the system is evolving towards multilateralism "à la carte". The declining ratio of core contributions provided to the multilateral development system shows that multilateral donors are progressively abandoning consensus-based approaches, while increasingly opting for ad-hoc funding decisions to address specific development challenges (Figure 4). This trend reflects, in large part, the increasingly diverging views and lack of collective vision among the main shareholders of the multilateral development system. Ultimately, there is a risk that this trend will result in a transfer of decision making and accountability from the governing boards of multilateral organisations to a narrower set of multilateral donors that can influence the priorities of multilateral organisations through their earmarked funding

(Barder, Ritchie and Rogerson, 2019[6]). A strategic rethink of DAC members' use of, and support to, the multilateral development system is thus necessary.

Figure 4. The rise of earmarked funding reflects a shift towards "à la carte" approaches

Evolution of the funding received by the multilateral development system as a share of core funding (vertical axis) and changes in multilateral contributions since 2000 (horizontal axis)

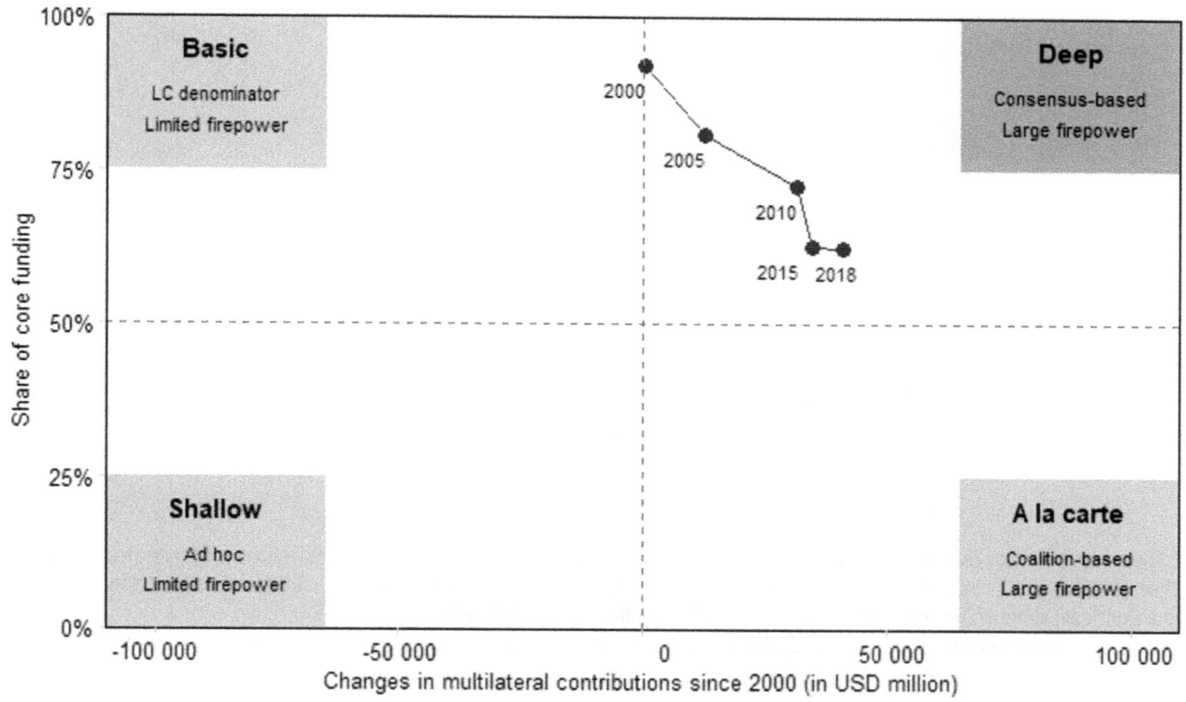

Note: Disbursements, 2018 prices. The changes in the volume of multilateral contributions (horizontal axis) are calculated as a five-year moving average.

Source: Authors' calculations based on 2000-2010 data from (Eichenauer and Reinsberg, 2017[1]), "What determines earmarked funding to international development organizations? Evidence from the new multi-bi aid data", https://www.ipz.uzh.ch/de/forschung/lehrstuehle/ep/research/internationaldevelopment/multi-bi-aid/data.html and 2011-2018 data from (OECD, 2020[4]) "Creditor Reporting System", https://stats.oecd.org/Index.aspx?DataSetCode=crs1.

StatLink https://doi.org/10.1787/888934177119

The analysis also reveals that some multilateral development organisations face a high degree of funding vulnerability. This is especially true of many UN agencies devoted to humanitarian aid, due to their relatively concentrated donor bases and a high share of earmarked funding (Figure 5). The recent announcement by the United States of its withdrawal from the World Health Organisation (WHO), following charges of the organisation's close ties with China, illustrates how a high degree of reliance on a few large donors and low funding quality can affect the independence of multilateral organisations and the sustainability of their programmes. These findings call for increased attention from DAC countries to ensure financial contributions are built around collective priorities and incorporate sufficient flexibility. This would ensure the sustainability of programmes, and allow organisations to maintain impartiality in delivering these priorities.

Figure 5. Several UN entities present high funding vulnerability

Concentration of multilateral organisations' donor base - scale from 0 (less concentrated) to 100 (most concentrated) and 2016-2018 share of earmarked funding

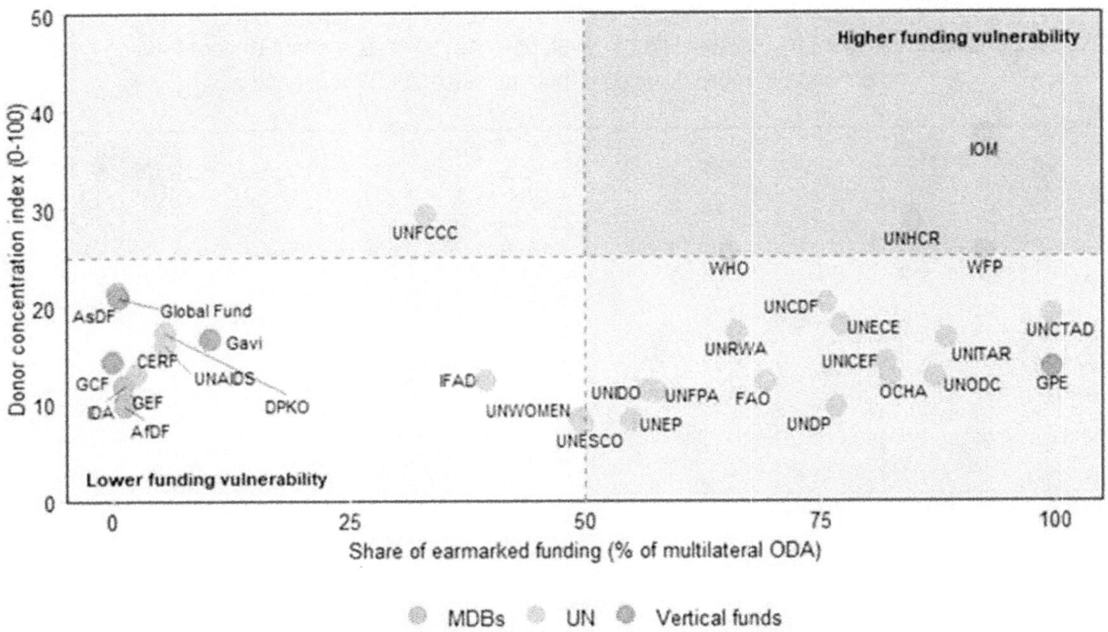

Note: The analysis focuses on multilateral organisations that are largely reliant on donors' multilateral contributions to finance their core functions and their operational activities. For this reason, the analysis excludes the non-concessional arms of multilateral development banks, which derive a significant share of their financing from other sources (e.g. from the capital markets).

Source: Authors' calculations based on (OECD, 2020[4]), "Creditor Reporting System", https://stats.oecd.org/Index.aspx?DataSetCode=crs1.

StatLink https://doi.org/10.1787/888934177138

Financing from the multilateral development system (outflows)

The multilateral system has remained a stable source of development finance over time: despite a slight drop in 2018, multilateral outflows have increased steadily since 2011, mainly driven by non-concessional lending from multilateral development banks (Figure 6). Multilateral outflows exceed inflows from contributions by DAC and non-DAC members reporting to the system because some organisations, notably multilateral development banks, have access to financing from capital markets.

Figure 6. Multilateral outflows have been steadily increasing since 2011

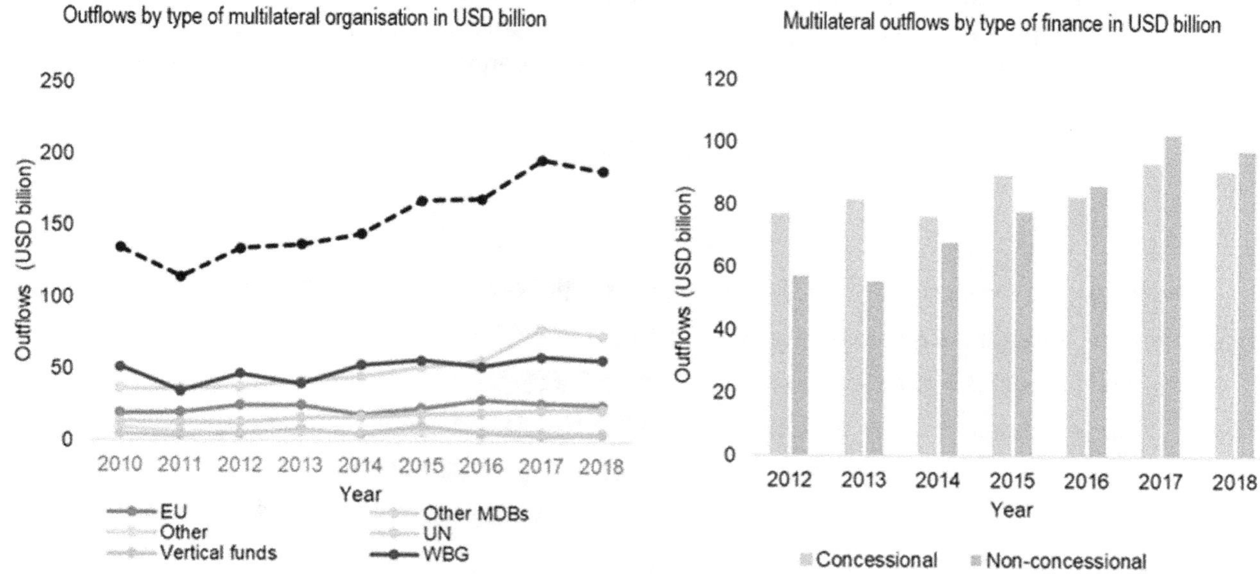

Note: Commitments in USD billion, 2018 prices.
Source: Authors' calculations based on (OECD, 2020[4]), "Creditor Reporting System", https://stats.oecd.org/Index.aspx?DataSetCode=crs1

StatLink https://doi.org/10.1787/888934177157

Infrastructure and production are still the primary beneficiaries of multilateral outflows. Infrastructure remains the largest recipient sector of multilateral outflows (accounting for 27% of total outflows in 2018). This is followed by the productive sectors (25%), which have seen a steep increase in recent years, in particular in the areas of banking and financial services, agriculture and industry. While humanitarian aid still receives a relatively small portion of total multilateral outflows, volumes have rapidly increased since 2012 as a consequence of the Syrian civil war and the refugee crises.

Middle-income countries are among the biggest beneficiaries of recent increases in multilateral outflows. The growth in non-concessional flows reflects an increased focus of multilateral finance on middle-income countries, especially upper middle-income ones (UMICs). On the other hand, multilateral finance appears less focused than in the past on least developed countries (LDCs) and other low-income countries (LICs), although the reclassification of many recipient countries in recent years largely explains this shift.

DAC members expect the multilateral development system to add value across a variety of development areas. The recent OECD survey on DAC members' policies and practices vis-à-vis the multilateral development system (OECD, 2020[7]) reveals that DAC members harbour particularly high expectations for the future role of legacy multilateral development banks (such as the World Bank, African Development Bank, Asian Development Bank, Islamic Development Bank and European Bank for Reconstruction and Development) to tackle global public "bads" and socio-economic challenges. They expect new MDBs, such as the Asian Infrastructure Investment Bank and the New Development Bank, to help close the gap in infrastructure investment, and anticipate a larger role for the UN in supporting peace and security, and delivering humanitarian aid.

Development effectiveness remains at the core of the multilateral value proposition. Improvements in multilateral effectiveness are also indispensable to increase the scale, efficiency and accountability of multilateral development finance. The 2018 monitoring round of the Global Partnership for Effective Development Co-operation (OECD/UNDP, 2019[8]) indicated a stronger performance of the multilateral system compared to bilateral providers in most areas of effective development co-operation, including alignment with partner countries' strategic priorities, and making forward expenditure and implementation plans available to partner countries (Figure 7). On the other hand, multilateral organisations' results for funding predictability were more mixed than those for bilateral partners.

Figure 7. Multilateral partners out-perform bilateral partners on most effectiveness indicators

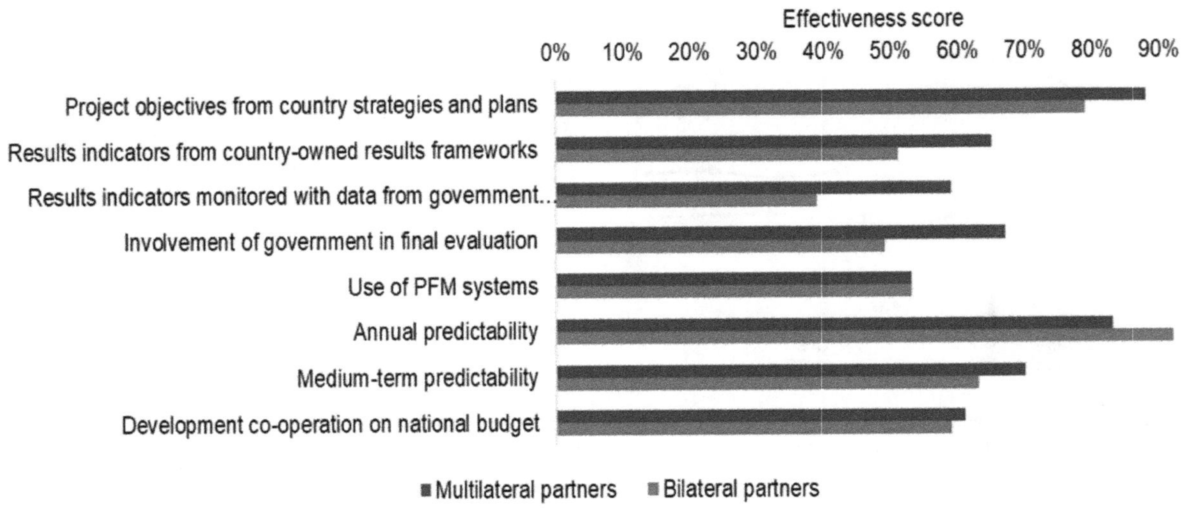

Note: PFM: public financial management. Detailed information on the calculation of effectiveness scores can be found at https://www.effectivecooperation.org/system/files/2020-09/Technical%20Companion%20-%20Final%20online.pdf.
Source: Analysis from Global Partnership for Effective Development Co-operation (GPEDC) based on raw data collated in (GPEDC, 2018[9]), 2018 Global Partnership Monitoring Round, https://www.effectivecooperation.org/content/gpedc-monitoring-excel-database.

StatLink https://doi.org/10.1787/888934177176

Finally, the financing patterns of multilateral organisations confirm their greater added value and complementarity compared to other development partners in several areas (Figure 8**).** For example, the analysis shows that the fragmentation of the multilateral development system has not eroded its scale advantages over bilateral aid. Multilateral organisations also exhibit a stronger degree of specialisation than bilateral development partners. The analysis also confirms that multilateral development finance makes greater use of government channels and that multilateral organisations devote a greater share of resources to fragile contexts than bilateral partners. Surprisingly, multilateral organisations devote a smaller share of their funds to multisector or cross-country activities than bilateral providers, reflecting a dichotomy between their global goals and their country-based engagement models.

Figure 8. Multilateral entities offer diverse and complementary comparative advantages

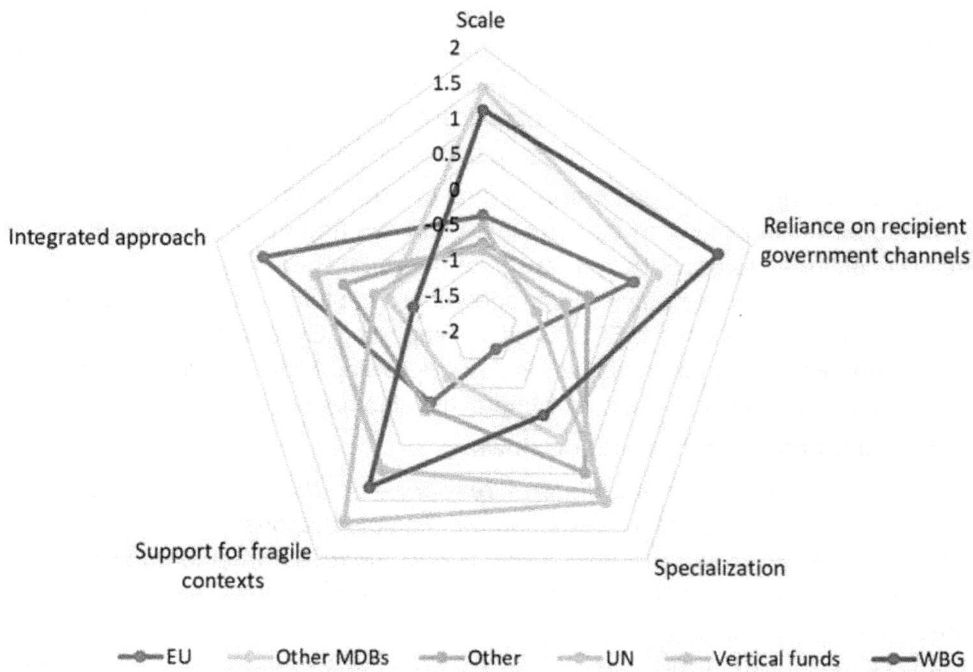

Note: The scores for the different indicators are calculated based on the average size of country portfolios and the share of specific types of projects in the overall outflows of multilateral organisations.
EU: European Union; MDBs: Multilateral development banks; UN: United Nations; WBG: World Bank Group; Other: all other multilateral organisations.
Source: Authors' calculations based on (OECD, 2020[4]), "Creditor Reporting System", https://stats.oecd.org/Index.aspx?DataSetCode=crs1.

StatLink https://doi.org/10.1787/888934177195

Main conclusions and policy recommendations

In line with the key reform areas and building blocks outlined in the first section, the following recommendations are made concerning multilateral inflows and outflows:

1. **Recommendations on multilateral inflows:**
   - ***Use the momentum generated by the COVID-19 crisis to increase DAC members' multilateral funding levels***, in particular their total support to the multilateral development system. The current international context calls for an unprecedented financial effort, and display of global solidarity, from the main shareholders and funders of the multilateral development system. While the economic and financial consequences of the crisis may make it hard for DAC members to safeguard their multilateral aid budgets, now is also the moment where their multilateral contributions are most needed and can have the most transformative impact.
   - ***Assess multilateral funding decisions based on multilateral effectiveness and good practice.*** Given the important implications of funding quality on the performance and governance of the multilateral development system, DAC members should carefully consider the trade-offs and alternatives to the different funding modalities at their disposal, and use a mix of core and earmarked funding in accordance with commitments made as part of the international reform agenda and good practice principles. The policy brief on DAC members' earmarked funding that accompanies this report provides initial pointers to determine the most

appropriate funding modalities according to the specific development objectives that are pursued.

- ***Ensure that DAC members' financial contributions provide multilateral organisations with sufficient independence and flexibility to carry out their activities.*** This calls for increased attention from the DAC to the volume and quality of funding provided to multilateral organisations, as well as the degree of concentration of their funding base, to ensure that they are not vulnerable to excessive influence by specific members.
- ***Improve the data collection on multilateral contributions from non-DAC members.*** As the multilateral funding provided by non-DAC countries and other stakeholders (such as private actors) continues to grow, both in absolute and relative terms, it is increasingly important to ensure that these contributions are adequately captured in existing ODA data collection mechanisms, such as the OECD Creditor Reporting System and the forthcoming TOSSD[1] framework. Failure to do so would result in a growing blind spot in multilateral stakeholders' vision and understanding of the multilateral development system.

2. **Recommendations on multilateral outflows:**
   - ***Draw lessons from the multilateral response to the COVID-19 crisis.*** Assessing the effectiveness of multilateral organisations' immediate response to the COVID-19 crisis should be a priority for multilateral stakeholders. This would reveal whether multilateral organisations are equipped to confront challenges of this type of magnitude, and could also help identify specific areas for improvement.
   - ***Develop statistical methodologies and tools to shed light on the financial leverage and mobilisation capacity of multilateral organisations.*** Evidence for this aspect of multilateral development finance is difficult to come by due to the lack of detailed data and information in the public domain. A better understanding of the financial leverage and mobilisation capacity of the multilateral development system could help identify specific measures to increase the scale of its impact. A first step for the OECD DAC could be to conduct an initial mapping and quantification of data gaps in multilateral development finance, which would help to prioritise and plan the improvements required in data collection.
   - ***Develop an analytical framework to assess and enhance the selectivity of multilateral organisations' operations.*** In a context of constrained resources, as is likely to emerge in the aftermath of the COVID-19 pandemic, better prioritisation of multilateral activities will be key to ensure the best possible use of the scarce resources available (e.g. by making sure that multilateral development finance targets the most in need). Work to assess and improve the selectivity of multilateral development finance should rely on a careful analysis of its complementarity with bilateral ODA and other sources of development finance.
   - ***Review the role, focus and contribution of multilateral organisations to specific development challenges deemed a priority for the "decade of action".*** An assessment of the contributions of multilateral organisations to some of these key development challenges could help to ensure an adequate focus, prioritisation and alignment of their operations with the expectations of multilateral stakeholders. Specific topics to explore could include multilateral organisations' contribution to: (i) the immediate response to the COVID-19 pandemic, (ii) the fight against climate change; and (iii) a green, resilient and inclusive COVID-19 recovery.

References

Barder, O., E. Ritchie and A. Rogerson (2019), *"Contractors or Collectives?" Earmarked funding of multilaterals, donor needs and institutional integrity: the World Bank as a case study*, Center for Global Development, pp. 1-37, https://www.cgdev.org/sites/default/files/contractors-or-collectives-earmarked-funding-multilaterals-donor-needs-and_0.pdf. [6]

Eichenauer, V. and B. Reinsberg (2017), "What determines earmarked funding to international development organizations? Evidence from the new multi-bi aid data", *The Review of International Organizations*, Vol. 12/2, pp. 171-197, http://dx.doi.org/10.1007/s11558-017-9267-2. [1]

GPEDC (2018), *2018 Global Partnership Monitoring Round*, https://www.effectivecooperation.org/content/gpedc-monitoring-excel-database. [9]

Gulrajani, N. (2016), *Bilateral versus multilateral channels: Strategic choices for donors*, Overseas Development Institute, London, https://www.odi.org/sites/odi.org.uk/files/resource-documents/10393.pdf. [2]

Kharas, H. (2019), *International financing of the Sustainable Development Goals*, Dag Hammarskjöld Foundation, https://www.daghammarskjold.se/wp-content/uploads/2019/08/financial-instr-report-2019-interactive.pdf#page=71. [5]

OECD (2020), *Creditor Reporting System (database)*, OECD, Paris, https://stats.oecd.org/Index.aspx?DataSetCode=crs1. [4]

OECD (2020), *Survey on DAC providers' policies and practices vis-a-vis the multilateral development system*, Unpublished. OECD, Paris. [7]

OECD/UNDP (2019), *Making Development Co-operation More Effective: 2019 Progress Report*, OECD Publishing, Paris, https://dx.doi.org/10.1787/26f2638f-en. [8]

Rudolph, A. (2017), *The Concept of SDG-Sensitive Development Co-operation: Implications for OECD-DAC Members*, German Development Institute, https://www.die-gdi.de/uploads/media/DP_1.2017.pdf. [3]

Notes

[1] TOSSD (total official support for sustainable development) is a new international statistical framework for monitoring official resources and private finance mobilised by official interventions for sustainable development. TOSSD is being developed by an international task force of experts; the OECD serves as the Secretariat to the Task Force.

1 Panorama of the multilateral development system

This chapter provides an overview of the multilateral development system: it presents the scope and purpose of multilateral development finance and describes its value proposition. The chapter also provides a historical perspective by retracing the evolution of the multilateral development system, starting with its inception in the aftermath of World War II, and describing the mix of development needs and geopolitical interests that have led to the creation of the complex multilateral finance system we see today. After analysing the implications of the 2030 Agenda and the COVID-19 pandemic for multilateral development finance, the chapter presents three key reform areas, and six related building blocks, with the potential to make multilateral development finance fit to address today's global development challenges.

1.1. The multilateral development finance system at a glance

1.1.1. Structure and scope

The multilateral development system encompasses all multilateral organisations conducting work of a development-related nature. This report defines the multilateral development system as the totality of multilateral organisations that are mandated by their members and shareholders to promote international development. The analysis in this report covers over 200 multilateral agencies and institutions, including entities from the United Nations Development System (UNDS), the World Bank Group (WBG), regional development banks, vertical funds, as well as other multilateral organisations included in the OECD Development Assistance Committee (DAC)'s list of official development assistance (ODA)-eligible international organisations that report to the OECD Creditor Reporting System (CRS).[1] The main organisations are shown in Figure 1.1.

Figure 1.1. Overview of the main organisations forming the multilateral development system

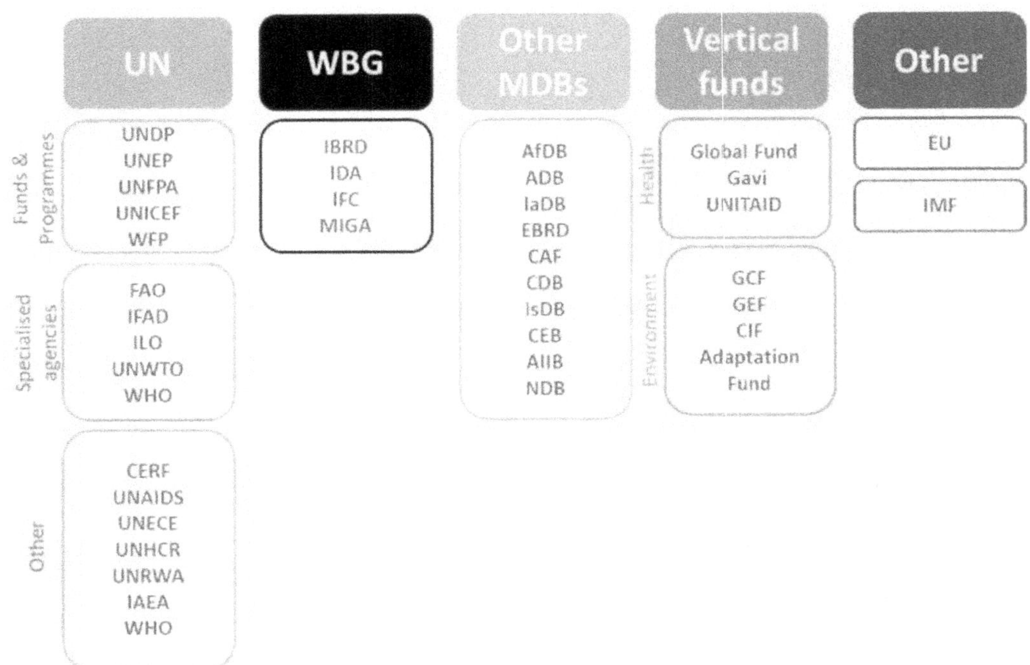

Source: Authors' design based on (OECD, 2020[1]), "OECD DAC Annex 2 - List of ODA-eligible international organisations", available at https://www.oecd.org/dac/financing-sustainable-development/development-finance-standards/annex2.htm.

Analysing multilateral development finance as a system can help assess whether multilateral efforts to finance development co-operation are effective. It helps to identify the specific areas where the system works well (for example through well-arranged co-ordination and division of labour among organisations), but can also help spot potential inefficiencies in the form of redundancies, inconsistencies and incoherence in the multilateral finance architecture.

As pointed out in previous editions, the term "system" can be somewhat misleading by suggesting the existence of a "perfectly cohesive and coherent system, which develops through an orderly process guided by simple principles" (OECD, 2018[2]). In reality, the multilateral development system is closer to a collection of living organisms that adapt to overarching shifts in the broader international order, the development landscape and the development of co-operation architecture.

This report analyses the multilateral development system through the lens of multilateral finance. In doing so, it looks both at (i) the funding that is directed to or channelled through, multilateral organisations – multilateral inflows (Chapter 2); and at (ii) how this financing is used by the multilateral development system to address specific development challenges – multilateral outflows (Chapter 3). Most of the analysis in this report is based on data from the OECD CRS. However, since the scope of multilateral development finance goes beyond the data available in the CRS, the report also presents an analysis based on alternative datasets and includes caveats where the available data may not provide a complete picture. For example, the OECD CRS does not include detailed data on the multilateral contributions provided by many non-DAC countries (e.g. People's Republic of China ["China"], Brazil, etc.) or the financing that multilateral development banks (MDBs) raise from the capital markets.

Figure 1.2. Multilateral development finance has grown into a complex ecosystem

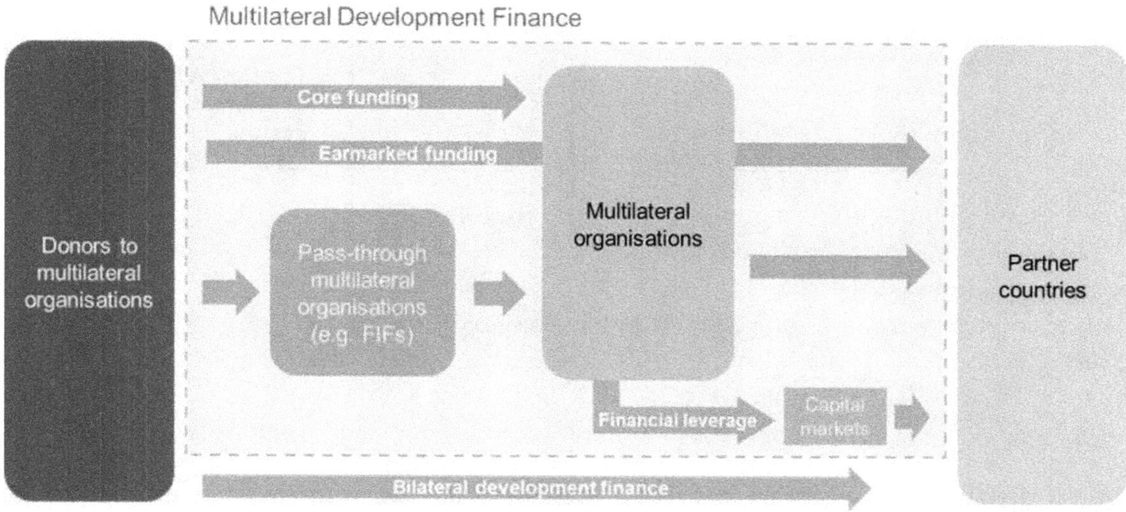

Note: FIFs: Financial intermediary funds.
Source: Authors' design adapted from (Eichenauer and Reinsberg, 2017[3]), "What determines earmarked funding to international development organizations? Evidence from the new multi-bi aid data", https://doi.org/10.1007/s11558-017-9267-2.

Multilateral ODA[2] **is the cornerstone of multilateral development finance (**Figure 1.2**).** It provides multilateral organisations with essential funding that they can pool and incorporate as part of their financial assets. The governing boards of multilateral organisations have the unqualified right to allocate these funds as they see fit within the limits prescribed by the organisation's mandate. In 2018, core multilateral ODA represented USD 46.4 billion. In addition to core multilateral ODA, development partners usually pass part of their bilateral funding through multilateral organisations by earmarking it for specific uses:[3] in 2018, earmarked contributions to multilateral organisations represented USD 25.5 billion. Total support to the multilateral development system, which combines both core and earmarked contributions, amounted to USD 71.9 billion in 2018 (Figure 1.3).

Figure 1.3. More than one-third of all ODA is channelled through the multilateral development system

DAC countries' and other official providers' bilateral, core and non-core (earmarked) multilateral ODA, 2018

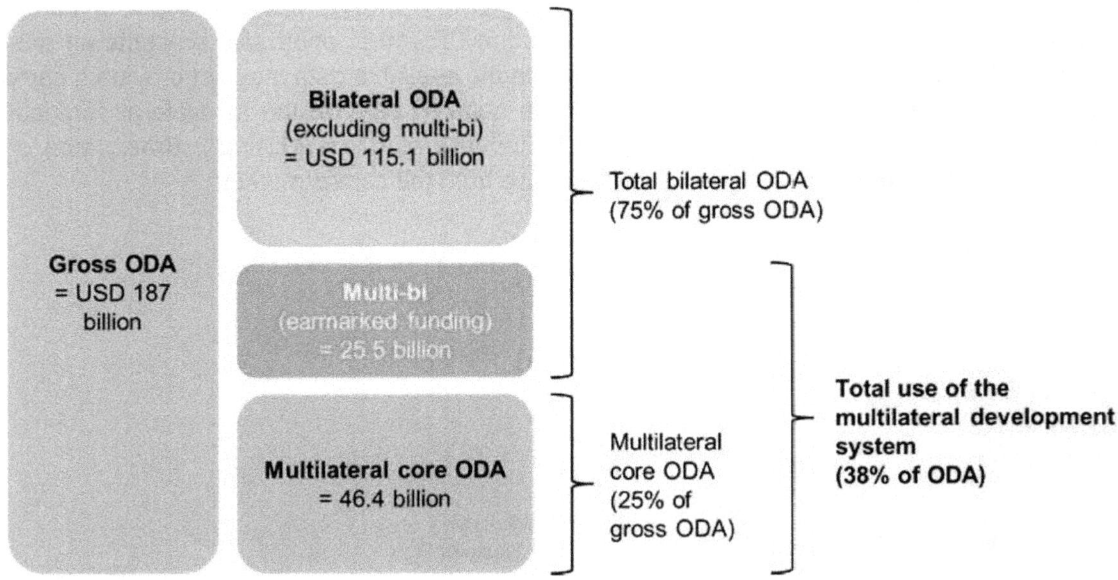

Note: Disbursements, in USD billion.
Source: Authors' design and calculations based on (OECD, 2020[4]), "Creditor Reporting System", https://stats.oecd.org/Index.aspx?DataSetCode=crs1.

Multilateral development institutions vary in their mandate, range and governance

Multilateral development institutions can be broadly classified into four categories: the United Nations Development System (UNDS), multilateral development banks (MDBs), vertical funds, and other organisations with specialised mandates or particular governance models, such as the International Monetary Fund (IMF) and the European Union (EU) (Figure 1.1). Each is described further below. Although they share broad characteristics, the organisations within each category can be further distinguished by their various mandates, governance structures and operational models. Depending on the type of analysis conducted, this report either refers to these four categories of multilateral actors, or specific multilateral organisations.

The UNDS consists of 34 entities (UN funds, programmes and agencies) that receive funding to carry out operational and standard-setting activities for development. The mandates of UN entities vary widely, ranging from service provision to policy development and norm-setting across a wide range of sectors (health, education, environment, food security, migration, etc.). The UNDS includes affiliate organisations such as the UN Development Programme (UNDP), the UN Children's Fund (UNICEF) and the World Food Programme (WFP), as well as specialised agencies such as the Food and Agriculture Organisation (FAO) and the World Health Organisation (WHO).

MDBs include entities with a global mandate, such as the World Bank Group or the New Development Bank, as well as organisations with a regional or subregional focus. MDBs are widely recognised for their role of providing financial and technical assistance for development in low-income and middle-income countries. A key characteristic of MDBs is that, unlike other types of multilateral entities relying primarily on multilateral ODA provided by bilateral donors, they have the capacity to leverage their balance sheets and borrow from the market to increase their lending and grant provision capacity. Financing raised from capital markets accounts for a sizable portion of MDBs' resources. The International Bank for Reconstruction and Development (IBRD), an entity of the World Bank Group, for example, had a borrowing portfolio amounting to USD 229 billion at the end of June 2019, compared to equity holdings of USD 45 billion, which includes capital contributions from member countries.

Most prominent among the MDBs is the World Bank Group, which is comprised of five entities: (i) the above-mentioned International Bank for Reconstruction and Development (IBRD); (ii) the International Development Association (IDA); (iii) the International Finance Corporation (IFC); (iv) the Multilateral Investment Guarantee Agency (MIGA); and (v) the International Centre for the Settlement of Investment-related Disputes (ICSID). MDBs also include regional development banks, such as the African Development Bank (AfDB), the Asian Development Bank (ADB), the European Bank for Reconstruction and Development (EBRD), the Islamic Development Bank (IsDB), and the Inter-American Development Bank (IADB).

The vertical funds have emerged as a new category of multilateral actors in recent decades. Vertical funds are multilateral financing mechanisms that pool finance from both public and private sector sources to target needs in specific development domains, such as health or the fight against climate change. The most prominent vertical funds operate in the health sector (the Global Fund to fight AIDS, Tuberculosis and Malaria, or the Vaccines Alliance – Gavi), the environment (the Green Climate Fund – GCF, the Adaptation Fund – AF, and the Global Environment Facility – GEF), and education (Global Partnership for Education – GPE).

Some important organisations with specialised mandates and governance structures do not fit in any of the above-mentioned categories. This is the case for the International Monetary Fund (IMF), which provides financial support to member countries facing balance-of-payments crises. Unlike the multilateral development banks, the IMF does not lend for specific projects and most of its lending is non-concessional, although concessional financial support is also provided through the Poverty Reduction and Growth Trust (PRGT). In addition to its lending activities, the IMF provides technical assistance and training in a wide range of areas, such as central banking, monetary and exchange rate policy, tax policy and administration, and official statistics.

The European Union (EU) holds a unique place in the multilateral development finance architecture due to its dual role in development assistance. The EU is a full DAC member and a provider of ODA in its own right, with its development policy and its own resources. The EU institutions by themselves ranked fifth amongst DAC members in 2019 for their official development assistance (ODA) volume, which amounted to USD 18 billion (OECD, 2019[5]). At the same time, the EU operates as a group of multilateral institutions. For analytical and statistical purposes, the EU is therefore often presented as a multilateral organisation in DAC publications, including in this report (OECD, 2018[2]). The EU funds its development assistance from several sources, including the: (i) EU budget: (ii) European Development Fund (EDF); (iii) European Investment Bank (EIB); (iv) European trust funds; and (v) European Fund for Sustainable Development (EFSD).

The multilateral development system forms a rich network of interlinked actors

Transfers of resources across multilateral organisations reveal the extensive collaboration and mutual dependence that characterises the multilateral development system. Multilateral organisations frequently channel their resources through other multilateral actors to increase their financial leverage, or to tap into the expertise of other institutions. Figure 1.4 illustrates the rich network that results from such cross-funding and collaboration among multilateral organisations.

The UNDS is a major hub of the multilateral development system, in line with its universal mandate. UN entities are highly interlinked, with some entities such as the Peacebuilding Fund often channelling funds to a range of other UN organisations with implementation capacity. Other UN entities, such as the WHO, UN Women or UN-Habitat, are on the receiving end of funding from multiple UN entities. The network graph reveals the centrality of some specific UN entities, such as UNDP, within the multilateral development network: UNDP is both at the giving and receiving end of cross funding within and outside of the UN development system, and has traditionally played a co-ordinating role in the UN ecosystem.

MDBs are vital players due to their large financing capacity, as well as their extensive field presence and operational capacities. The World Bank, for example, receives funds from diverse actors, including UN entities and vertical funds, looking to benefit from its operational infrastructure and expertise. The Asian Infrastructure Investment Bank (AIIB), as a relatively new player, is not yet reflected in this network, which is based on OECD CRS data for the period 2011-2018.

Vertical funds are financially dependent on traditional multilateral institutions due to their specific governance and business models. Since global vertical funds usually lack implementing capacity and field presence, they tend to channel funds to a range of actors across the multilateral development system to fulfil their mandates. This is true of all the main climate and health-related vertical funds. The Global Environment Facility (GEF), for instance, which was created in 1991 as a programme hosted by the World Bank, continues to channel most of its resources through the World Bank, UNDP and the UN Environment Programme (UNEP) for implementation, despite gaining considerable autonomy since its inception and attaining a high profile as a standalone body.

Figure 1.4. Multilateral organisations are highly interconnected

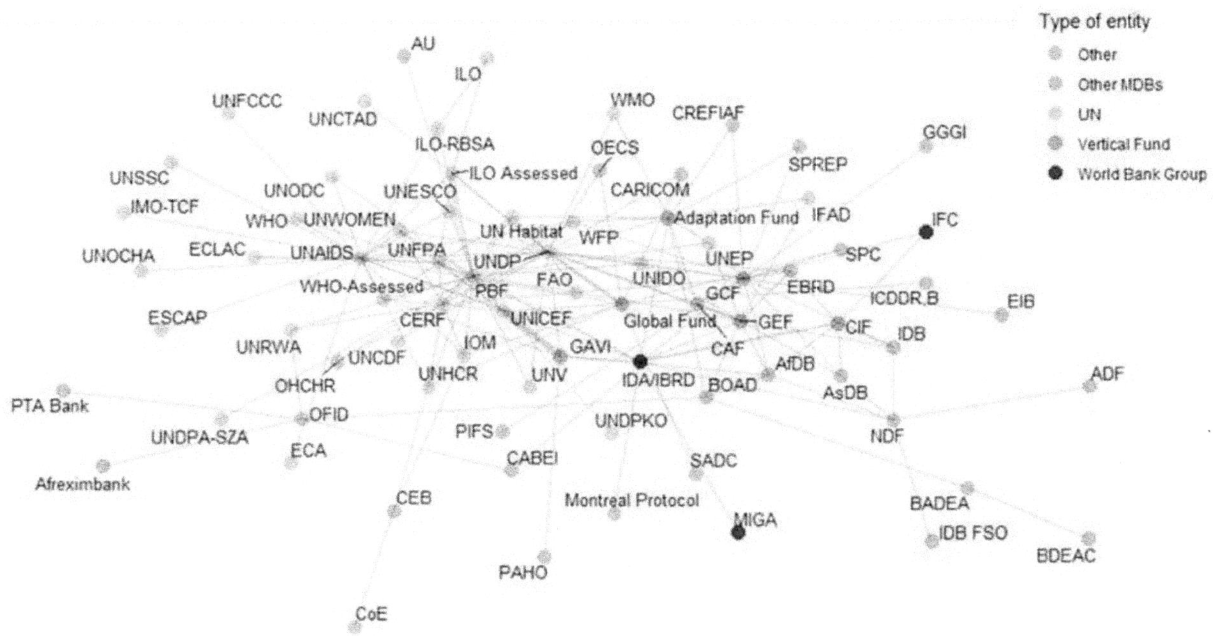

Note: This graph shows transfers of resources among multilateral organisations between 2011 and 2018, but does not capture other forms of collaboration (e.g. co-financing). Multilateral organisations, and MDBs in particular, frequently collaborate as part of co-financing arrangements, which are not captured by the OECD Creditor Reporting System.
Source: Authors' calculations based on (OECD, 2020[4]), "Creditor Reporting System", https://stats.oecd.org/Index.aspx?DataSetCode=crs1.

StatLink https://doi.org/10.1787/888934177214

Despite the creation of new multilateral entities in recent decades, legacy multilateral organisations such as the UN and the main MDBs seem to retain a key and central role in the system. Vertical funds have often been presented as a new and more effective way to channel funds to address global development challenges than traditional multilateral organisations. However, the analysis shows that vertical funds continue to rely on traditional multilateral institutions (especially MDBs) for their implementing capacity and operational infrastructure, as well as their convening power, geographical presence and expertise in financial and trustee services. The fact that these vertical funds still rely on the traditional multilateral system suggests that DAC members' support to new or emerging multilateral channels should always go hand in hand with continued and sustained support to the rest of the multilateral development system.

1.1.2. Multilateral institutions add value to the development co-operation landscape

The multilateral development system is an essential and diverse source of development solutions

The sizable portion of ODA channelled through multilateral entities reflects the widespread recognition of the strengths and relevance of the multilateral system. Previous editions of this report (OECD, 2011[6]) have highlighted that donors' motives for channelling development finance through the multilateral development system can be manifold. Some of the motives frequently invoked are the efficiency gains and enhanced effectiveness resulting from multilateral organisations' characteristics, such as (i) economies of scale and scope, and reduced transaction costs from resource pooling; (ii) financial leverage; (iii) thematic and geographical expertise (e.g. in fragile contexts); (iv) global reach and large field presence; and (v) large operational and implementing capacities. In Chapter 3 of this report, we analyse whether multilateral organisations still enjoy a comparative advantage in some of these key areas.

Efficiency is often presented as one key value proposition of the multilateral development system. By allowing development partners to pool their resources to address specific development challenges, multilateral organisations are believed to offer substantial economies of scale (efficiencies of volume) and scope (efficiencies of variety). However, research shows that concrete evidence to verify claims of comparative efficiency is generally difficult to find (Gulrajani, 2016[7]).[4]

The system is also said to add qualitative value to development finance. Multilateral organisations are increasingly recognised as providers of technical assistance and as knowledge hubs; they are also valued for their normative, standard-setting and policy advisory roles (Gulrajani, 2016[7]). Moreover, their global presence and convening power allow them to disseminate international best practice, either as part of their country work or through international surveys, forums and conferences. A recent survey conducted among DAC member countries (OECD, 2020[8]) showed that they appreciate multilateral entities for their technical expertise and knowledge, financing capacity, convening power, as well as support to global public goods (Figure 1.5). For example, the UNDS is generally viewed as having great convening power, an ability to respond to crises promptly, as well as an extensive reach and country presence. MDBs and vertical funds, on the other hand, are widely recognised for their capacity to mobilise additional public and private resources.

Multilateral organisations complement one another in their thematic strengths and specialisation. For example, in the recent survey of DAC members' policies and practices vis-à-vis the multilateral system (OECD, 2020[8]), DAC members were very positive about the UN's work in humanitarian aid, food security and peace and security. The World Bank Group and other MDBs were viewed as performing well in infrastructure financing and support to inclusive growth and in their advisory role on tax and fiscal matters, as well as trade and financial sector policy and regulation. Overall, DAC members also had a positive perception of the multilateral system's performance in addressing global public goods (e.g. climate and environmental issues) and cross-cutting issues (e.g. gender mainstreaming).

Some experts note that there is scope to build further on these key strengths, for example by focusing more on localised and contextualised knowledge (Kharas, 2016[9]). Given their large field presence and operational experience, multilateral organisations seem uniquely positioned to cross-fertilise knowledge and to actively promote South-South and triangular co-operation in their knowledge-based work. Development practitioners, for example, refer to the "hummingbird" role of the World Bank Group to describe its capacity to leverage knowledge and good practice across different countries and regions (Canuto, 2018[10]; Peters, 2006[11]).

Figure 1.5. DAC members recognise UN entities for their convening power, standard-setting role and ability to react quickly to crises

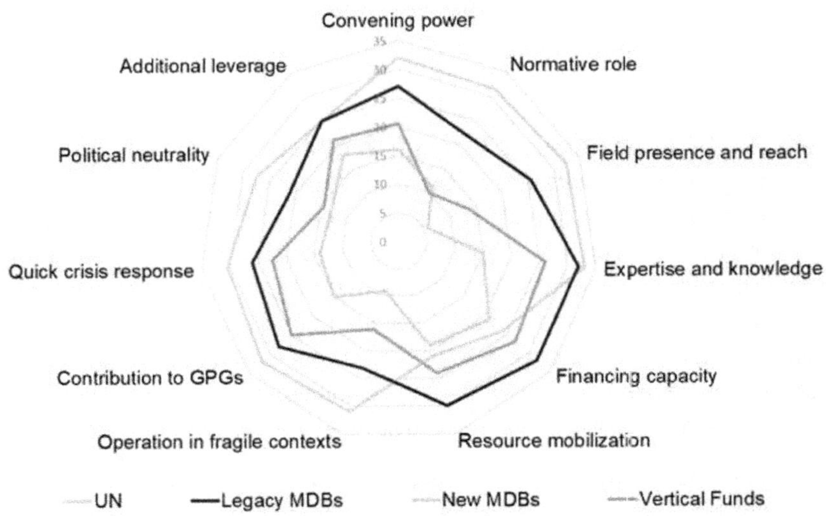

Note: The scores shown on the graph correspond to the number of survey respondents indicating that they think multilateral organisations add value vis-à-vis bilateral channels in the specific category.
Source: (OECD, 2020[8]), "Survey on DAC providers' policies and practices vis-a-vis the multilateral development system" (unpublished).

StatLink https://doi.org/10.1787/888934177233

The multilateral development system is also a financial innovator. Multilateral organisations offer a wide range of financial instruments that can be tailored to the needs of countries across the development spectrum. Figure 1.6 provides an overview of the wide array of financing instruments made available by different categories of multilateral organisations. The key and unique role of multilateral development banks in multilateral development finance is visible through the large variety of financing instruments that these institutions offer to their client countries, allowing for a tailored response to their financing needs.

Figure 1.6. Multilateral institutions offer a wide range of financing instruments

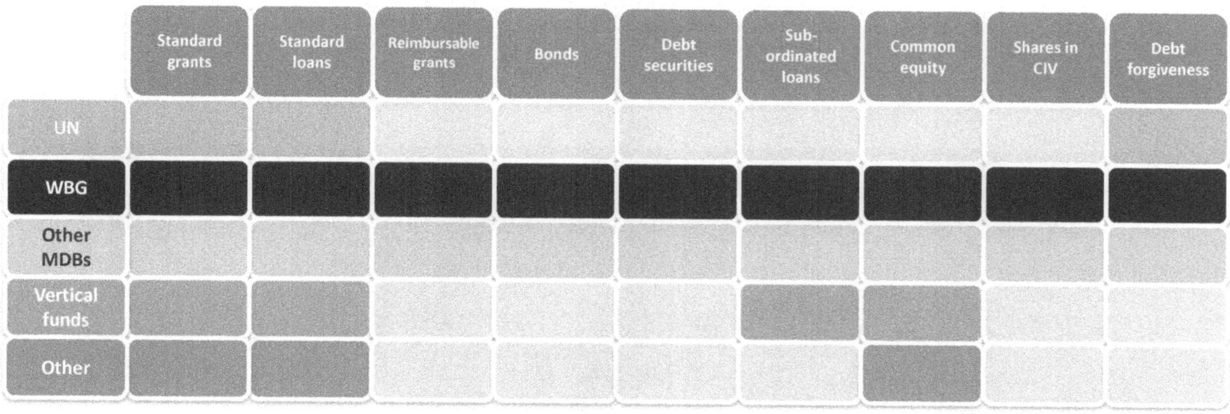

Source: Authors' design based on (OECD, 2020[4]), "Creditor Reporting System", https://stats.oecd.org/Index.aspx?DataSetCode=crs1.

Multilateral organisations' potential to mobilise and engage with the private sector is seen as another key asset of the multilateral development finance system. In recent years, policy makers and researchers have increasingly called upon multilateral organisations to scale up their private sector development efforts (Nielson, 2017[12]) and pointed to private sector finance as an indispensable component to achieve the Sustainable Development Goals (OECD, 2018[2]). This includes the mobilisation of private sector resources for development, but also partnerships with the private sector (including in recipient countries) to foster their positive impact on sustainable development. However, progress in this area has so far been complex to track and measure because of the difficulty of obtaining comprehensive and comparable data. Data and information on amounts mobilised from the private sector by multilateral organisations, for example, are often subject to disclosure exceptions because of commercial sensitivity and the need to protect business interests.

Despite recurrent criticism, multilateral institutions still benefit from significant political support and legitimacy

In recent years, multilateral organisations have been under close scrutiny. One recurring criticism is their alleged lack of effectiveness and accountability. The growing complexity of the multilateral development system, made up of a constellation of entities with different mandates, geographical scope and expertise, has also spurred concerns over a possible lack of coherence across the system. While the global reach of multilateral organisations is a core strength, it also raises questions regarding potential mandate overlaps. Our analysis shows that there are, on average, 20 active multilateral entities in each developing country (Figure 1.7). Uganda is the country receiving support from the largest number of active multilateral entities (30), closely followed by other eastern African countries: Ethiopia, United Republic of Tanzania and Kenya (29 each). Africa is the continent featuring the largest average number of active multilateral entities per country, at around 23.

Figure 1.7. There are on average 20 active multilateral organisations in each partner country

Note: This map, as well as any data, included herein, are without prejudice to the status of, or sovereignty over, any territory, to the delimitation of international frontiers and boundaries and the name of any territory, city or area.
Source: Authors' calculations based on (OECD, 2020[4]), "Creditor Reporting System", https://stats.oecd.org/Index.aspx?DataSetCode=crs1.

StatLink https://doi.org/10.1787/888934177252

However, surveys show that there is still broad trust in the multilateral development system among the general public. Recent studies confirm that multilateral organisations retain a generally positive view and image in most countries. The Pew Research Center's 2019 Global Attitudes Survey, based on opinions of 34 904 respondents, finds that a median of 61% respondents from across 32 surveyed countries have a positive view of the UN, while a median of just 26% expressed a negative view (Pew Research Center, 2019[13]). The views of the multilateral development system tend to be especially positive among young people: in 19 of the 32 countries, respondents between 18 to 29 years old are more positively inclined towards the UN than those aged 50 and older. Another survey of millennials in the United States confirmed the broadly favourable view of the multilateral development system among younger people (Edelman, 2019[14]). The Ipsos group's 2019 Global Influence Report finds that a majority of citizens across 28 countries believe that multilateral organisations such as the United Nations (71% of respondents positive), EU (70%), the World Bank Group (61%) and IMF (58%) have a positive influence in the world (Bricker, 2019[15]).

1.2. Evolution of the multilateral development system to date: 75 years of relevance

1.2.1. From Bretton Woods to the SDG Summit

This section provides a concise historical perspective on the evolution of the multilateral development system over its 75 years of existence. In doing so, it illustrates the consecutive movements of expansion and fragmentation of the multilateral development system. (Figure 1.8)

The multilateral development system is an increasingly crowded and fragmented space. Since its inception more than 75 years ago, the proliferation of new multilateral organisations and the progressive expansion of their mandates in response to new global development challenges has profoundly transformed the multilateral development landscape.

Four main waves have marked the evolution of the multilateral development system; each wave tried to address the shortcomings of the previous one. The first wave, at the end of World War II, was a response to the absence of multilateralism and a system of alliances that had led to the war. It resulted in the creation of the modern multilateral development system, led by the UN and the Bretton Woods institutions. The second wave, from the 1960s to the 1970s, coincided with a call for increased decentralisation and regionalisation of multilateral governance and resulted in the establishment of the first regional development banks. The third wave, during the 1990s and early 2000s, emerged as a consequence of the rise in prominence of sector-specific global development issues. It was characterised by the creation of the global vertical funds, as well as rapid growth in the number of trust funds hosted by multilateral organisations. The fourth wave, observable since the early 2010s, saw the creation of new multilateral development banks in response to major geopolitical and economic shifts in the international order, in particular the emergence of the BRICS (Brazil, Russian Federation, India, China, and South Africa). Each wave is analysed below.

Post-World War II: foundations of the modern multilateral development system

The multilateral development system as we know it was born in the aftermath of World War II. The United Nations and the Bretton Woods institutions (the International Bank for Reconstruction and Development – IBRD – and the International Monetary Fund - IMF) were created from the ashes of World War II.

The United Nations (UN) officially came to existence on 24 October 1945. While the UN is best known for its mission to maintain international peace and security through international co-operation, the preamble of the UN charter also mentions the promotion of "social progress and better standards of life" as one of the main goals of the organisation and vows to "employ international machinery for the promotion of the economic and social advancement of all peoples". At present, 187 UN agencies, funds, programmes and commissions are included in the OECD DAC List of ODA-eligible International Organisations. Beyond its purely development-related work, the UN also co-ordinates humanitarian relief operations in support of national authorities and helps enforce global norms and standards.

In parallel to the creation of the UN, the Bretton Woods conference held in July 1944 established the IBRD and the IMF. The initial mandate of the IBRD was to extend loans for economic development to finance the reconstruction of post-war Europe, although its focus shifted to development activities and developing countries in subsequent years. Over time, a new set of specialised entities was also created alongside the IBRD to constitute what is now known as the World Bank Group: these entities are the International Development Association (IDA), the International Finance Corporation (IFC), the Multilateral Investment Guarantee Agency (MIGA), and the International Centre for the Settlement of Investment-related Disputes (ICSID). In 2013, the World Bank Group adopted two goals to guide its work: (i) ending extreme poverty by 2030; and (ii) boosting the shared prosperity of the poorest 40% of the population in every country.

Figure 1.8. The multilateral system has significantly evolved since the end of World War II

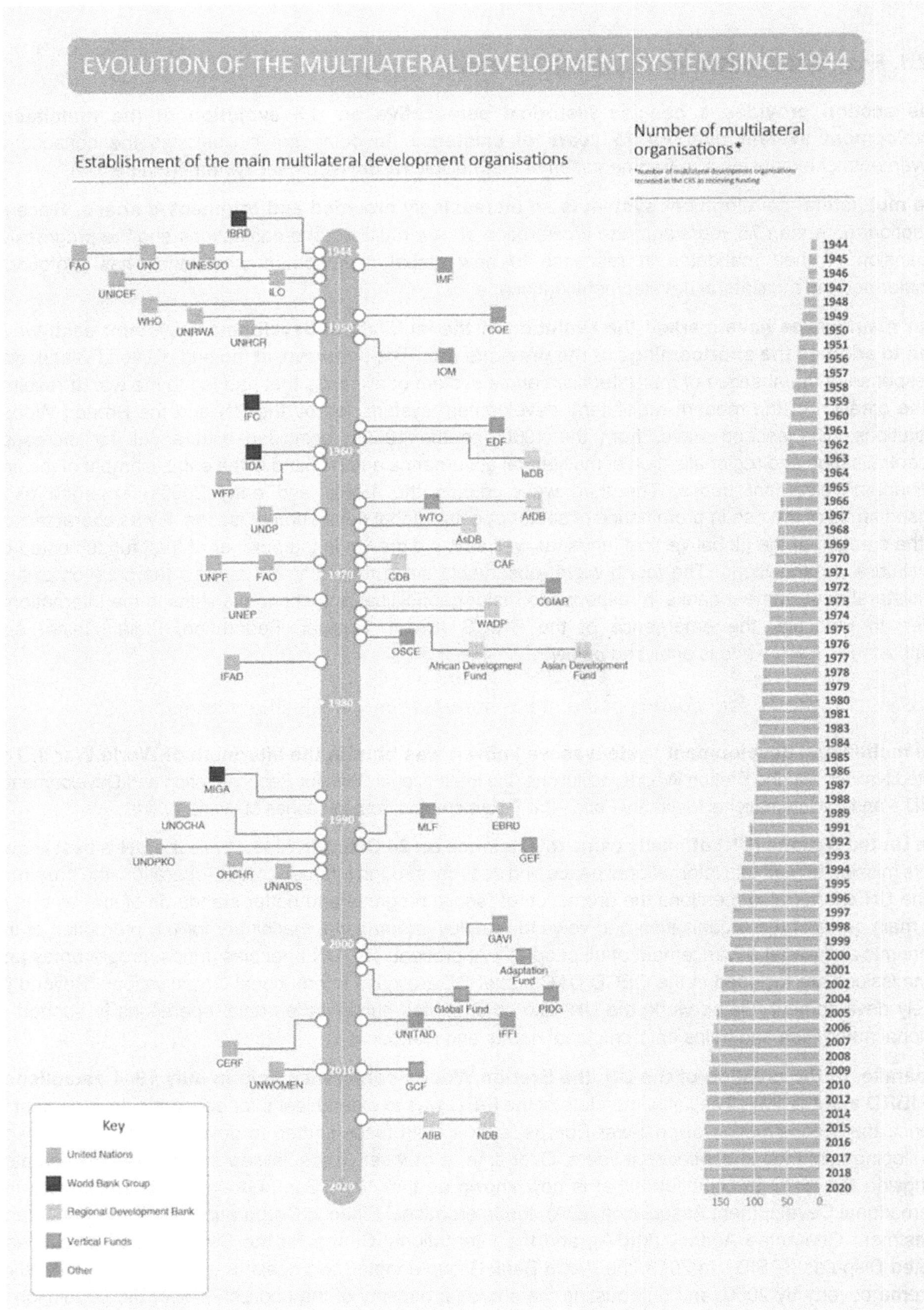

The 60s-70s: adaptation to regional realities

The rise of regional development banks originated from a call for greater decentralisation of the multilateral development system. This movement implied a radical shift of multilateral development finance from a global to a regional, and even sub-regional, focus. The creation of the Inter-American Development Bank (1959), African Development Bank (1964), and Asian Development Bank (1966) was primarily a consequence of the rising discontent among developing countries with the aid and development policies of global institutions (Ben-Artzi, 2016[16]). However, the geopolitical realities of the time, characterised by the Cold War and decolonisation processes, also played a crucial role in the emergence of these organisations (Engen and Prizzon, 2018[17]). In the 1970s the rising economic power of oil-producing Arab states led to the establishment of new banks, such as the Islamic Development Bank (IsDB) in 1975.

The governance framework of regional development banks mirrors the World Bank's, with a large role devolved to traditional donors. However, a major difference exists between the ownership of the World Bank and that of the first generation of regional development banks: the IaDB, ADB, and AfDB all count more borrowers than donors among their shareholders – the exact opposite of the World Bank Group. This is true not only in absolute terms but also in terms of voting shares, as borrowers also retain the majority of percentage voting shares in all three organisations.

The mandate of most regional development banks builds on two pillars: (i) fostering sustainable economic development; and (ii) supporting regional co-operation, economic integration and within-region or among-member states trade (Engen and Prizzon, 2018[17]). Nonetheless, a handful of these organisations have an additional specialisation, such as Shari'ah-compliant finance for the Islamic Development Bank (IsDB), or infrastructure investments in the case of the East African Development Bank (EADB).

End of the 20th century: the emergence of vertical funds

The third wave in the evolution of the multilateral development system shifted the focus from regional to thematic specialisation. An early example is the establishment of the Consultative Group on International Agricultural Research (CGIAR) in 1971 to support successful public-private research partnerships to help developing countries achieve food self-sufficiency.

In the late 1990s and early 2000s, the increased attention by the international community on new global challenges coincided with the emergence of the global vertical funds. This movement was accelerated by the adoption of the Millennium Development Goals (MDGs) in 2000: vertical funds appeared as appropriate tools to advance the MDGs as they allowed donors to eschew the classic horizontal, country-based model of traditional international financial institutions and to instead allocate funds to specific sectors (such as health, education, agriculture) (Gartner and Kharas, 2013[18]).

The list of vertical funds has grown considerably over the past few decades. Nowadays, it includes high-profile entities such as the Global Environment Facility (GEF, established in 1992), the Vaccine Alliance (Gavi, established in 2000), the Adaptation Fund (created in 2001), the Global Fund to Fight AIDS, Tuberculosis and Malaria (set up in 2002) and the Green Climate Fund (GCF, launched in 2010).

Owing to their governance and operational model, vertical funds have taken an increasingly prominent role in support of global public goods. Their thematic orientation and global mandate are expected to facilitate the shift away from country-based solutions and approaches, towards interventions that target the under-provision of global public goods and the over-production of global public bads. However, most of these funds still rely in part on traditional multilateral organisations (UN entities and multilateral development banks) for implementation.

The early 2000s was also a period of internal fragmentation within the multilateral development system. Development partners significantly increased their volume and share of non-core (earmarked) funding, leading to rapid growth in the number of trust funds hosted by multilateral organisations. Since then, several multilateral organisations have launched reforms to limit this proliferation (see Box 2.1. in Chapter 2).

The 21st century: towards a new multilateral order

The emergence of new multilateral entities at the turn of the 21st century reflects major shifts in the international economic order. The global geopolitical context has changed significantly since the end of the Cold War in the early 1990s, with the BRICS, and China, in particular, taking an increasingly important role in the global economic landscape. Between 1990 and 2019, the size of China's GDP relative to the world's total income increased from 1.7% to 16.3% in real terms. In aggregate, the BRICS' contribution to global GDP grew from 7.9% to 24.1% over the same period.

The creation of the Asian Infrastructure Investment Bank (AIIB) and the New Development Bank (NDB) responded to the need to fill the huge infrastructure gap in developing countries. Filling this gap, which has been estimated to be in the range of USD 3 billion to USD 5 billion annually, is considered as a prerequisite to the achievement of many SDGs. The AIIB is almost unique in multilateral development finance by bringing geographical (Asia) as well as sectoral (infrastructure) considerations under the same roof (Chin, 2019[19]). However, beyond the purely developmental motives, the establishment of these new institutions is also often interpreted as a move by developing countries to gain greater representation and weight in the multilateral aid architecture (Wang, 2019[20]).

The entry of new actors in the multilateral landscape was initially met with mixed reactions. While some experts highlighted their potential complementary role in international development financing (Gu, 2017[21]), others depicted the NDB and the AIIB as a threat to traditional multilateral development banks, with largely redundant mandates and geographic coverage (Subacchi, 2015[22]). In the case of the AIIB, the creation of the institution also raised concerns that it would promote China's geopolitical agenda. In its first few years of existence, however, the institutional growth of the AIIB has confirmed the global nature of its membership: four years after its launch, the AIIB counts more than 100 member countries.[5] In comparison, the ADB, established in 1966, counts 68 members after its 54 years of existence.

The AIIB and the NDB have brought some innovation to the multilateral development system. These two organisations combine the classic institutional structure of traditional MDBs with some innovations derived from their shareholders' 75 years of experience across the multilateral development landscape. Compared to traditional MDBs, for example, the governance of the NDB reflects a commitment to the equality of its five members, most evident in the equal distribution of their voting power. Another of its distinctive feature lies in NDB's decision to offer local currency lending to its client countries. The AIIB, for its part, was designed with a non-resident Board of Directors (unlike the World Bank, the AfDB and the ADB, but similar to the EIB and Development Bank of Latin America or CAF). Another innovative feature of the AIIB's governance model resides in its charter (Chin, 2019[19]), which provides the AIIB with the flexibility to adapt to changes in the global development context, for example by introducing new types of financing, or extending its support to non-members. These are only some examples, among many, of characteristics that differentiate these new institutions both from traditional MDBs, and from each other (Table 1.1).

Table 1.1. A close comparison between the AIIB and the NDB reveals significant differences

	New Development Bank	Asian Infrastructure Investment Bank
Origin	BRICS initiative based on Indian proposal	China-led initiative
Scale	USD 50 billion in subscribed capital	USD 100 billion in subscribed capital
	Limited access to international capital markets	Access to international capital markets
Governance	Equal shares and voting power among members No member has veto power	Different shares and voting power among members China has veto power on major issues
Transparency	Limited information about projects	Detailed information about projects, including safeguards
Safeguards	Country systems	International 'best practice'
Main partners	National authorities and banks	Traditional MDBs
Board residency	Non-resident	Non-resident

Source: (Wang, 2019[20]), "The New Development Bank and the Asian Infrastructure Investment Bank: China's Ambiguous Approach to Global Financial Governance", https://onlinelibrary.wiley.com/doi/full/10.1111/dech.12473.

1.2.2. The 2030 Agenda puts the multilateral system under increased pressure to deliver

The 2030 Agenda and the Sustainable Development Goals revitalised the demand for multilateral approaches to support the global development agenda. Multilateral actors received a pivotal role and expanded mandate with the adoption of the 2015 Addis Ababa Action Agenda (AAAA), which provided a blueprint to finance the implementation of the 2030 Agenda. The recognition of the integrated and interlinked nature of the SDGs helped to put multilateral collaboration at the heart of the agenda (Rudolph, 2017[23]). Due to the breadth of their activities, multilateral organisations have positioned themselves as key contributors to the SDGs. Figure 1.9 shows that the activities of multilateral organisations span the whole range of the 17 SDGs, with most categories of multilateral organisations providing support across multiple SDGs.

The 2030 Agenda also challenged the traditional approaches of multilateral development finance. The AAAA called for the mobilisation and alignment of all financing flows – including domestic public resources, private investment, remittances as well as official development finance – with the SDGs. As a result, the mobilisation of private finance for sustainable development has become an important function of the multilateral development system. Central to this is the vision to move from "billions to trillions" and use the multiplier effect of multilateral finance by leveraging investment from business, venture capital, sovereign wealth funds and other non-state sources (AfDB, ADB, EBRD, EIB, IADB, IMF; WBG, 2015[24]).

The extensive financial resources, field presence and expertise of multilateral organisations make them indispensable to address global challenges such as the SDGs. From its very inception, the multilateral development system has been created as an instrument for global burden-sharing and joint action (Martens, 2005[25]; Milner and Tingley, 2013[26]). As such, it provides an ideal platform to tackle development challenges whose impacts spread across large geographical areas, socioeconomic groups and generations (Gulrajani, 2016[7]). By co-ordinating interventions, harmonising approaches and promoting common standards and procedures, multilateral organisations can act as a powerful conduit for collective action. They are also uniquely positioned to tackle the collective action problems arising in the production and maintenance of public goods,[6] such as free riding, the prisoner's dilemma and the tragedy of the commons (Kharas, 2016[9]).

Figure 1.9. The activities of multilateral organisations span all 17 SDGs

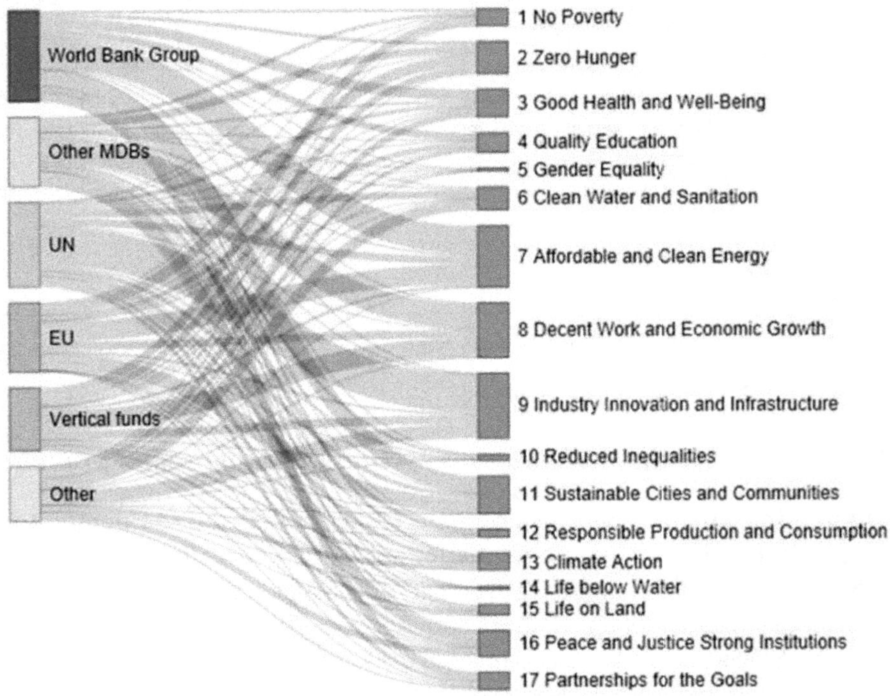

Note: The OECD SDG Financing Lab uses artificial intelligence to link official development flows (ODF) spending to the SDGs.
Source: Authors' calculations based on (OECD, 2020[4]) "Creditor Reporting System", https://stats.oecd.org/Index.aspx?DataSetCode=crs1, and (OECD, 2019[27]), "SDG Financing Lab", https://sdg-financing-lab.oecd.org.

StatLink https://doi.org/10.1787/888934177271

However, the 2030 Agenda has also exposed some inherent limitations of the multilateral development system that hamper its contribution to the provision and maintenance of global public goods. While many multilateral organisations have significantly stepped up their activities to support global public goods (GPGs) since 2015, their work has also revealed some basic shortcomings of their approach (Kaul, 2017[28]; McDade et al., 2019[29]). These shortcomings include: (i) the absence of clear strategies within and across multilateral organisations to collectively address cross-border issues; and (ii) the country-based operating models of traditional multilateral organisations, which are often perceived as restraining their ability to contribute to GPGs. In some instances, this has led to calls for overarching reforms to improve how multilateral organisations deal with cross-border issues. Proposals run the whole gamut from creating new institutions devoted to GPG provision, to adapting the mandates, operational models and governance structures of existing organisations in a way to better accommodate this increasingly important function (Kaul et al., 2015[30]; Kanbur, 2015[31]).

The financial capacity of multilateral organisations is another key limitation. In the years following the adoption of the 2030 Agenda, the magnitude of the SDG funding gap led policymakers to call for innovative financial reforms in multilateral development banks (G20, 2015[32]). As a result, the main MDBs implemented a series of measures aimed at optimising their balance sheets, for example by merging their concessional and non-concessional windows or by deploying exposure exchange mechanisms to diversify their portfolios (World Bank Group, 2016[33]). Despite these advances, a growing chorus of voices still points out the need to adjust the scale of multilateral development finance to the magnitude of the global development challenges (Humphrey, 2017[34]). According to the 2020 OECD survey on DAC members' policies and practices vis-à-vis the multilateral development system (OECD, 2020[8]), the lack of financial resources was perceived to be one of the key constraints that hampered an effective response of the multilateral system to the COVID-19 crisis.

1.2.3. Global COVID-19 crisis: time for multilateral innovation?

The multilateral development system was quick to step into the sustainable development finance vacuum generated by the crisis

The COVID-19 pandemic, with its profound economic, social and human impacts, is a wake-up call for multilateralism. Although all countries are, in one way or another, affected by the recent COVID-19 crisis, the situation of developing countries is particularly worrisome. Unlike industrialised countries, which can rely on relatively strong healthcare systems and financial buffers to deal with the immediate impact of the crisis through fiscal or monetary measures, most developing countries have seen their access to finance severely compromised following the global economic slowdown. Early research points to record capital flight, accompanied by a drop in remittances and negative projections for domestic finance (OECD, 2020[35]). The measures implemented by governments around the world to deal with the devastating effects of the virus have also led to a temporary, albeit severe, rollback of globalisation. Yet, at the same time, the global scale of the virus has highlighted the interdependence of nations and people around the world, demonstrating that the need for international co-operation and solidarity is greater than ever.

The multilateral development system is in a unique position to meet the vast and pressing financial needs of developing countries during the crisis. The multidimensional and global nature of the COVID-19 crisis calls for leveraging the comparative advantages of the multilateral development system, and to let it assume a central role both in the immediate response to the pandemic and in the medium to long-term efforts to mitigate its social, economic and human impacts. The global reach of multilateral organisations – combined with their broad mandates and expertise, convening power, large array of financing instruments, and knowledge of local contexts – makes them ideal candidates to lead and co-ordinate global efforts to address the current crisis (Table 1.2). The added value of multilateral partners' financing, including its effectiveness, is discussed in more detail in Section 3.2 of this report.

Table 1.2. The multidimensional nature of the COVID-19 crisis calls for leveraging the strengths of the multilateral development system

Key areas of strength	Description
Global reach	Thanks to their universal membership, multilateral organisations have a global reach and are well-positioned to tackle cross-border challenges. This also gives them legitimacy to work with stakeholders from around the world, and the capacity to operate in all sorts of environments, including fragile contexts or post-disaster situations.
Wide-ranging mandate and expertise	The multisector knowledge and mandate of international development organisations allows them to design and implement comprehensive responses to multidimensional challenges, such as the COVID-19 crisis. It also allows them to deal with their complex – and sometimes indirect – social, economic and human consequences.
Convening power	The strong convening power of the multilateral development system can play a key role in sparking collective action on global issues, and to help co-ordinate and monitor the individual actions of member countries and development partners. This is particularly relevant in a context of a pandemic, which calls for co-operative, transparent and co-ordinated responses.
Flexible and diverse financing mechanisms	Thanks to the diverse and complementary nature of multilateral entities (UN agencies, funds and programmes, multilateral development banks, vertical funds, etc.), the multilateral development system can offer a wide range of public and private financing instruments. This lends the multilateral system a considerable amount of flexibility, allowing it to propose tailored responses to the specific financing needs of member countries.
Promotion of evidence-based international best practices	The universal membership and mandate of the multilateral development system make it an ideal conduit for knowledge exchange and information-sharing among member countries in times of crises. Besides, some multilateral organisations have a specific mandate to promote the use of international best practices among member countries or to design and articulate

	norms that can guide the actions of national governments.
Field presence and knowledge of local contexts	Multilateral organisations have a strong field presence, and the ability to operate in fragile and conflict-affected contexts. The UN is the perfect example, with its global mandate and the work of its agencies, funds and programmes spanning 182 countries. This gives these organisations an in-depth knowledge of local contexts, as well as access to a strong network of country partners – both of which are considered key to address the COVID-19 crisis.
Operational infrastructure	As a result of its 75 years of experience, the multilateral development system counts an extensive operational infrastructure, including a strong logistical and procurement capacity, as well as well-established policies and processes. This enables multilateral organisations to respond to emergencies with unmatched scale and speed in times of crisis.

Source: Authors' design based on (UN, 2020[36]), "A UN framework for the immediate socio-economic response to COVID-19", https://unsdg.un.org/resources/un-framework-immediate-socio-economic-response-covid-19 and (World Bank Group, 2020[37]), "Saving Lives, Scaling-Up Impact and Getting Back on Track: World Bank Group Covid-19 Crisis Response Approach Paper", http://documents1.worldbank.org/curated/en/136631594937150795/pdf/World-Bank-Group-COVID-19-Crisis-Response-Approach-Paper-Saving-Lives-Scaling-up-Impact-and-Getting-Back-on-Track.pdf.

A large part of the financing made immediately available to developing countries during the crisis was channelled through the multilateral system. Multilateral development organisations have reacted swiftly to the crisis, launching a timely response to step into the financial vacuum generated by the global pandemic. The recent replenishments of some MDB concessional windows, such as the IDA and the African Development Fund, turned out to be particularly timely and put the system in a strong position to respond to the crisis. This allowed the multilateral development system to make available nearly USD 250 billion for the immediate response to the crisis in the weeks following the declaration of the pandemic. This compares to an estimated USD 5.5 billion reported as COVID-19 response by DAC members and other official providers, as of the end of May 2020 (OECD, 2020[38]). Considering the challenging context in which multilateral organisations had to operate, characterised by numerous operational constraints (travel restrictions, lockdown measures, disruption of supply chains, and volatility of the international capital markets), their ability to ensure business continuity and to mobilise large volumes of financing in record time is an impressive feat.

A number of flexible financing mechanisms allowed the IMF and the main MDBs to rapidly deploy their resources at scale. The IMF, for example, provided emergency financial assistance to developing countries through its Rapid Credit Facility (RCF) and Rapid Financing Instrument (RFI). It also provided grants for debt relief through the Catastrophe Containment and Relief Trust (CCRT), a facility that had already been used to support Guinea, Liberia, and Sierra Leone during the 2014 Ebola outbreak. The World Bank Group and the main regional development banks used fast-track financing facilities and repurposed part of their existing portfolio to provide rapid support to their client countries. The flexibility demonstrated by multilateral development banks in reallocating resources and repurposing their portfolios played a key role in the speed at which these organisations were able to respond to the demand and needs of developing countries.

The UN put in place a two-track response plan to address the humanitarian and development aspects of the crisis. To combat the social and economic dimensions of the crisis, the UN launched a Global Humanitarian Response Plan (GHRP), which aims to address the urgent health and humanitarian needs of populations already caught up in humanitarian crises. A strong focus of the UN response was to provide support to and through local health systems, especially in fragile contexts characterised by weak institutions. The UN further announced the creation of a COVID-19 Response and Recovery Fund (RRF) to help low and middle-income developing countries to combat the virus[7] and called for an unprecedented global stimulus to be provided to developing countries to help them cope with the economic and social fallout (UN, 2020[36]).

In addition, the multilateral system was instrumental in promoting collective action and supply-side co-ordination to mitigate the impact of the pandemic in developing countries. For example, multilateral actors, such as the World Bank Group and the IMF, have been actively promoting and facilitating the G20 debt moratorium to alleviate the burden of debt repayment for the most vulnerable countries.

As well as scale and speed, the effectiveness of the current multilateral response to the crisis will also be determined by its capacity to adequately prioritise its interventions. Given the limited resources available and the magnitude of the challenge posed by COVID-19, the multilateral development system needs to exercise careful selectivity to ensure it is able to serve the most in need while taking into consideration each country's absorptive capacity (including debt sustainability considerations). It is worth noting the efforts made by multilateral organisations to better understand the needs and vulnerabilities generated by the crisis at the global level.[8] Once data and information related to the immediate response to the COVID-19 crisis become available, a review of the activities financed by the multilateral development system would be welcome to shed light on the sectoral and geographic focus of the response, and analyse how multilateral organisations prioritised their interventions.

1.3. An agenda for reform of the multilateral development system

In the years preceding the COVID-19 crisis, the multilateral system was already facing numerous stress factors. Many of these factors appeared to be exogenous, originating from changes in the global development landscape rather than from the failings of multilateral organisations. In the recent OECD survey on DAC members' policies and practices vis-à-vis the multilateral development system, for example, respondents pointed to the changes in the global geopolitical landscape as the main stress factor affecting the multilateral development system, with 58% of respondents rating it as a highly significant factor (Figure 1.10) (OECD, 2020[8]). In order of importance, the next stress factors highlighted as highly significant by respondents were the emergence of new global development challenges (43%), and the declining trust among member countries (37%). Most factors related to the performance of multilateral entities, such as public perceptions of multilateral effectiveness (21%), the expanding mandates of multilateral organisations (16%) and their operational models (11%), ranked last. These results suggest that in order to be effective, any reform of the multilateral development system should be contextual (i.e. take into account changing circumstances), inclusive (i.e. address the deficiencies of all multilateral stakeholders – not only multilateral organisations) and holistic (i.e. consider the whole chain of multilateral development finance – not only the final link in the chain)

Figure 1.10. According to DAC members, external factors put greatest stress on the multilateral development system

Which factors put the multilateral development system under increased stress?

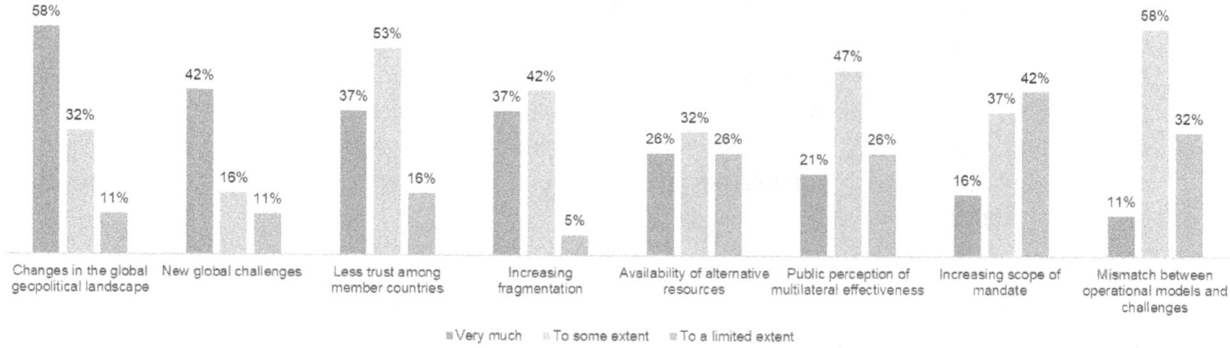

Source: (OECD, 2020[8]), "Survey on DAC providers' policies and practices vis-a-vis the multilateral development system",(unpublished) .

StatLink https://doi.org/10.1787/888934177290

The COVID-19 pandemic is a test of the multilateral system's ability to address global development challenges. The crisis has already exposed the fragility of the multilateral system, with many countries reacting to the crisis in an uncoordinated fashion, and a few governments raising concerns over the competency and impartiality of some multilateral organisations. By challenging the multilateral development system and pushing it to its limits, the crisis can help to identify potential deficiencies that should be solved to prepare the system for other challenges of the magnitude posed by climate change and the COVID-19 pandemic.

The international call to "build back better" should also apply to the multilateral development system. Given the magnitude of the challenges lying ahead, the shareholders of the multilateral development system should explore ways to make the system fit for purpose to deal with these new and emerging development challenges. If the target of achieving the SDGs by 2030 seemed daunting before the COVID-19 crisis, the added challenge posed by the pandemic requires a move away from business as usual to engage in changes that help maximise the impact of multilateral finance.

Achieving this will require the multilateral system to improve in three key dimensions. This section presents three key reform areas, and six related building blocks, with the potential to make multilateral development finance fit to address global development challenges:

- **Key reform area 1 – Scale of impact:** To stay relevant in the context of the 2030 Agenda and the global development challenges such as the COVID-19 pandemic, multilateral development finance needs a change of scale (Humphrey, 2020[39]). Maximising the impact of multilateral finance requires a rethink of the financial and operational model of the various institutions comprising the multilateral development system to ensure it is able to meet the ever-growing demand and needs (Bhattacharya et al., 2018[40]). This is especially relevant in times of crisis, when other financing sources (e.g. tax revenues, foreign direct investment, remittances, commercial lending, etc.) available to developing countries tend to dry up (UN, 2020[41]). At such times the multilateral system needs to use its funding strategically and catalytically.
- **Key reform area 2 – Efficiency:** The socio-economic consequences of the COVID-19 pandemic have widened the already large gap in funding required to achieve the SDGs (OECD, 2020[35]; Inter-agency Task Force on Financing for Development, 2020[42]). In the resource constrained environment that is likely in the aftermath of the crisis, the multilateral development system must demonstrate that it constitutes an efficient channel to address new and emerging development challenges. Achieving progress in this area will require building on the comparative advantages of the multilateral system (Le Drian and Maas, 2019[43]).
- **Key reform area 3 – Accountability:** Long before the pandemic, the perceived lack of accountability of the multilateral development system was already considered an area requiring increased attention from multilateral stakeholders. Over the past decades, the growing complexity of the system, made up of a large number of entities with various and sometimes overlapping mandates, has contributed to an increased sense of remoteness and opacity surrounding the governance and activities of multilateral organisations (OECD, 2011[6]). It is thus key for multilateral stakeholders to push for greater accountability in order to restore trust in the multilateral development system: this will require better communication of its results and impact, as well as clarifying the role of each stakeholder in the system, and ensuring a transparent and effective division of labour.

Progress in these three areas requires multilateral stakeholders to address existing constraints affecting the multilateral development finance process. Over the years, researchers and policymakers have highlighted a number of constraints limiting the scale of impact, efficiency and accountability of multilateral development finance (Figure 1.11). These constraints, which span all stages of the multilateral development finance process and concern all its stakeholders, call for a holistic and inclusive set of reforms.

Figure 1.11. Reforming the multilateral system requires to address key constraints across the multilateral development finance process

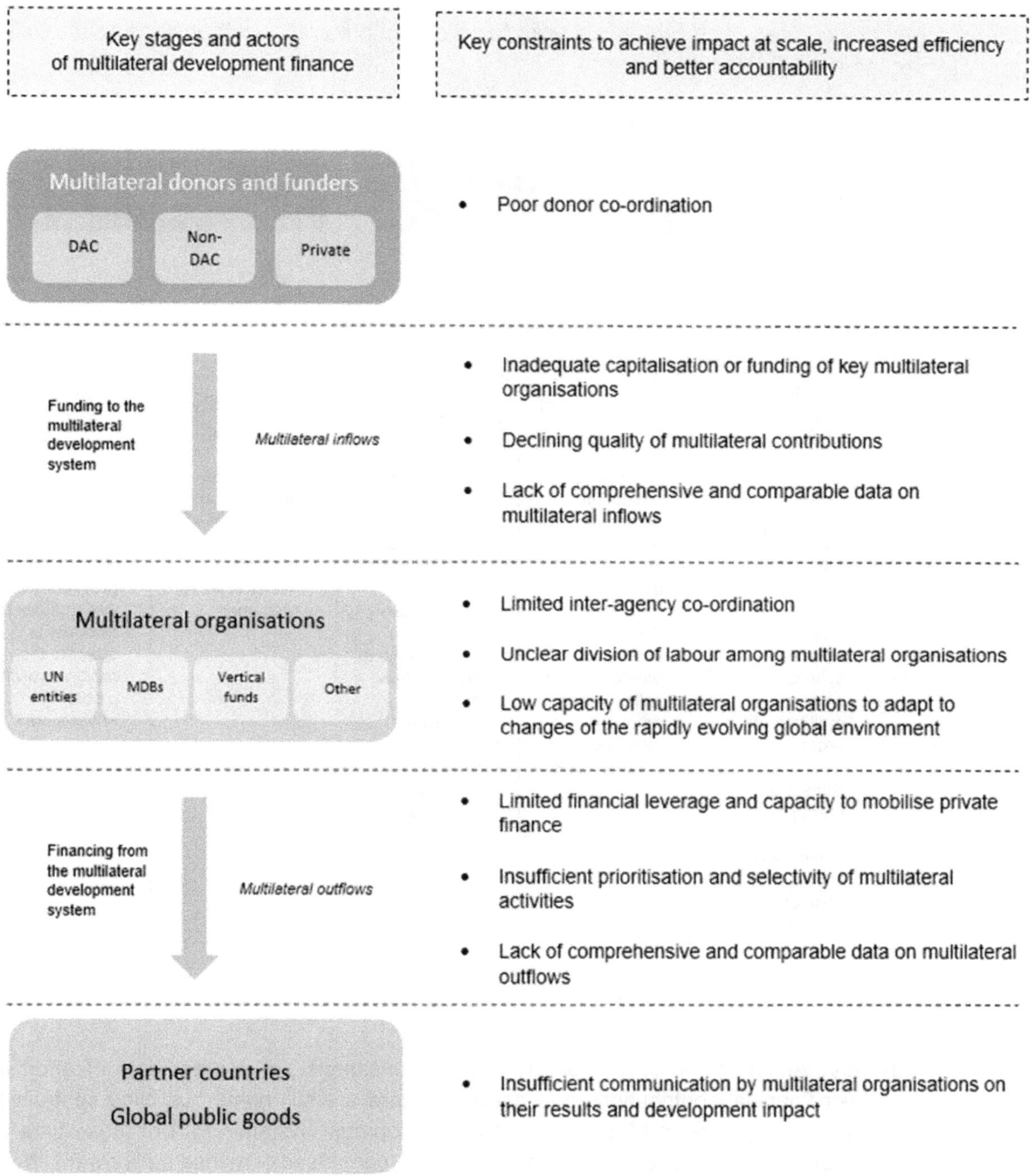

Source: Authors' design.

Removing these constraints requires action grouped into six building blocks. Together these outline a possible research agenda on the reform of the multilateral development system. The six building blocks aim to respond to structural, operational and financial shortcomings in the multilateral development system that are constraining its ability to respond to new global challenges (Figure 1.12). Most of them, however, warrant more research and analysis before they can be translated into actionable solutions. Where possible, the section highlights specific areas that would benefit from more in-depth research, analyses or reviews by the OECD DAC and other stakeholders. Since many of the building blocks are not new, further research could also be useful to understand what has so far prevented or deferred reform efforts to date.

Figure 1.12. Key reform areas and building blocks to adapt multilateral development finance to 21st century development challenges

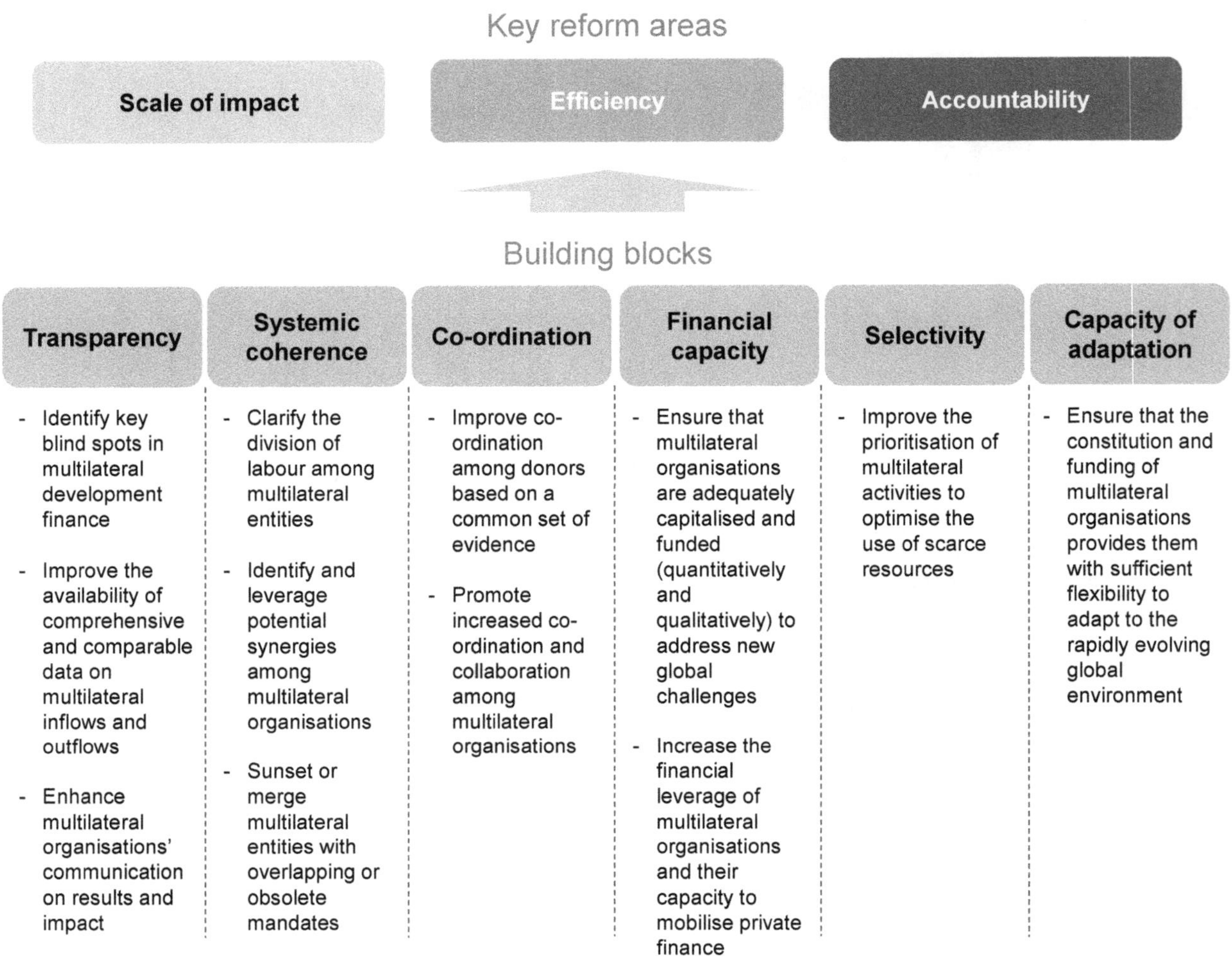

Source: Authors' design.

1. **Transparency:** Although multilateral donors and organisations put a great deal of effort into disclosing their financial contributions and activities, there are still numerous blind spots in the financing flows and operations of the multilateral development system.[9] Part of these data and information gaps stem from the complexity of the system, comprised of myriad actors with different funding and operational models. The complexity of the multilateral development system makes the production of comprehensive and comparable data a costly and time-consuming task that also requires co-ordination among a multitude of multilateral stakeholders, including non-state actors. In the absence of such data, however, it is difficult to hold multilateral stakeholders accountable, as well as to identify and eliminate inefficiencies in the system. The emergence of new actors, whose financial flows are not yet captured in existing data collection and disclosure mechanisms, also affects the comprehensiveness of the data available. These data gaps are likely to increase over time as the multilateral system continues to grow in volume and complexity.

2. **Coherence:** Recent research points to the need to make the multilateral development finance architecture more coherent. This would help avoid overlapping mandates that result in inefficiencies and duplication of efforts and contribute to opacity in the system. Such an endeavour would require comprehensive reviews of the various functions and specialisations of multilateral organisations to clarify their mandate and scope of responsibility in tackling new development challenges, and ultimately ensure an improved division of labour. In the longer term, once sufficient analytical evidence has been collected, multilateral stakeholders could determine whether systemic adjustments are needed, such as: (i) adjusting the mandates and division of labour to address potential gaps; or conversely (ii) consolidating, ramping down or sunsetting organisations that have already fulfilled their missions, or whose mandates are deemed obsolete, nonessential or redundant. The coherence of donors' multilateral policies and practices should also be considered. Specific areas of interest could include donors' internal coherence (e.g. the coherence between their multilateral and bilateral programmes; the coherence of their programming on acute humanitarian relief, development, and peacebuilding[10]; or their use of whole-of-government approaches) as well as their external coherence (e.g. coherence across donors' funding decisions).
3. **Co-ordination:** The COVID-19 crisis has exposed a lack of collective leadership and co-ordination among both multilateral institutions and multilateral donors, making it clear that multilateral stakeholders still have a long way to go to "work as a system". While most multilateral organisations have ample experience collaborating with their peers (e.g. UN inter-agency collaboration, or project co-financing between multilateral development banks), the magnitude and multidisciplinary dimension of the COVID-19 pandemic calls for broader and more inclusive partnerships between stakeholders with very different mandates and governance models (for example between UN entities and MDBs, or between vertical funds with diverse sectoral mandates). Increasing the impact and efficiency of the multilateral development system calls for symbiotic partnerships (instead of purely opportunistic ones), building on the comparative advantages of each stakeholder across the variety of institutions which make up the multilateral development system. An in-depth review of the strengths and comparative advantages of multilateral actors engaged in the response to the COVID-19 crisis could be a good start to identify synergies and potential for increased collaboration and co-ordination.
4. **Financial capacity:** New development challenges require a change of scale in development finance. While the Addis Ababa Action Agenda has already alluded to the need to turn billions into trillions, the COVID-19 pandemic and its socio-economic implications have intensified the urgency of scaling up the impact of development finance. Building on some of its comparative advantages, the multilateral development system can do so by (i) helping to pool resources from multiple donors for greater impact; (ii) offering a variety of financing instruments that can be tailored to the evolving needs of developing countries; and (iii) mobilising and aligning private finance with the SDGs. For this to happen at the required scale, however, a number of issues currently constraining multilateral development finance need to be solved. For example, the donor community needs to ensure that multilateral organisations are adequately capitalised and funded – both in terms of funding quantity and quality – and that their financial models are well suited to the type of challenges they are asked to address (e.g. country challenges or global public goods). This also means providing them with funding that is predictable, flexible and aligned with their core mandates, and ensuring that multilateral organisations are not vulnerable to the influence of small groups of donors. Finally, donors should push for a more catalytic use of the funding they provide to multilateral organisations in order to tap into the large pool of private finance necessary to reach the trillions target.
5. **Selectivity:** The pandemic implies a double risk for the multilateral development system: it could destroy hard-won development gains while at the same time reducing donors' funding, ultimately increasing the challenge of achieving the SDGs. In this context, a key objective of the multilateral development system should be to optimise the resources made available by multilateral donors by allocating them where they are likely to achieve the greatest impact. This entails improving project

prioritisation to better target those most in need, while keeping in mind demand-side constraints such as the limited absorptive or implementing capacity of some developing countries (including considerations linked to debt sustainability). An important but difficult question is whether the allocation criteria currently used by multilateral organisations are still valid to address challenges that transcend national boundaries, such as the COVID-19 pandemic.[11]

6. **Capacity to adapt:** The pandemic has exacerbated the uncertainty already present in the development landscape and caused by factors such as the shifting multilateral order and the increased probability of extreme events resulting from climate change. In this new context, flexibility must become a key feature in the design and funding of the future multilateral development system. Multilateral organisations need to be able to adapt swiftly to emerging challenges and to a rapidly evolving environment: they should be able to adjust their list of eligible recipients (e.g. to support non-member countries), to establish new partnerships with different types of stakeholders (e.g. private actors), to provide novel types of financing, or to adapt their thematic and geographic priorities. The experience of those multilateral organisations to have already undergone such transformations shows that engaging in such changes can be arduous and time-consuming when a certain degree of flexibility has not been incorporated from the inception in the governance framework and the funding of the organisation.[12] Additional research would be welcome to assess whether the governance and funding modalities of the existing multilateral organisations give them sufficient capacity to adapt quickly to shifting contexts, and to determine whether specific changes in their governance framework could increase their capacity to adapt.

The next two chapters of the report provide insights into the two key phases of the multilateral development finance process within which these reforms should materialise. Chapter 2 focuses on the funding that donors provide to multilateral organisations (multilateral inflows), and outlines the systemic implications of their individual funding decisions. Chapter 3, on the other hand, sheds light on the development activities financed by multilateral organisations, and identifies areas where multilateral entities are expected to increase their contribution.

References

AfDB, ADB, EBRD, EIB, IADB, IMF; WBG (2015), *From billions to trillions: transforming development finance*, World Bank, Washington D.C., http://pubdocs.worldbank.org/en/622841485963735448/DC2015-0002-E-FinancingforDevelopment.pdf. [24]

Ben-Artzi, R. (2016), "Origins, Politics, and Structure of Regional Development Banks", in *Regional Development Banks in Comparison*, Cambridge University Press, Cambridge, http://dx.doi.org/10.1017/cbo9781316681398.005. [16]

Bhattacharya, A. et al. (2018), "The new global agenda and the future of the multilateral development bank system", *Economics Discussion Papers, Kiel Institute for the World Economy* No 2018-26, https://www.brookings.edu/wp-content/uploads/2018/02/epg_paper_on_future_of_mdb_system_jan301.pdf. [40]

Bricker, D. (2019), *World Affairs: Citizens in 24 countries assess engagement in international affairs for a global perspective*, Ipsos, https://www.ipsos.com/sites/default/files/ct/news/documents/2019-11/future-of-the-world-order-2019.pdf. [15]

Canuto, O. (2018), *The World Bank as hummingbird: Leveraging knowledge for development finance*, https://blogs.worldbank.org/eastasiapacific/world-bank-hummingbird-leveraging-knowledge-development-finance. [10]

Chin, G. (2019), "The Asian Infrastructure Investment Bank – New Multilateralism: Early Development, Innovation, and Future Agendas", *Global Policy*, Vol. 10/4, pp. 569-581, http://dx.doi.org/10.1111/1758-5899.12767. [19]

Edelman (2019), "UN Youth Perception Survey", https://www.edelman.com/news-awards/new-survey-reveals-strong-support-of-united-nations-from-millennials. [14]

Eichenauer, V. and B. Reinsberg (2017), "What determines earmarked funding to international development organizations? Evidence from the new multi-bi aid data", *The Review of International Organizations*, Vol. 12/2, pp. 171-197, http://dx.doi.org/10.1007/s11558-017-9267-2. [3]

Engen, L. and A. Prizzon (2018), *A Guide to Multilateral Development Banks`*, Overseas Development Institute, London, https://www.odi.org/sites/odi.org.uk/files/resource-documents/12274.pdf. [17]

G20 (2015), *Multilateral development banks: Action plan to optimize balance sheets*, G20, http://www.g20.utoronto.ca/2015/Multilateral-Development-Banks-Action-Plan-to-Optimize-Balance-Sheets.pdf. [32]

Gartner, D. and H. Kharas (2013), *Scaling up impact: vertical funds and innovative governance*, Brookings, https://www.brookings.edu/wp-content/uploads/2014/11/getting-to-scale-chapter-4.pdf. [18]

Gu, B. (2017), "Chinese Multilateralism in the AIIB", *Journal of International Economic Law*, Vol. 20/1, pp. 137-158, http://dx.doi.org/10.1093/jiel/jgx006. [21]

Gulrajani, N. (2016), *Bilateral versus multilateral channels: Strategic choices for donors*, Overseas Development Institute, London, https://www.odi.org/sites/odi.org.uk/files/resource-documents/10393.pdf. [7]

Humphrey, C. (2020), "All hands on deck: how to scale up multilateral financing to face the Covid-19 crisis", *ODI Briefing Paper*, https://www.odi.org/publications/16832-all-hands-deck-how-scale-multilateral-financing-face-coronavirus-crisis. [39]

Humphrey, C. (2017), "Six proposals to strengthen the finances of multilateral development banks", *ODI Working Paper*, https://www.odi.org/publications/10780-six-proposals-strengthen-finances-multilateral-development-banks. [34]

Inter-agency Task Force on Financing for Development (2020), *Financing for Sustainable Development Report 2020*, United Nations, New York, https://developmentfinance.un.org/fsdr2020. [42]

Kanbur, R. (2015), *What is the World Bank Good For? Global Public Goods and Global Institutions*, https://ssrn.com/abstract=2988848. [31]

Kaul, I. (2017), *Providing global public goods: What role for the multilateral development banks?*, Research Reports and Studies, April 2017, Overseas Development Institute, https://www.odi.org/publications/10784-providing-global-public-goods-what-role-multilateral-development-banks. [28]

Kaul, I. et al. (2015), "Policy debate: Financing the SDGs: Global vs Local Public Goods", *Revue internationale de politique de développement*, Vol. 6.2, https://doi.org/10.4000/poldev.2068. [30]

Kharas, H. (2016), *Rethinking the roles of multilaterals in the global aid architecture*, Brookings, https://www.brookings.edu/wp-content/uploads/2016/07/09_development_aid_kharas2.pdf. [9]

Le Drian, J. and H. Maas (2019), *Who, if not us? An alliance for multilateralism*, https://onu.delegfrance.org/Who-if-not-us-An-alliance-for-multilateralism. [43]

Lichtenstein, N. (2019), "AIIB at Three: A Comparative and Institutional Perspective", *Global Policy*, Vol. 10/4, pp. 582-586, https://doi.org/10.1111/1758-5899.12703. [45]

Martens, B. (2005), "Why Do Aid Agencies Exist?", *Development Policy Review*, pp. 643-663, https://doi.org/10.1111/j.1467-7679.2005.00306.x. [25]

McDade, K. et al. (2019), "Aligning multilateral support for global public goods for health under the Global Action Plan", *Duke Global Working Paper Series*, http://DOI 10.2139/ssrn.3448704. [29]

Milner, H. and D. Tingley (2013), "The Choice for Multilateralism: Foreign Aid and American Foreign Policy", *Review of International Organizations*, Vol. 8/3, pp. 313-341, http://dx.doi.org/10.1007/s11558-012-9153-x. [26]

Nielson, D. (2017), "International organizations and development finance: Introduction to the special issue", *The Review of International Organanizations*, Vol. 12, pp. 157–169, https://doi.org/10.1007/s11558-017-9270-7. [12]

OECD (2020), *Annex 2 - List of ODA-eligible international organisations*, https://www.oecd.org/dac/financing-sustainable-development/development-finance-standards/annex2.htm. [1]

OECD (2020), *COVID-19 Survey - Main Findings*, DAC Working Party on Development Finance Statistics, https://one.oecd.org/document/DCD/DAC/STAT(2020)35/en/pdf. [38]

OECD (2020), *Creditor Reporting System (database)*, OECD, Paris, https://stats.oecd.org/Index.aspx?DataSetCode=crs1. [4]

OECD (2020), *Survey on DAC providers' policies and practices vis-a-vis the multilateral development system*, Unpublished. OECD, Paris. [8]

OECD (2020), *The impact of the coronavirus (COVID-19) crisis on development finance*, OECD Policy Responses to Coronavirus (COVID-19), OECD, Paris, http://www.oecd.org/coronavirus/policy-responses/the-impact-of-the-coronavirus-covid-19-crisis-on-development-finance-9de00b3b/. [35]

OECD (2019), "European Union institutions", in *Development Co-operation Profiles*, OECD Publishing, Paris, https://dx.doi.org/10.1787/c0ad1f0d-en. [5]

OECD (2019), *SDG Financing Lab*, https://sdg-financing-lab.oecd.org/. [27]

OECD (2018), *Multilateral Development Finance: Towards a New Pact on Multilateralism to Achieve the 2030 Agenda Together*, OECD Publishing, Paris, https://doi.org/10.1787/9789264308831-en. [2]

OECD (2011), *Multilateral Aid 2010*, OECD Publishing, Paris, https://dx.doi.org/10.1787/9789264046993-en. [6]

Peters, K. (2006), *Reform And Growth: Evaluating the World Bank Experience*, Routledge, https://www.routledge.com/Reform-and-Growth-Evaluating-the-World-Bank-Experience/Peters/p/book/9781412805230. [11]

Pew Research Center (2019), "Spring 2019 Global Attitudes Survey", https://www.pewresearch.org/wp-content/uploads/2019/09/FT_19.09.23_ViewsOfUN_PewResearchCenter_UNGA_TOPLINE_FOR_RELEASE_Sept_23_2019.pdf. [13]

Reisen, H., M. Soto and T. Weithöner (2004), *Financing Global and Regional Public Goods through ODA: Analysis and Evidence from the OECD Creditor Reporting System*, Working Paper No. 232, OECD Development Centre, Paris, https://www.oecd.org/development/pgd/24482500.pdf. [44]

Rudolph, A. (2017), *The Concept of SDG-Sensitive Development Co-operation: Implications for OECD-DAC Members*, German Development Institute, https://www.die-gdi.de/uploads/media/DP_1.2017.pdf. [23]

Subacchi, P. (2015), *The AIIB is a Threat to Global Economic Governance*, Foreign Policy, https://foreignpolicy.com/2015/03/31/the-aiib-is-a-threat-to-global-economic-governance-china/. [22]

UN (2020), *A UN framework for the immediate socio-economic response to COVID-19*, United Nations, New York, https://unsdg.un.org/resources/un-framework-immediate-socio-economic-response-covid-19. [36]

UN (2020), *Shared responsibility, global solidarity: responding to the socio-economic impacts of Covid-19*, United Nations, New York, https://unsdg.un.org/sites/default/files/2020-03/SG-Report-Socio-Economic-Impact-of-Covid19.pdf. [41]

Wang, H. (2019), "The New Development Bank and the Asian Infrastructure Investment Bank: China's Ambiguous Approach to Global Financial Governance", *Development and Change*, Vol. 50/1, pp. 221-244, http://dx.doi.org/10.1111/dech.12473. [20]

World Bank Group (2020), *Saving Lives, Scaling-Up Impact and Getting Back on Track: World Bank Group Covid-19 Crisis Response Approach Paper*, World Bank Group, Washington D.C., http://documents1.worldbank.org/curated/en/136631594937150795/pdf/World-Bank-Group-COVID-19-Crisis-Response-Approach-Paper-Saving-Lives-Scaling-up-Impact-and-Getting-Back-on-Track.pdf. [37]

World Bank Group (2016), *Statement by Multilateral Development Banks: Delivering on the 2030 Agenda*, World Bank Group, Washington D.C., https://www.worldbank.org/en/news/press-release/2016/10/09/delivering-on-the-2030-agenda-statement. [33]

Notes

[1] For the complete list, see the OECD DAC Annex 2 – List of ODA-eligible international organisations, available at https://www.oecd.org/dac/financing-sustainable-development/development-finance-standards/annex2.htm.

[2] Multilateral ODA are core contributions provided by governments to multilateral organisations. It includes both assessed and voluntary core (unearmarked) contributions.

[3] Earmarked funding, also known as multi-bi or non-core funding, are resources channelled through multilateral organisations over which donors retain some degree of control, and which can be earmarked for a specific country, project, region, sector or theme.

[4] Some recent studies claim that multilaterals no longer enjoy major cost advantages compared to bilateral ones, as their compliance procedures have become more cumbersome and costly while technology has helped smaller donors operate with lower transaction costs (Kharas, 2016[9]; Gulrajani, 2016[7]).

[5] Made up of 44 full regional members, 37 full non-regional members and 20 prospective members (as of 29 June 2020).

[6] Reisen, Soto, & Weithöner (2004[44]) define public goods as follows: "A public good is "a commodity, measure, fact or service which can be consumed by one person without diminishing the amount available for consumption by another person (non-rivalry); which is available at zero or negligible marginal cost to a large or unlimited number of consumers (non-exclusiveness); and which does not bring about disutility to any consumer now or in the future (sustainability). A global public good is an international public good which, while not necessarily to the same extent, benefits consumers all over the world."

[7] At the time of publication of this report, the RRF had received total commitments amounting to USD 2 billion.

[8] OCHA, UNDP and the main international financial institutions (IFIs) have for example been collaborating on this.

[9] Examples of current data gaps include: (i) funding flows to multilateral organisations from non-DAC actors (some data can be obtained on an individual basis from multilateral organisations but not in harmonised and comparable formats); (ii) data on outflows from multilateral organisations (varying quality across multilateral entities reporting to the OECD CRS); (iii) data on private finance mobilised by multilateral organisations (disclosure of such data is currently restricted due to commercial sensitivity and protection of business interests); and (iv) data regarding co-financing arrangements and other forms of collaboration among multilateral organisations (currently not captured in the OECD CRS). The mapping and quantification of existing data gaps in multilateral development finance could be the subject of a forthcoming policy brief.

[10] See the 2019 OECD DAC Recommendations on the Humanitarian-Development-Peace nexus: https://legalinstruments.oecd.org/en/instruments/OECD-LEGAL-5019

[11] In the case of global public bads such as climate change, for example, larger and more sustainable gains may be achieved for those most in need by addressing the root cause of the problem (e.g. reducing CO_2 emissions in high and middle-income countries) than by focusing only on addressing the downstream consequences in low-income countries.

[12] The IADB and AfDB charters, for example, have experienced several rounds of amendments to introduce changes such as opening their membership to countries from outside the region (Lichtenstein, 2019[45]). Building on their 75 years of experience, multilateral shareholders have made flexibility a key feature in the design of the AIIB to ensure that the organisation can adapt to changing circumstances and remain relevant over time.

2 Funding to the multilateral development system

Multilateral organisations rely on the financial contributions of their members, shareholders and other stakeholders to function and carry out their operations. The volume and quality of funding they receive have crucial implications for their capacity to deliver. This chapter presents four key trends in recent funding to the multilateral development system. It also proposes an analytical framework to map the broader implications of the individual funding decisions made by Development Assistance Committee (DAC) members and other multilateral stakeholders. The DAC, whose members remain the largest shareholders and funders of the multilateral development system, retains a central role in multilateral development finance. It needs to make strategic and effective use of its multilateral contributions. The chapter analyses official providers' multilateral portfolio strategies, and explores how the funding base of multilateral organisations can affect their independence and the sustainability of their programmes.

2.1. Key trends of multilateral inflows

2.1.1. Key trend 1: continued growth in funding to multilateral organisations despite growing tensions in the multilateral space

Multilateral contributions from Development Assistance Committee (DAC) and other official providers amounted to USD 71.9 billion in 2018, representing 38% of gross official development assistance (ODA). This represents a 3% increase in real terms over 2017 and a 32.4% increase over the period 2011-2018 (Figure 2.1). DAC members' funding to multilateral organisations amounted to USD 69 billion in 2018 (Figure 2.1, left-hand graph). The 2018 increase was largely driven by rising contributions from some of the largest donors to the multilateral system, such as France (10.7%), the United Kingdom (1.5%), and Germany (0.8%). The increase in their multilateral contributions was strong enough to offset the decline in the contributions of 11 other DAC countries since 2017.

Figure 2.1. Multilateral contributions are growing while the share of bilateral aid is declining

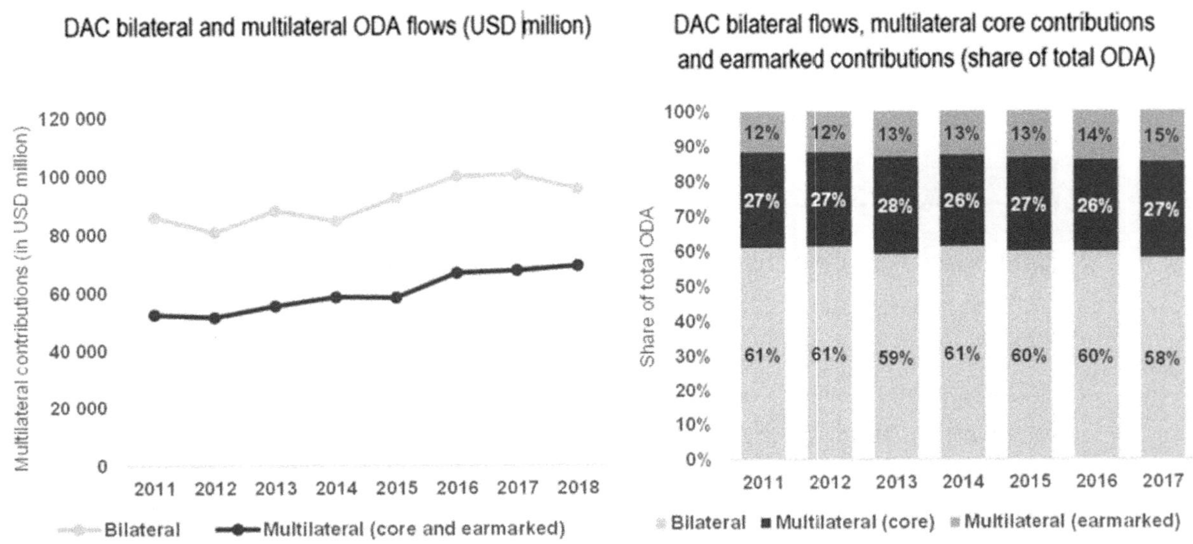

Note: Core contributions are funds added to multilateral organisations' general budgets, while earmarked contributions are tied to projects for specific regions, countries, themes or sectors.
Source: Authors' calculations based on (OECD, 2020[1]), "Creditor Reporting System", https://stats.oecd.org/Index.aspx?DataSetCode=crs1.

StatLink https://doi.org/10.1787/888934177309

The multilateral development system is gaining in importance as a channel of official development assistance. Funding to the multilateral system has followed a steady upwards trend since 2012, with the exception of a brief slowdown between 2014 and 2015. In 2016, the year the 2030 Agenda, the Addis Ababa Action Agenda (AAAA) and the Paris Agreement came into effect, inflows to the multilateral development system grew by 16% (from USD 59.7 billion to USD 69.3 billion). In 2018, the sustained rise of multilateral ODA contrasted with a slight, yet tangible, decrease in bilateral ODA.[1] As a consequence, multilateral ODA accounts for a growing share of development co-operation: while the share of total ODA channelled through multilateral organisations amounted to less than 34% in 2008, it had risen to 38% in 2018. In the case of DAC members specifically, multilateral contributions accounted for 42% of their development co-operation in 2018 (Figure 2.1, right-hand graph).

Funding earmarked through the multilateral system seems to have grown at the expense of pure bilateral ODA. Between 2011 and 2018, the share of earmarked funding to multilateral organisations in DAC members' total ODA rose from just 11% to 15%, while the share of bilateral ODA receded from 62% to 58% over the same period (Figure 2.1, right-hand graph). The share of core contributions, on the other hand, remained stable, at around 27%. This suggests that DAC members' earmarked funding may not be at the expense of core contributions to the multilateral development system, and instead may be additional funding used by DAC members to substitute bilateral aid in areas where multilateral aid can have more impact (e.g. humanitarian response).

2.1.2. Key trend 2: multilateral organisations face increased competition for resources

The United Nations and the World Bank Group are the two main pillars of the multilateral development system, receiving more than three-quarters of multilateral funding. In 2018, they received respectively 49.5% and 28.3% of total funding to multilateral development organisations (Figure 2.2). The various entities that make up the United Nations Development System have experienced a steady increase of multilateral funding contributions since 2012: this is likely driven by their role in addressing recent humanitarian crises, such as the Syrian civil war and the recent refugee crises. Funding to the World Bank Group (WBG), which had been stable since 2012, saw an increase in 2018, due in part to the 2018 International Bank for Reconstruction and Development (IBRD) capital increase.[2] Although they still receive a large share of the funding to the multilateral system, these institutions are increasingly competing for resources with other types of entities.

Regional development banks and vertical funds are slowly gaining ground in the multilateral development finance landscape. Funding to regional development banks grew by 12.2% between 2011 and 2018 (from USD 4.3 billion to USD 6.4 billion), driven by increased contributions to the concessional lending arms of the African Development Bank and Asian Development Bank (the African Development Fund and the Asian Development Fund), and the capital subscriptions to the new Asian Infrastructure Investment Bank (AIIB). Despite the predominant position of the UN and multilateral development banks, vertical funds have also experienced a considerable rise in their volume of funding in recent years, securing an important role in the multilateral development finance space. Between 2012 and 2017, the growth of multilateral contributions to vertical funds was mainly driven by additional funding provided to health and climate-related organisations, such as the Global Fund to Fight AIDS, Tuberculosis and Malaria, the Vaccine Alliance (Gavi), and the recently created Green Climate Fund (GCF).

Figure 2.2. Contributions to the United Nations have increased steadily since 2011

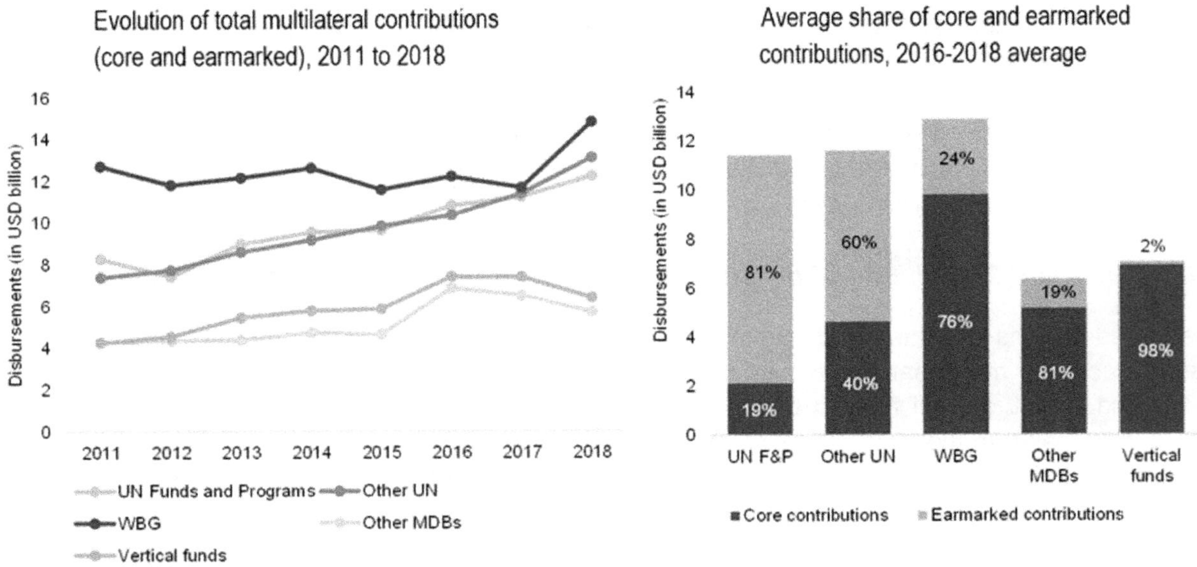

Note: Core contributions are funds added to multilateral organisations' general budgets, while earmarked contributions are tied to projects for specific regions, countries, themes or sectors. UN F&P: United Nations Funds and Programmes; WBG: World Bank Group; MDBs: multilateral development banks.

Source: Authors' calculations based on (OECD, 2020[1]), "Creditor Reporting System", https://stats.oecd.org/Index.aspx?DataSetCode=crs1,

StatLink https://doi.org/10.1787/888934177328

2.1.3. Key trend 3: non-DAC actors account for a growing share of multilateral funding

DAC providers are still the majority shareholders of the multilateral development system. In 2018, DAC donors' contributions made up more than three-quarters of total multilateral funding to the UN Development System. In addition, the share of their core contributions (assessed and voluntary) was considerably higher than that of non-DAC donors, making DAC members a reliable funding source for UN entities.

Although DAC donors retain a central role, emerging economies are becoming increasingly important funders of the multilateral development finance system. This is most apparent in the declining share of DAC funding to the UN system, which decreased from 78% to 71% between 2008 and 2017, despite a rebound to 76% in 2018. Growing contributions from the BRICS to the UN system, coupled with their establishment of new multilateral organisations of which they are main shareholders, such as the AIIB and the New Development Bank, attest to their rise in influence. Their share of total multilateral contributions to the UN system, while still relatively low at around 4% in 2018, has increased steadily over the past decade (Figure 2.3).

Figure 2.3. The share of non-DAC funding to the UNDS increased from 22% to 29% between 2008 and 2017

Volume and share of DAC and non-DAC multilateral contributions to the UNDS, 2008-2017 (USD million, 2018 prices)

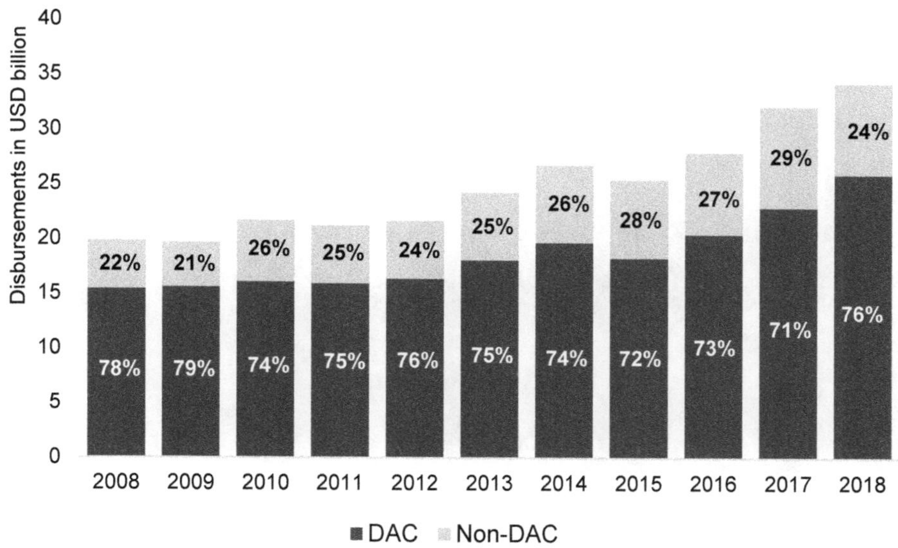

Source: Authors' calculations based on (UNDESA, 2018[2]), unpublished dataset provided by the United Nations Department of Economic and Social Affairs (UNDESA).

StatLink https://doi.org/10.1787/888934177347

Philanthropic foundations and other private actors represent a sizeable source of multilateral finance in some sectors. Despite the record-setting contributions of DAC donors to the multilateral system in 2018, multilateral organisations are gradually broadening their donor base beyond sovereign states, towards the private sector and philanthropic funding (Graham, 2017[3]). The increasing involvement of non-state actors in funding the multilateral system gives these emerging stakeholders influence in multilateral organisations' priorities. Although the level of funding from non-state actors varies across multilateral organisations, the weight of private funders is generally increasing. In aggregate, private actors provided USD 1.97 billion in contributions to the UN system in 2018 (nearly 6% of total contributions to the UN), making them the sixth overall contributor to UN entities (Figure 2.4).

Figure 2.4. Private actors are the sixth biggest contributor to the UN Development System

Top 25 contributors to the United Nations Development System in 2018

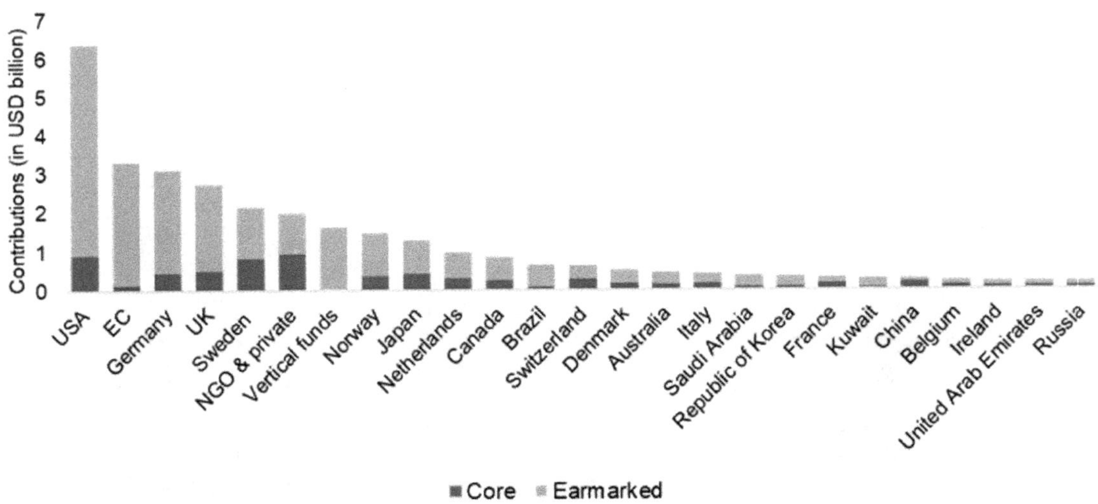

Note: Disbursements in USD billion, 2018 prices.
Source: Authors' calculations based on (UNDESA, 2018[2]), unpublished dataset provided by the United Nations Department of Economic and Social Affairs.

StatLink https://doi.org/10.1787/888934177366

2.1.4. Key trend 4: earmarked contributions are rising, prompting concerns over the quality of multilateral funding

Both core and earmarked contributions to the multilateral system have increased over the 2011-2018 period. Core contributions rose from USD 37.9 billion to USD 46.4 billion, while earmarked contributions grew from USD 16.4 billion to USD 25.5 billion over the same period. However, the analysis reveals that earmarked funding has been growing at a faster pace (+7.8%) than multilateral core contributions (+3.8%), and now represents 35% of multilateral contributions (up from 30% in 2011).

The growth of multilateral funding is primarily driven by the rise of earmarked aid channelled through the multilateral system. Although historical data on earmarked flows are scarce, recent research suggests that earmarked aid has quadrupled since the early 2000s (Eichenauer and Reinsberg, 2017[4]). In parallel, multilateral organisations have witnessed a surge in the number of trust funds created to channel and manage the rising flows of earmarked funding: the World Bank is a textbook case, seeing the number of active trust funds it manages skyrocket to reach more than 1 000 by the early 2010s (OECD, 2015[5]; Reinsberg, 2017[6]).[3] However, similar trends can be observed for other multilateral organisations.

The rise of earmarked contributions spurs concerns over a growing "bilateralisation" of multilateral aid. Several studies have pointed out that continued growth of earmarked aid could undermine multilateral effectiveness, especially if it is not accompanied by an increase in core resources. Possible negative implications mentioned in recent research include: (i) a mismatch between the allocation of earmarked flows and the strategic priorities of multilateral organisations (OECD, 2018[7]); (ii) the use of earmarked funding to steer multilateral programmes towards donors' geopolitical interests – a trend labelled as "Trojan multilateralism" by Sridhar and Woods (2013[8]); (iii) reduced partner country ownership, in particular for non-country-specific earmarked funding (Reinsberg, 2017[9]); and (iv) lack of donor co-ordination and accountability (Weinlich et al., 2020[10]).

The rise of earmarking is mainly attributable to the spike in humanitarian interventions of the past decade. Humanitarian interventions account for a large share of the funding earmarked by DAC members through the multilateral development system. In 2018, humanitarian aid made up 44% of DAC members' total earmarked funding, followed by social (17%) and governance interventions (13%). Taken together, these three sectors accounted for almost 75% of the earmarked contributions received by the multilateral development system in 2018. Figure 2.5 shows that earmarked funding for humanitarian purposes has accelerated since 2013, and peaked at USD 10.6 billion in 2017.

Figure 2.5. Humanitarian aid experienced a sharp increase between 2012 and 2017

Evolution of earmarked contributions by sector

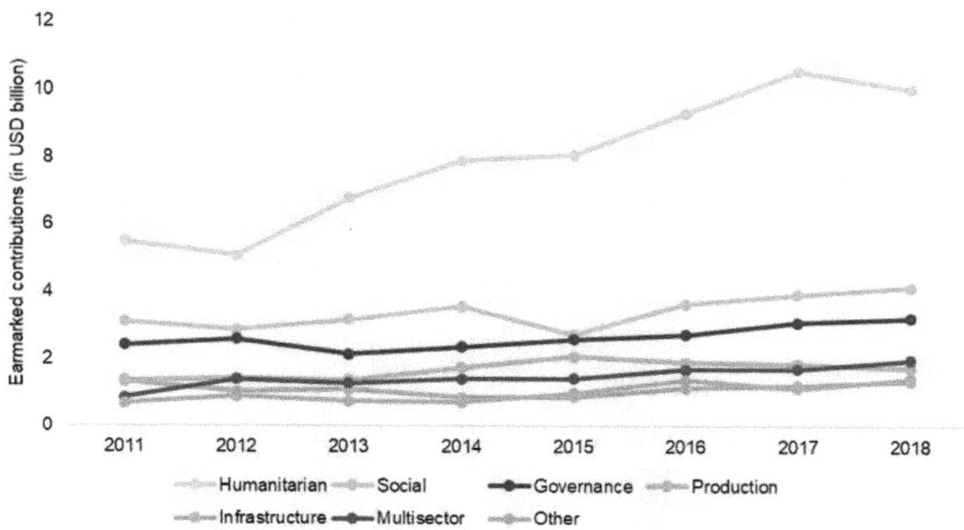

Note: Disbursements, in USD billion, 2018 prices.
Source: Authors' calculations based on (OECD, 2020[1]), "Creditor Reporting System", https://stats.oecd.org/Index.aspx?DataSetCode=crs1.

StatLink https://doi.org/10.1787/888934177385

2.2. Strategic relevance and role of DAC members' funding to multilateral organisations

2.2.1. Donors' funding policies and practices are reshaping the multilateral development landscape

DAC members' multilateral contributions are vital to the multilateral development system. They provide the financial resources necessary to allow multilateral organisations to function and to carry out their operational activities. Some multilateral organisations are also able to use the ODA received from their members and shareholders as a financial lever to raise additional resources. For example, multilateral development banks use their balance sheets for financial leverage.

The quantity and quality of DAC multilateral funding have strategic implications for the performance of the multilateral development system. The funding modalities used by multilateral donors affect the governance of multilateral organisations, influence their strategic priorities and their allocations of funds, and condition their operational capacities (Figure 2.6). This, in turn, has implications for the level of ambition and agility of the multilateral development system, and its ability to respond effectively to global development challenges. **As the largest funders and shareholders of the multilateral development system, DAC members hold a responsibility to ensure the system is adequately equipped to deliver global development solutions.** It is, therefore, necessary for DAC members to develop funding approaches that support the DAC's collective vision, and expectations, of the multilateral development system. Figure 2.6 depicts the impact that some key parameters of multilateral ODA – the volume of funding and the relative level of core contributions – can have on the multilateral development system. While the characteristics of multilateral funding go well beyond these two parameters, this simple framework depicts the implications of DAC members' funding decisions for the system.

Figure 2.6. The volume and characteristics of multilateral aid influence the multilateral system

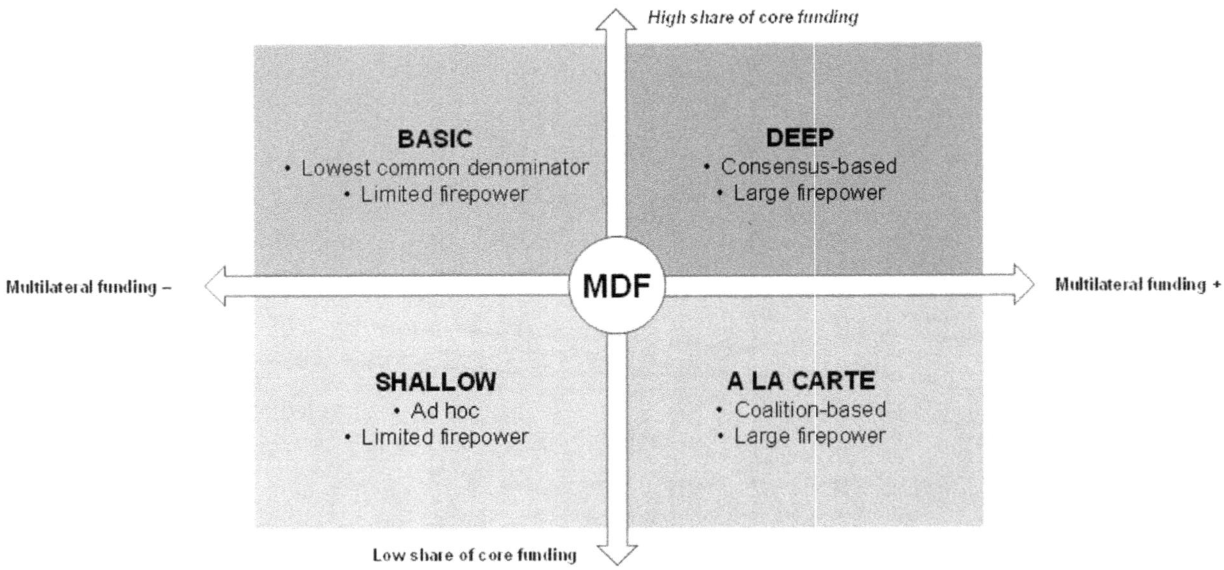

Source: Authors' design, adapted from (Grimm and Weinlich, 2020[11]), "Multilateralism without future – or the future of multilateralism?", https://blogs.die-gdi.de/2020/01/08/multilateralism-without-future-or-the-future-of-multilateralism/.

The quadrant presents four possible funding models for the multilateral development system based on the two parameters mentioned above:

Quadrant 1: Deep multilateralism:

- Funding characteristics: multilateral donors provide large volumes of funding to the multilateral development system, mostly as core contributions.
- Implications: the multilateral development system has significant financial firepower to address global development challenges. Strategic decisions are taken based on consensus among members or shareholders in the governing boards of multilateral organisations, while multilateral organisations retain significant programmatic and operational control, and agility, in the design of their operations and the allocation of funds.

Quadrant 2 : Multilateralism "à la carte":

- Funding characteristics: multilateral donors provide large volumes of funding to the multilateral development system but earmark a large share of these contributions.
- Implications: the multilateral development system has significant financial firepower to address global development challenges, but its shareholders retain significant control over the design of operations and the allocation of funds. This funding model could favour the formation of coalitions

whereby donors pool resources with like-minded peers and channel them through the multilateral development system to address specific development challenges.

Quadrant 3: Basic multilateralism:

- Funding characteristics: multilateral donors provide limited volumes of funding to the multilateral development system, mostly as core contributions.
- Implications: the multilateral development system has limited financial firepower to respond to global development challenges. Decisions are taken by its members or shareholders based on consensus reflecting the least common denominator. This funding model entails a focus on a narrower set of strategic priorities that enjoy consensual support from the majority shareholders or funders of the multilateral development system.

Quadrant 4: Shallow multilateralism:

- Funding characteristics: multilateral donors provide limited volumes of funding to the multilateral development system, with a relatively low share of core funding.
- Implications: this limits the multilateral development system's financial firepower to respond to global development challenges, and its shareholders earmark a relatively high share of their contributions to retain control over the design of operations and the allocation of funds. This results in a multilateral development system with minimal ability to contribute to global development challenges, and whose agenda is largely driven, and possibly influenced, by ad-hoc funding decisions by a few large donors.

Towards an "à la carte" multilateral development system?

Though the past two decades have seen a significant rise in the total volume of funding provided to multilateral organisations, the share of core funding has decreased. Between 2000 and 2018, multilateral funding more than doubled, from USD 33 billion to USD 71.9 billion. Due to the increased use of earmarking modalities, the share of earmarked (non-core) contributions in total multilateral ODA rose by 29 percentage points, from 6% to 35%.

The analysis suggests that the system is evolving towards an approach increasingly based on ad-hoc coalitions. The growing use of earmarked funding shows that multilateral donors are progressively forsaking the search for consensus, and increasingly choosing to join forces on an ad hoc basis with a narrower set of donors to address specific development challenges. Recent research points to the risk of seeing the emergence of a hollow and less inclusive multilateral development system, where decision making and accountability are transferred from the wider collective (e.g. governing boards) to contracting relationships between bilateral donors and multilateral agencies (Barder, Ritchie and Rogerson, 2019[12]).

This trend towards "à la carte" approaches largely reflects the growing divide among the main funders of the multilateral development system. As long as donors to the multilateral system share a common vision of the system, they are more inclined to provide core (unearmarked) contributions since they are confident that the strategic priorities of multilateral organisations reflect this broad consensus. Yet in recent years, the shareholders and funders of the multilateral development system have expressed increasingly diverging views on the roles, strategic priorities and performance of multilateral organisations.[4] This is likely to influence their funding decisions and in particular their choice of funding modalities. This divergence may also in part explain the growing use of funding modalities that allow them to retain control over funding allocations (such as contributions tightly earmarked for specific projects or locations), thus bypassing the strategic directions set by the governing boards of multilateral organisations.

Yet the sustained rise of DAC members' multilateral contributions attests to the continued relevance of multilateral organisations in the global development landscape. The volume of ODA that donors choose to provide to, or channel through, the multilateral development system is in part conditioned by their trust in the relevance and effectiveness of multilateral organisations. Donors are more likely to increase their funding to multilateral organisations if they consider that they deliver effectively and provide good value for money. Deeper multilateralism can therefore only be achieved if multilateral stakeholders trust in and share a common vision for the multilateral development system.[5]

Figure 2.7. The rise of earmarked funding reflects a shift towards "à la carte" approaches

Evolution of the funding received by the multilateral development system as share of core funding (vertical axis) and changes in multilateral contributions since 2000 (horizontal axis)

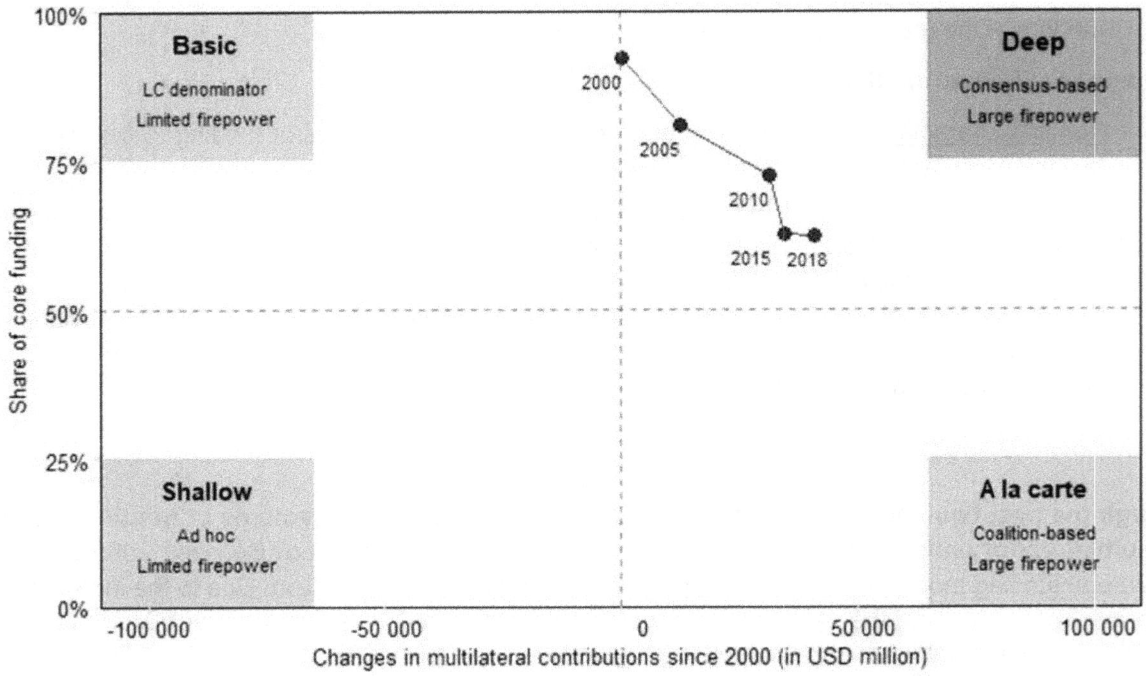

Note: The changes in the volume of multilateral contributions (horizontal axis) are calculated as a five-year moving average.
Source: Authors' calculations based on 2000-2010 data from (Eichenauer and Reinsberg, 2017[4]), "What determines earmarked funding to international development organizations? Evidence from the new multi-bi aid data", https://www.ipz.uzh.ch/de/forschung/lehrstuehle/ep/research/internationaldevelopment/multi-bi-aid/data.html, and on 2011-2018 data from (OECD, 2020[1]), "Creditor Reporting System", https://stats.oecd.org/Index.aspx?DataSetCode=crs1.

StatLink https://doi.org/10.1787/888934177404

Access to, and quality of, funding is uneven across multilateral organisations

UN funds and programmes are high-profile institutions that tend to receive large volumes of multilateral ODA. For example, this is the case for the World Food Programme, which received contributions amounting to USD 10 795 million between 2017 and 2018, and to a lesser extent UNICEF (USD 7 057 million) and UNHCR (USD 6 310 million). However, these organisations receive a large part of their funding as earmarked contributions, providing them with little funding stability or flexibility, and limiting their control over the allocation of funds or the design of their operations, meaning they fall into the "à la carte" category (Figure 2.7 and Figure 2.8). Other UN entities (outside of the UN funds and programmes) present a more varied profile, both in terms of the volume and quality of their funding (Figure 2.8).

Owing to their particular business model, the concessional arms of multilateral development banks receive large volumes of funding, a significant share of which are core (unearmarked)

contributions. The World Bank's IDA, for instance, received a total of USD 18 296 million between 2017 and 2018, 99% of which was provided as core contributions. The concessional arms of the African Development Bank and the Asian Development Bank follow the same pattern: the African Development Fund (ADF) received USD 4 088 million in 2017-2018, of which 99% corresponded to core contributions, and the Asian Development Fund (AsDF) received USD 1 299 million and a similar share of core funding.

Vertical funds receive most of their funding as core contributions, but the amounts involved vary largely according to the profile of the organisation. For example, the Global Fund received USD 6 455 million over the period 2017-2018, compared to less than USD 208 million in the case of the Adaptation Fund. Although many vertical funds fall within the quadrant of "deep multilateralism", these results should be interpreted with caution since core funding to vertical funds is sometimes viewed as an implicit way for development partners to earmark their multilateral contributions to specific development themes or challenges.

Figure 2.8. UN Funds and Programmes receive high shares of earmarked (non-core) contributions, placing them in the "à la carte" quadrant

Share of core contributions in total multilateral funding (vertical axis) and 2017-2018 volume of multilateral funding, disbursements in USD million, 2018 prices (horizontal axis)

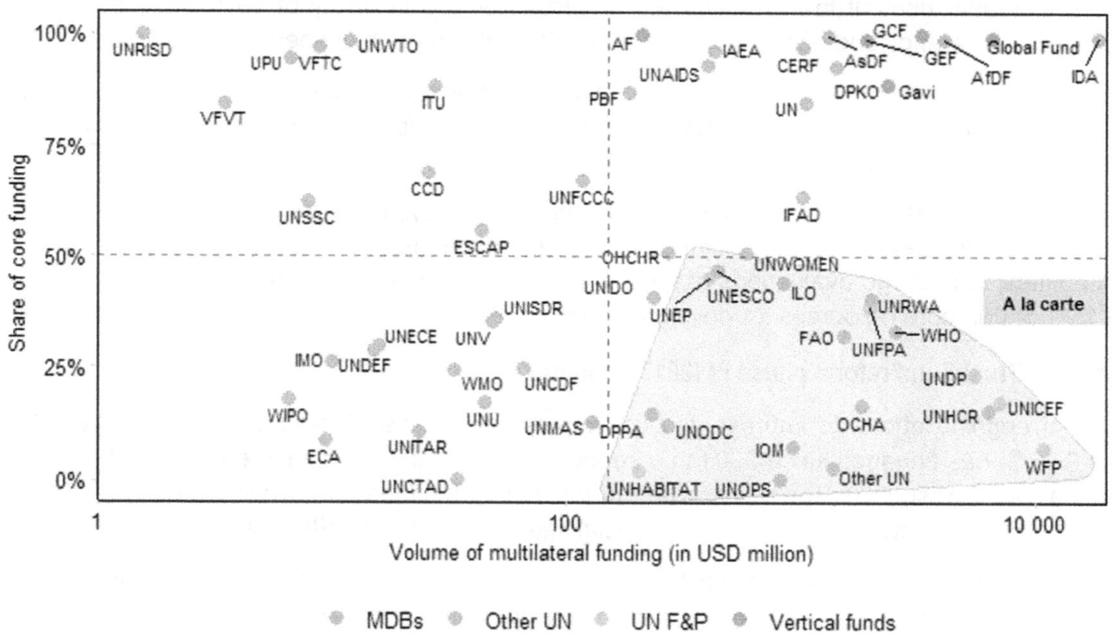

Note: The analysis excludes the non-concessional windows of multilateral development banks, as these entities finance a significant share of their operations from other sources of financing (e.g. by leveraging their balance sheets and borrowing from the international capital markets).
Source: Authors' calculations based on (OECD, 2020[1]), "Creditor Reporting System", https://stats.oecd.org/Index.aspx?DataSetCode=crs1.

StatLink https://doi.org/10.1787/888934177423

Funding patterns depend largely on the mandate and governance structure of multilateral organisations. The funding model and governance of the multilateral development banks' concessional windows (e.g. IDA, ADF and AsDF), for example, explains in large part their position in the quadrant: these entities are replenished on a multiannual basis following the negotiation of financing and policy packages that determine the volume of funding committed by their members and define a set of strategic priorities for the windows in a spirit of consensus. On the other hand, the fact that UN entities receive a relatively large share of their funding as earmarked contributions owes in part to their traditional role in crisis and emergency response, which by nature is more contingent and less predictable (even though the UN also makes available to development partners contingency funds accepting core funding to counter the growing use of earmarked funding).

In recent years, the growing concerns over the quality of donors' contributions have prompted multilateral organisations to launch a set of institutional reforms. Most prominent among these initiatives is the UN Funding Compact launched by the United Nations Secretary General in 2019, and the World Bank Trust Fund reform, which is currently in its fourth phase (Box 2.1).

Box 2.1. The UN and the World Bank are leading the recent reform drive to improve the quality of multilateral aid

UN Funding Compact (2019)

The UN Funding Compact is an initiative proposed in July 2017 by the UN Secretary-General, Mr Antonio Guterres, to address the deteriorating quality of the funding received by UN entities, and the growing fragmentation of the UN system. The Funding Compact is a pact between the UN Development System – UNDS – (also known as UN Sustainable Development Group) and its member states, whereby the latter commit to increasing the predictability and flexibility of their funding in return for increased transparency and accountability from UNDS entities on their spending and results.

More specifically, UN members commit to increase the share of their core contributions to at least 30% by 2023 and to double their contributions to interagency pooled funds (to a total of USD 3.4 billion) and entity-specific thematic funds (to USD 800 million) over the same period.

The UNDS, for its part, commits to provide annual reporting on system-wide results by 2021; to enhance the visibility of member states' core contributions; to enhance the transparency of financial information for all entities; to undergo evaluations of results; to further harmonise cost recovery; and to allocate at least 15% of non-core resources for development joint activities.

World Bank Trust Fund reform phase IV (2017-ongoing)

As part of ongoing efforts to improve its business model and development impact, the World Bank Group (WBG) has engaged since 2001 in a series of reforms of its management of trust funds. These reforms aimed to respond to the rapid growth of the WBG trust fund portfolio in the early 2000s, which saw the number of active trust funds and financial intermediary funds (FIFs) skyrocket.

The first three phases of the reform process focused respectively on: strengthening financial controls and oversight (phase I: 2001-2007); mainstreaming trust funds in WBG processes and procedures (phase II: 2007-2013); and improving the strategic oversight and management of the entire trust fund life cycle (phase III: 2013-2017). In addition, the second and third phases also tried to reduce the inefficiencies caused by the proliferation of small trust funds by progressively raising the minimum threshold to establish new trust funds to USD 1 million first (phase II), and USD 2 million (phase III).

Phase IV of the trust funds reform process, which was launched in 2017 and is still ongoing, aims to align the World Bank Groups' portfolio of trust fund and FIFs with the organisation's priorities. It also aims to further reduce the fragmentation of its portfolio, which still counts a large number of small trust funds representing relatively small financial amounts: at the end of FY18, for example, 90% of WBG trust funds accounted for less than 26% of the organisation's total portfolio value).

The current reforms revolve around three key pillars: (i) the creation of "Umbrella 2.0" Programs that can include multiple "associated" trust funds to reduce fragmentation; (ii) the strengthening of trust funds' integration into World Bank strategy, planning and budgeting processes; and (iii) the implementation of efficiency measures to streamline internal processes for the management of trust funds.

Source: (UN, 2019[13]), "Funding Compact: Report of the Secretary-General", https://www.un.org/ecosoc/sites/www.un.org.ecosoc/files/files/en/qcpr/SGR2019-Add%201%20-%20Funding%20Compact%20-%2018%20April%202019.pdf, and (World Bank Group, 2019[14]), "2018-2019 Trust Fund Annual Report: Value proposition of World Bank Group trust funds", http://documents.worldbank.org/curated/en/461611570786898020/Trust-Fund-Annual-Report-for-2018-2019.

2.2.2. DAC members use their funding strategically to support and influence the multilateral development system

DAC members' multilateral contributions reveal a large variety of portfolio strategies

In 2018, the United Kingdom surpassed the United States as the largest donor to the multilateral development system in absolute terms, owing both to the growth of its multilateral contributions from USD 10.7 billion in 2017 to USD 10.9 billion in 2018 (+3.3%) and to the concurrent drop of US multilateral funding over the same period, from USD 11.4 billion to USD 10.2 billion (-11%). In comparison, the 2018 DAC average stood at USD 2.4 billion (+2% compared to 2017), and Iceland remained the smallest DAC multilateral donor, at USD 39 million (Figure 2.9).

Figure 2.9. In 2018, the United Kingdom surpassed the United States as the largest funder of the multilateral development system

Multilateral contributions of the eight largest funders of the multilateral development system (2011-2018)

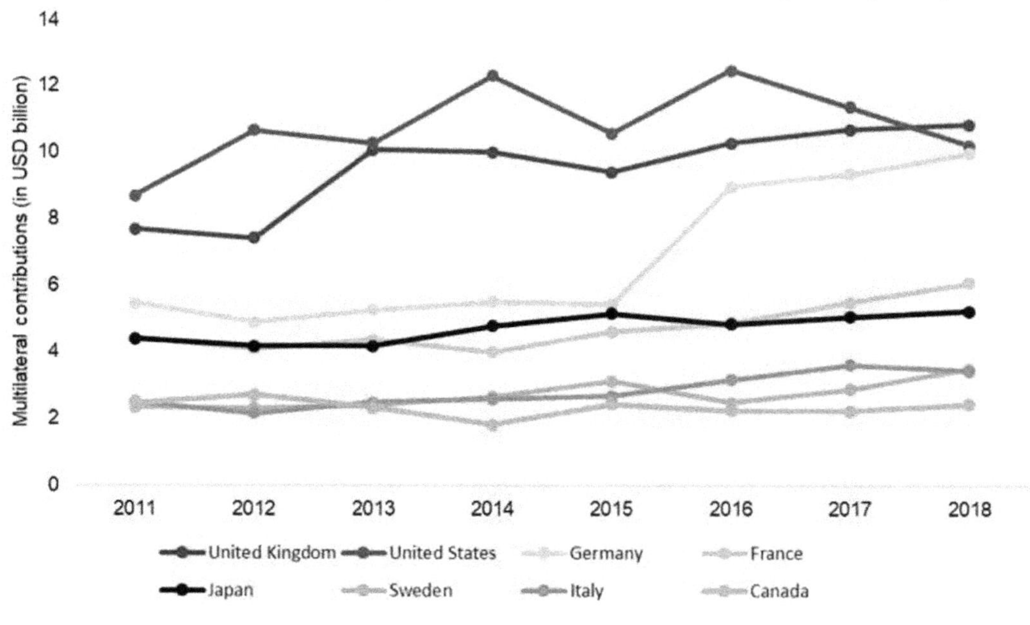

Note: Note: Disbursements, in USD billion, 2018 prices.
Source: Authors' calculations based on (OECD, 2020[1]), "Creditor Reporting System", https://stats.oecd.org/Index.aspx?DataSetCode=crs1.

StatLink https://doi.org/10.1787/888934177442

Large providers of multilateral aid tend to have large and diversified portfolios, reflecting their search for influence in the global development landscape. This is the case for the United Kingdom, the United States, Germany, France and Japan, for example. (Figure 2.10) shows the volume of DAC members' multilateral

ODA and the level of concentration of their multilateral portfolio, measured as a Herfindahl-Hirschman Index (HHI). The high level of diversification observed in the multilateral portfolios of the main ODA providers attests to their willingness to weigh in on a wide range of issues and development challenges in order to position themselves as major actors on the multilateral stage.

Small providers, on the other hand, present more diverse portfolio strategies. For small ODA providers, concentrated portfolios reduce the transaction costs involved in maintaining a large number of multilateral partnerships. This is the case for many small European countries, which tend to have highly concentrated portfolios as they channel a large share of their multilateral ODA through the European Union. Other small multilateral funders, however, choose to maintain diversified multilateral portfolios: for example, Denmark, Ireland, Finland, Korea, New Zealand and Switzerland all have portfolio concentration indices inferior to 10.

Figure 2.10. The financial clout of multilateral donors plays a key role in their portfolio management strategies

Concentration of DAC providers' multilateral portfolio: scale from 0 (less concentrated) to 100 (most concentrated) and volume of multilateral contributions 2017-2018 (disbursements in USD million, 2018 prices)

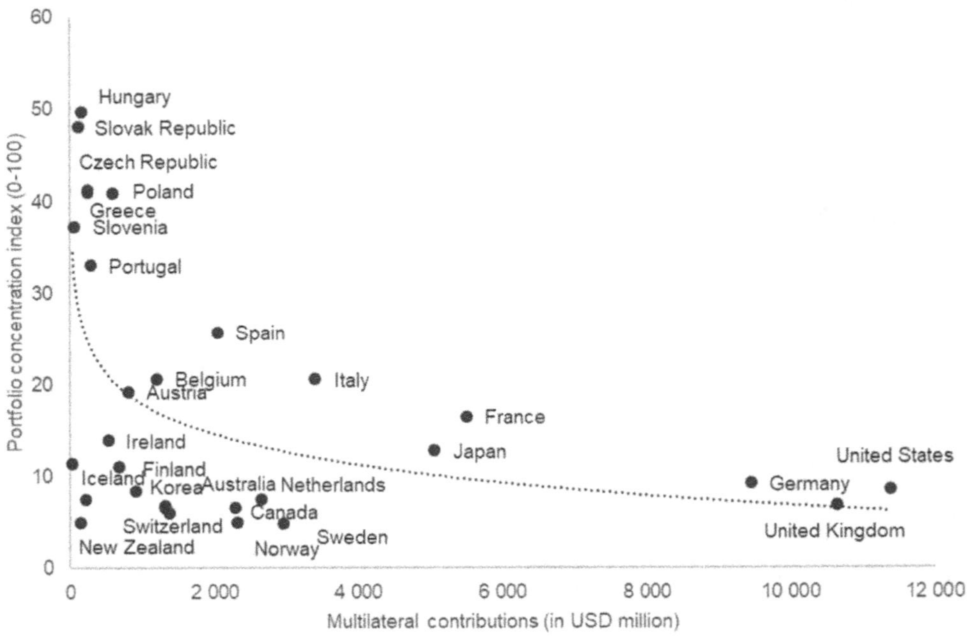

Note: The concentration index (vertical axis) is calculated as a Herfindahl-Hirschman Index (HHI), a commonly accepted measure of market concentration. The index takes into consideration both (i) the number of multilateral organisations that each donor contributes to; and (ii) the relative weight of each organisation in its portfolio. Multilateral contributions (horizontal axis) include both core and earmarked funding.
Source: Authors' calculations based on (OECD, 2020[1]), "Creditor Reporting System", https://stats.oecd.org/Index.aspx?DataSetCode=crs1.

StatLink https://doi.org/10.1787/888934177461

Multilateral contributions also reflect DAC providers' varying levels of effort to support the multilateral development system. Considering DAC providers' total support to the multilateral system in light of their share of the DAC gross national income (GNI) helps to distinguish countries that punch above their weight and those that provide less than their equal share of multilateral ODA. The Nordic countries, the United Kingdom, Switzerland, Luxembourg and the Netherlands perform well on this measure. Sweden, Norway and Luxembourg stand out in particular, contributing more than three times their share of multilateral funding (Figure 2.11). This analysis shows, among other things, that the largest multilateral donors are not necessarily the most generous in their support for the multilateral development system.

Figure 2.11. Nordic countries are particularly generous multilateral supporters

Annual funding to multilateral organisations relative to countries' share in overall DAC GNI (2016-2018 average)

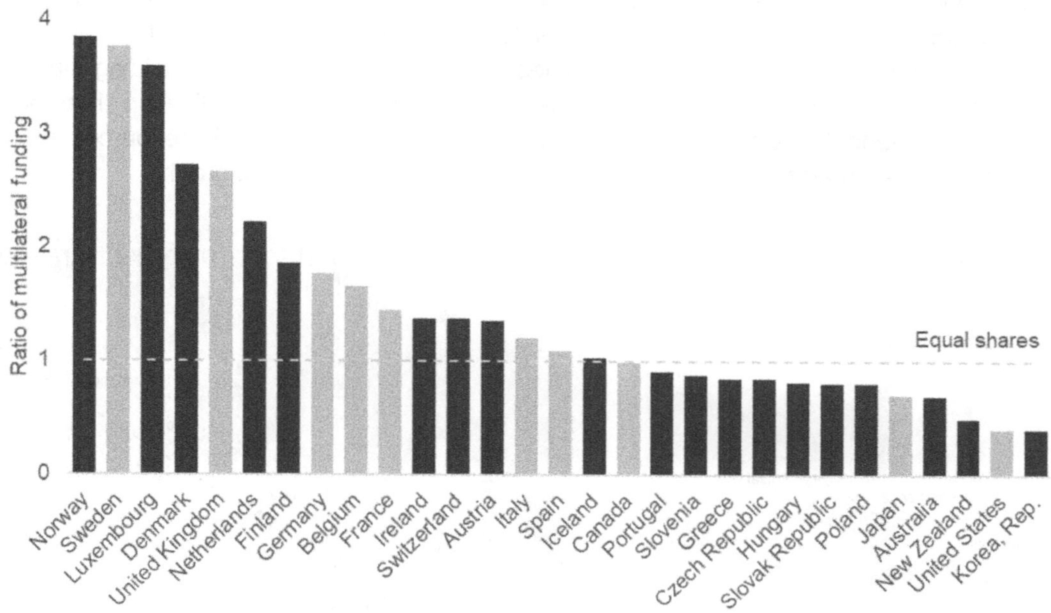

Note: The top 10 DAC multilateral donors are shown in light blue, while all other DAC countries are shown in dark blue. The calculations include both core and earmarked contributions.
Source: Authors' calculations, adapted from (McArthur and Rasmussen, 2017[15]), "Who funds which multilateral organizations?", https://www.brookings.edu/research/who-funds-which-multilateral-organizations/ and based on data from (OECD, 2020[1]), "Creditor Reporting System", https://stats.oecd.org/Index.aspx?DataSetCode=crs1.

StatLink https://doi.org/10.1787/888934177480

DAC members use a strategic mix of funding modalities to diversify their multilateral portfolios

Donors use different funding modalities in their engagement with multilateral organisations. While multilateral funding has traditionally been provided as core contributions, recent decades have seen a surge in the use of earmarked contributions (also known as non-core or multi-bi contributions). Earmarked multilateral funding is often presented as a "third way", combining the advantages and shortcomings of bilateral and multilateral approaches. However, recent research has emphasised that, far from being a monolithic bloc, multilateral earmarked contributions span a wide range of funding modalities (Eichenauer and Reinsberg, 2017[4]; Weinlich et al., 2020[10]). The policy brief on DAC members' earmarking practices that accompanies this report provides some insights into the different types of earmarking modalities used by DAC members (OECD, 2020[16]). It also includes a set of interactive data visualisations to explore the earmarking practices of individual DAC countries, and a decision tree to guide donors in their choice of funding modalities, drawing on recent research and evidence gathered through OECD development co-operation peer reviews (OECD, 2020[17]).

Core and earmarked contributions to the multilateral development system have different purposes and sectoral targets. An analysis of the multilateral activities funded from core and earmarked contributions reveals that DAC providers often use earmarked contributions to carry out urgent and highly specialised interventions, such as humanitarian aid (emergency response, reconstruction, relief and rehabilitation). Figure 2.12 shows that humanitarian aid accounts for 37% of DAC members' portfolio of earmarked contributions, compared with 17% for social sectors, 14% for governance-related interventions, 11% for production and only 8% for infrastructure (Figure 2.12, left-hand graph).

Activities funded from multilateral organisations' core resources seem to focus overwhelmingly on sectors requiring longer-term interventions, such as infrastructure (28% of core resources), social sectors (23%), and production (19%). Governance is the only sector that is equally targeted by core and earmarked resources (14%), although this is likely related to the mixed nature of activities falling within this category, which include both crisis response activities (conflict prevention, peace-building, human rights) and longer-term ones (public financial management, domestic resource mobilisation, macroeconomic policy). On the other hand, the activities funded by multilateral organisations' core resources appear to be largely aligned with DAC members' direct bilateral aid (Figure 2.12, right-hand graph).

Figure 2.12. Donors tend to favour earmarked contributions for short-term, emergency responses

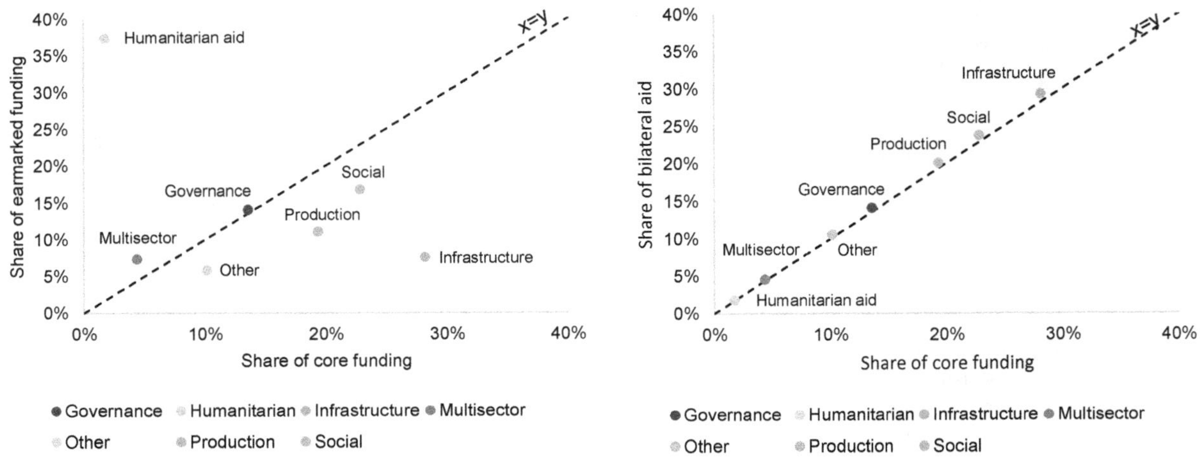

Note: These charts show the 2016-2018 share of DAC multilateral core funding (horizontal axis), multilateral earmarked funding (left-hand graph, vertical axis) and bilateral funding (right-hand graph, vertical axis) devoted to each sector. The line of equality corresponds to cases where the sector represents the same share of DAC bilateral and earmarking portfolios.
Source: Authors' calculations based on (OECD, 2020[1]), "Creditor Reporting System", https://stats.oecd.org/Index.aspx?DataSetCode=crs1.

StatLink https://doi.org/10.1787/888934177499

2.2.3. Multilateral organisations' funding base influences their level of dependence and vulnerability

Multilateral organisations tend to have highly concentrated funding bases. In 2018, for example, the United Nations Development System received USD 34.3 billion in funding, more than one-third of which (36%, or USD 12.3 billion) was provided by only three of the UN's 195 members: the United States, the United Kingdom and Germany. This suggests that, despite the progressive diversification of multilateral funding sources observed in recent years, the funding of traditional multilateral organisations remains dependent on a "vital few". This also means that some donors to the multilateral system (whether public or private) may find themselves in a position to influence the thematic or geographical priorities of specific multilateral entities, either directly (e.g. by earmarking their funding to specific topics, regions or projects) or indirectly (e.g. by using the threat of funding cuts like a sword of Damocles).

Entities with highly concentrated donor bases and poor funding quality are more vulnerable to the influence of individual donors. Figure 2.13 uses a Herfindahl-Hirschman Index (HHI) as a measure of donor concentration, and the ratio of core funding received by multilateral organisations as a proxy for funding quality. Multilateral entities with a highly concentrated donor base and a large share of funding as earmarked contributions appear particularly vulnerable to the influence of their funders (upper right-hand quadrant). **The WHO is a case in point (**Box 2.2**).** Conversely, entities with a diversified donor base and a substantial portion of their funding provided as core contributions are likely to receive funding flows that are both more stable over time and more predictable, and should also be less easily diverted from the strategic priorities set by their governing boards (lower left-hand quadrant).

Figure 2.13. Several UN entities present high funding vulnerability

Concentration of multilateral organisations' donor base - scale from 0 (less concentrated) to 100 (most concentrated) 2016-2018 share of earmarked funding

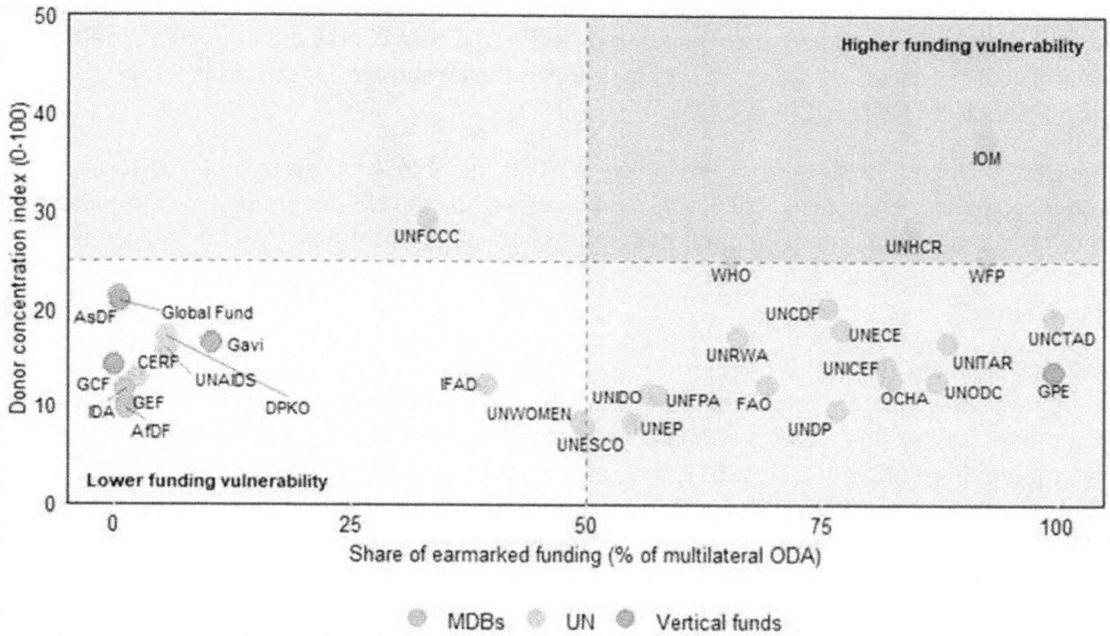

Note: The analysis focuses on multilateral organisations that are largely reliant on donors' multilateral contributions to finance their core functions and their operational activities. For this reason, the analysis excludes the non-concessional arms of multilateral development banks, which derive a significant share of their financing from other sources (e.g. by borrowing from the market).
Source: Authors' calculations based on (OECD, 2020[11]), "Creditor Reporting System", https://stats.oecd.org/Index.aspx?DataSetCode=crs1.

StatLink https://doi.org/10.1787/888934177518

The multilateral organisations' funding bases vary largely according to their governance model. Figure 2.13 shows that multilateral development banks tend to have diversified donor bases, owing to their relatively large membership base. The Development Bank of Latin America (CAF) is an exception, as it counts only 19 country shareholders. UN entities also have, on average, a relatively diversified funding base, although those UN entities are known to receive a high share of earmarked funding (e.g. IOM, WHO, UNHCR and WFP) seem to lose in financial independence what they gain in volume of operations by accepting large quantities of earmarked funding. Finally, vertical and thematic funds appear to have relatively concentrated funding sources. While this may be in part explained by their narrower thematic focus, it also raises questions regarding their potential vulnerability to the influence of their funders (including non-state actors, which have become significant funders, and influencers, of the multilateral development system).

These findings call for increased attention from the DAC and other multilateral stakeholders to ensure that multilateral organisations retain sufficient independence. The funding vulnerability of multilateral organisations also warrants more in-depth research: future analyses should explore how the governance and business models of the different multilateral organisations affect their funding vulnerability. For instance, the fact that some institutions are able to leverage their balance sheets and borrow from the market is likely to provide them with a higher degree of independence.

Box 2.2. Funding vulnerability: the case of the World Health Organisation

The World Health Organisation (WHO), a specialised agency of the United Nations system with the mandate to direct and co-ordinate international public health, has attracted a lot of public attention since the outbreak of the COVID-19 crisis. The organisation has been criticised by several countries for its handling of the pandemic. It has also been at the centre of a controversy after being charged by its top funder, the United States, for being slow to respond to the threat and for being biased in favour of the People's Republic of China ("China").

As a result, the United States announced in July 2020 its intent to withdraw from the WHO – a decision that should come into effect on 6 July 2021 – and declared that the US government would cut all funding to the organisation. This announcement has spurred concerns from policy makers and development practitioners over the potential financial and operational implications of a funding cut in the middle of a major pandemic.

The WHO's biannual budget is funded from two main sources: (i) the assessed contributions of its members (equivalent to countries' membership fees); and (ii) the voluntary contributions received from WHO member states and other stakeholders (such as philanthropies, the private sector, or other multilateral organisations). In 2018-2019, the United States was the top funder of the WHO, with total contributions amounting to USD 893 million (about 15% of the WHO's biennial budget). Of this total, USD 237 million, or 27%, were assessed contributions, while the remaining 73% were voluntary contributions. While the UN has stated that the procedure to withdraw from the WHO requires the United States to complete the payment of its assessed financial obligations, a substantial degree of uncertainty remains surrounding the impact the withdrawal could have on the country's voluntary contributions.

In the medium to long term, the US withdrawal would undoubtedly result in a significant reduction of the WHO's budget. Several countries have announced their intention to increase their own contributions in response to the US funding cut: for example, China pledged an additional USD 30 million in funding, Finland announced an additional USD 5.5 million, and Ireland promised to quadruple its contribution. However, these additional commitments are unlikely to fill the gap left by the US contributions. Since a large share of US funding was provided as tightly earmarked voluntary contributions, the programmes most affected by the withdrawal are likely to be those that constituted strategic priorities for the US in recent years, such as polio eradication, crisis-response, vaccine-preventable disease, HIV, hepatitis and tuberculosis. In addition, the US withdrawal could also profoundly change the funding base of the global health agency: the Bill & Melinda Gates Foundation, a non-state stakeholder, would, for example, become the agency's largest contributor.

While previous research has already pointed to the funding vulnerability of the WHO (OECD, 2018[7]), this case is a perfect illustration of the funding vulnerability analysis presented in this section. It shows how the concentration of multilateral organisations' donor base (e.g. their high degree of reliance on a few large donors) and the quality of their funding (e.g. the large share of funding received as voluntary non-core contributions) can ultimately affect their financial exposure and the sustainability of their programmes.

2.3. Conclusions and policy recommendations

As the majority shareholders and funders of the multilateral development system, DAC members' funding decisions have strategic implications for its performance and governance. DAC members thus need to develop funding policies and practices that support the DAC's collective vision, and expectations, of the multilateral development system. The following basic recommendations could help ensure a more strategic and effective use of DAC members' multilateral contributions:

- ***Use the momentum generated by the COVID-19 crisis to increase DAC members' multilateral funding levels***, in particular their total support to the multilateral development system. While it is too early for a full assessment of the multilateral response to the COVID-19 crisis, early observations indicate that multilateral organisations have responded with unprecedented scale and speed. However, there are also indications that the current financial capacity of multilateral organisations will be insufficient to respond to the needs and demands of developing countries in the medium to long term. The current international context thus calls for an unprecedented financial effort, and display of global solidarity, from the main shareholders and funders of the multilateral development system. While the economic and financial consequences of the crisis may make it hard for DAC members to safeguard their multilateral aid budgets, now is also the moment where their multilateral contributions are most needed and can have the most transformative impact.
- ***Assess multilateral funding decisions based on multilateral effectiveness and good practice.*** Given the important implications of funding quality on the performance and governance of the multilateral development system, DAC members should ensure that their funding decisions are aligned with principles of aid effectiveness and good practice. This implies, among other things, avoiding the default use of earmarked funding modalities, employing them only when they are the best option to achieve the intended development impact. The policy brief on DAC members' earmarked funding that accompanies this report provides initial pointers to determine the most appropriate funding modalities according to the specific development objectives that are pursued.
- ***Ensure that DAC members' financial contributions provide multilateral organisations with sufficient independence and flexibility to carry out their activities.*** This calls for increased attention from the DAC to the volume and quality of funding provided to multilateral organisations, as well as the degree of concentration of their funding base, to ensure that they are not vulnerable to excessive influence by specific members.
- ***Improve the data collection on multilateral contributions from non-DAC members.*** As the multilateral funding provided by non-DAC countries or other stakeholders (such as private actors) continues to grow, both in absolute and relative terms, it becomes increasingly important to ensure that these contributions are adequately captured in existing ODA data collection mechanisms, such as the OECD Creditor Reporting System and the forthcoming TOSSD[6] framework. Failure to tackle this problem would result in a growing blind spot in multilateral stakeholders' vision and understanding of the multilateral development system. A first step for the OECD DAC could be to map and quantify the existing data gaps in multilateral development finance, which would allow for prioritising and planning the improvements required in data collection.

References

Barder, O., E. Ritchie and A. Rogerson (2019), *"Contractors or Collectives?" Earmarked funding of multilaterals, donor needs and institutional integrity: the World Bank as a case study*, Center for Global Development, pp. 1-37, https://www.cgdev.org/sites/default/files/contractors-or-collectives-earmarked-funding-multilaterals-donor-needs-and_0.pdf. [12]

Eichenauer, V. and B. Reinsberg (2017), "What determines earmarked funding to international development organizations? Evidence from the new multi-bi aid data", *The Review of International Organizations*, Vol. 12/2, pp. 171-197, http://dx.doi.org/10.1007/s11558-017-9267-2. [4]

Graham, E. (2017), "Follow the Money: How Trends in Financing Are Changing Governance at International Organizations", *Global Policy*, Vol. 8, pp. 15-25, http://dx.doi.org/10.1111/1758-5899.12450. [3]

Grimm, S. and S. Weinlich (2020), *Multilateralism without future – or the future of multilateralism?*, Blog, German Development Institute, 8 January 2020, https://blogs.die-gdi.de/2020/01/08/multilateralism-without-future-or-the-future-of-multilateralism/. [11]

McArthur, J. and K. Rasmussen (2017), *Who funds which multilateral organizations?*, Brookings, https://www.brookings.edu/research/who-funds-which-multilateral-organizations/. [15]

OECD (2020), *Creditor Reporting System (database)*, OECD, Paris, https://stats.oecd.org/Index.aspx?DataSetCode=crs1. [1]

OECD (2020), *DAC countries' earmarked funding to the multilateral development system: how is it used, and what constitutes good practice?*. [16]

OECD (2020), *Partnering, funding and influencing the multilateral development system: rethinking how to assess good practice*, http://www.oecd.org/officialdocuments/publicdisplaydocumentpdf/?cote=DCD/DAC(2020)47&docLanguage=En. [17]

OECD (2018), *Multilateral Development Finance: Towards a New Pact on Multilateralism to Achieve the 2030 Agenda Together*, OECD Publishing, Paris, https://doi.org/10.1787/9789264308831-en. [7]

OECD (2015), *Multilateral Aid 2015: Better Partnerships for a Post-2015 World*, OECD Publishing, Paris, https://dx.doi.org/10.1787/9789264235212-en. [5]

Reinsberg, B. (2017), *Five steps to smarter multi-bi aid: a new way forward for earmarked finance*, Overseas Development Institute, London, https://www.odi.org/sites/odi.org.uk/files/resource-documents/11497.pdf. [9]

Reinsberg, B. (2017), "Organizational reform and the rise of trust funds: Lessons from the World Bank", *The Review of International Organizations*, Vol. 12/2, pp. 199-226, http://dx.doi.org/10.1007/s11558-017-9268-1. [6]

Sridhar, D. and N. Woods (2013), "Trojan multilateralism: global cooperation in health", *Global Policy*, Vol. 4/4, pp. 325-335, https://doi.org/10.1111/1758-5899.12066. [8]

UN (2019), *Funding Compact: Report of the Secretary-General*, United Nations, New York, https://www.un.org/ecosoc/sites/www.un.org.ecosoc/files/files/en/qcpr/SGR2019-Add%201%20-%20Funding%20Compact%20-%2018%20April%202019.pdf. [13]

UNDESA (2018), *Statistical annex - QCPR (unpublished).* [2]

Weinlich, S. et al. (2020), *Earmarking in the Multilateral Development System: Many shades of grey*, German Development Institute, Bonn, http://dx.doi.org/10.0.92.109/s101.2020. [10]

World Bank Group (2019), *2018-2019 Trust Fund Annual Report: Value proposition of World Bank Group trust funds*, World Bank Group, Washington D.C., https://www.worldbank.org/en/publication/trust-fund-annual-report-2019. [14]

World Bank Group (2016), *IDA18 Replenishment*, World Bank Group, Washington D.C., https://ida.worldbank.org/replenishments/ida18-replenishment. [18]

Notes

[1] Excluding bilateral flows earmarked through multilateral organisations.

[2] While the IDA18 replenishment round may also have played a role, partner contributions received for IDA18 were less than for IDA17. However, the total IDA18 envelope was larger and set a record high in the 56-year history of the organisation due to the leveraging of equity (World Bank Group, 2016[18]).

[3] The World Bank Group has since engaged in a wide set of reforms to consolidate its trust fund portfolio (Box 2.1 in this chapter).

[4] The Alliance for Multilateralism, for example, was created in 2017 by Germany and France, in reaction to a wave of criticism emanating from several governments against the rules-based international order.

[5] Initiatives such as the Multilateral Organisation Performance Assessment Network (MOPAN), which provide an independent view of multilateral organisations' performance, are a positive development towards achieving this common vision. A follow-on challenge is the uptake and co-ordinated use of this performance data to inform engagement and funding decisions; evidence of progress here remains anecdotal.

[6] TOSSD (total official support for sustainable development) is a new international statistical framework for monitoring official resources and private finance mobilised by official interventions for sustainable development. TOSSD is being developed by an International Task Force of experts; the OECD serves as the Secretariat to the Task Force.

3 Financing from the multilateral development system

The magnitude of the development challenges facing the world on the threshold of the "decade of action" requires a strong and effective multilateral response. This chapter sheds light on the development activities financed by multilateral organisations in recent years. Capitalising on recent research, the chapter also identifies specific areas in which multilateral development finance is expected to add value. Finally, the chapter assesses how multilateral entities perform in key dimensions of development effectiveness, and whether they make the best possible use of their respective business models and comparative advantages.

3.1. Key trends of multilateral outflows

3.1.1. Key trend 1: the multilateral system has remained a stable source of development finance over time

Funding from the multilateral system increased steadily from 2011, before falling slightly in 2018. Multilateral outflows to developing countries rose steadily between 2011 and 2017 (Figure 3.1). The increase was especially steep in 2015, a year marked by landmark multilateral agreements such as the 2030 Agenda and the Paris Agreement. However, after reaching a record high of USD 197 billion in 2017, multilateral outflows declined slightly to USD 189 billion in 2018.

Figure 3.1. Multilateral outflows have been steadily increasing since 2011

Commitments in USD billion, 2018 prices

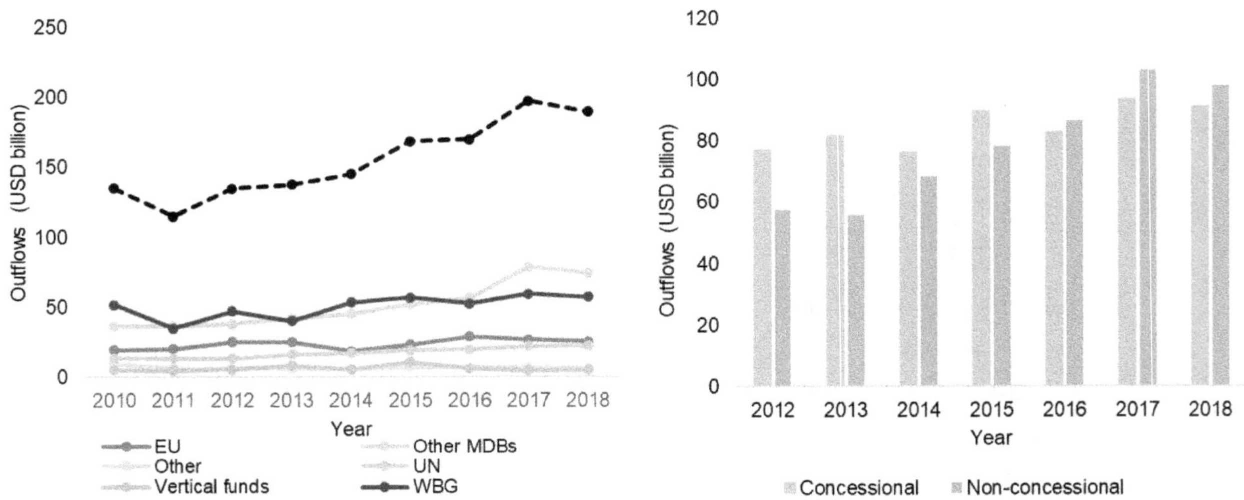

Source: Authors' calculations based on (OECD, 2020[11]), "Creditor Reporting System", https://stats.oecd.org/Index.aspx?DataSetCode=crs1.

StatLink https://doi.org/10.1787/888934177537

The upward trend in multilateral outflows is largely driven by the activity of the main multilateral development banks. The steady increase observed during the 2010s, and the uptick observed in 2017, are mainly attributable to the soaring lending volume of multilateral development banks, in particular the Asian Development Bank (ADB) and the newly established Asian Infrastructure Investment Bank[1] (AIIB). Likewise, the decrease in 2018 is partially due to a decline in outflows from some regional MDBs, in particular the African Development Bank (AfDB) and the Islamic Development Bank (IsDB).

The growth of MDBs' non-concessional flows from 2013 onwards was a key contributor to multilateral outflows. Figure 3.1 shows that non-concessional finance has constantly exceeded concessional flows since 2016. In 2018, non-concessional flows amounted to USD 98 billion (compared to USD 91 billion for concessional finance), accounting for 52% of total multilateral outflows. This again shows the increasing weight of MDBs in overall multilateral outflows, as those organisations are the main providers of non-concessional loans.

3.1.2. Key trend 2: multilateral outflows mainly target infrastructure and production, though humanitarian funding is rising

The infrastructure sector is the largest recipient of multilateral outflows (Figure 3.2**).** This pattern is predominantly driven by the major multilateral development banks' (MDBs) traditional focus on infrastructure; together the MDBs account for the largest portion of total multilateral outflows. Outflows to infrastructure-related sectors increased on average by 3% over the 2012-2018 period, although the share of infrastructure investments in overall multilateral development finance slightly decreased (from 31% in 2012 to 27% in 2018).

Outflows to productive sectors have increased steeply, in particular banking and financial services, agriculture and industry. Multilateral finance to productive sectors increased from USD 30 billion in 2012 to USD 55 billion in 2017, before declining slightly in 2018, to USD 48 billion. As a consequence, the share of productive sectors in multilateral finance rose from 23% to 25% between 2012 and 2018.

Multilateral development finance to social sectors peaked at USD 33 billion in 2015 before falling back below previous levels. The peak observed in 2015, probably driven by momentum at the end of the Millennium Development Goal era, coincided with a spike in financing from the Global Fund to end AIDS, Tuberculosis and Malaria.

Although it still represents a relatively small portion of total multilateral outflows, financing for humanitarian purposes has rapidly increased since 2012 (from USD 9 billion in 2012 to USD 14 billion in 2018, Figure 3.2). This increase can partially be attributed to the 2015-2016 refugee crisis, since most of the additional humanitarian funding targeted emergency response and reconstruction and relief.

Figure 3.2. Infrastructure and production remain the main focus of multilateral outflows

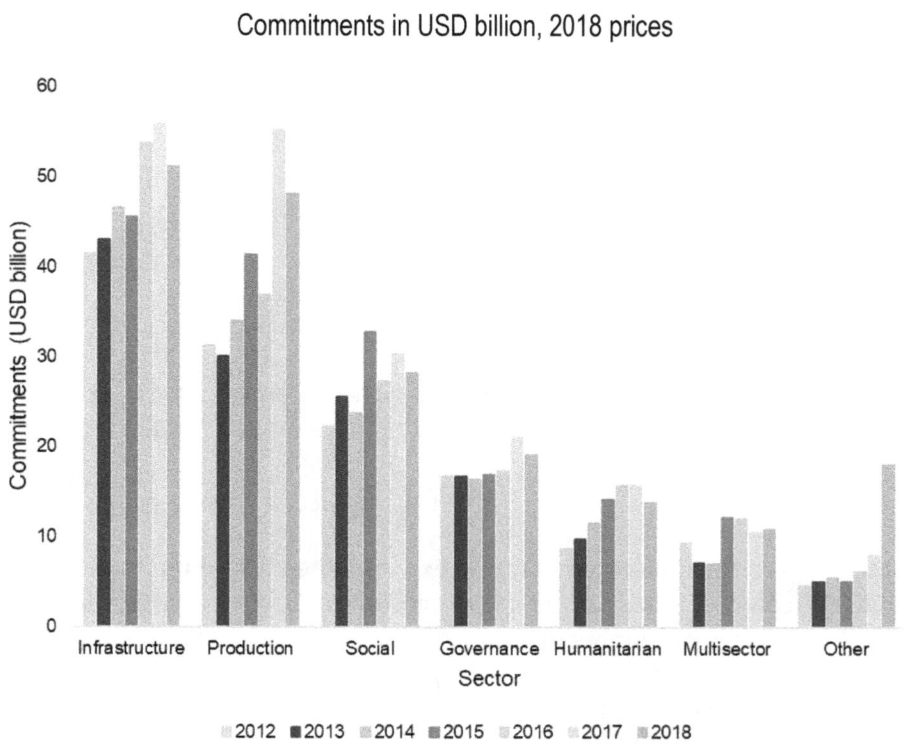

Source: Authors' calculations based on (OECD, 2020[1]), "Creditor Reporting System", https://stats.oecd.org/Index.aspx?DataSetCode=crs1.

StatLink https://doi.org/10.1787/888934177556

3.1.3. Key trend 3: middle-income countries benefit most from recent increases in multilateral outflows

The growth in non-concessional outflows reflects multilateral finance's increased focus on middle-income, and especially upper middle-income, countries (UMICs). Multilateral outflows to UMICs increased from USD 16 billion in 2001 to USD 56 billion in 2018. In relative terms, UMICs accounted for 30% of multilateral outflows in 2018.

Multilateral finance appears to be less focused on least developed countries (LDCs) and other low-income countries (LICs) than in the past. In 2004, the share of multilateral outflows to LDCs and other LICs peaked at 47% of total multilateral outflows. Although contributions to LDCs and LICs continued to increase in volume in subsequent years, their share has steadily declined: in 2018, they have come to represent only 23% of total multilateral outflows.

Figure 3.3. The focus of multilateral finance has shifted from low-income to middle-income countries

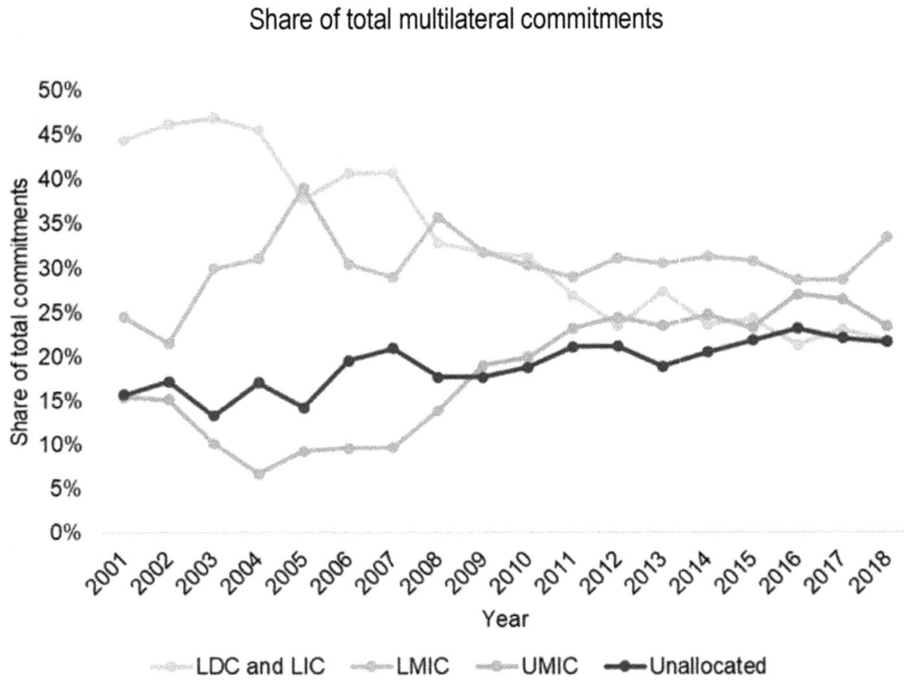

Note: LDC: least developed country; LIC: lower-income country; LMIC: lower middle-income country; UMIC: upper middle-income country.
Source: Authors' calculations based on (OECD, 2020[1]), "Creditor Reporting System", https://stats.oecd.org/Index.aspx?DataSetCode=crs1.

StatLink https://doi.org/10.1787/888934177575

The reclassification of recipient countries largely explains the shift of multilateral finance towards UMICs. The number of countries classified as upper middle-income by the World Bank Group rose from 47 in 2009 to 60 in 2018, while the number of low-income countries decreased from 40 to 31. In addition, three countries have graduated from the LDC category since 2010. Based on the previous categorisation of countries, the share of outflows to upper middle-income countries has actually declined, while flows to LDCs, LICs and LMICs have increased.

3.2. Joining the dots between the value proposition of multilateral development finance and its impact

Development partners' engagement with multilateral organisations rests on the assumption that multilateral approaches can complement their portfolios of bilateral aid. The unique strengths of the multilateral development system have come into renewed focus with the COVID-19 crisis. As the pandemic hits societies and economies across the world, countries find themselves faced with challenges of such a magnitude that they cannot be solved through unilateral action.

Now is a crucial time to assess whether, and how, multilateral stakeholders are able to leverage the comparative advantages of the multilateral development system to address present-day development challenges. This section explores the nature and extent of these comparative advantages by drawing from a variety of sources. First, it looks at findings from the 2020 survey on Development Assistance Committee (DAC) members' policies and practices vis-à-vis the multilateral development system to explore DAC members' perceptions of the comparative advantages of multilateral approaches (OECD, 2020[2]). Second, findings from the 2018 Global Partnership for Effective Development Co-operation (GPEDC) monitoring exercise (OECD/UNDP, 2019[3]) (Box 3.1) are examined to detect differences between multilateral and bilateral development co-operation, and between multilateral entities, in their alignment with development effectiveness principles. Finally, a comparative analysis of multilateral and bilateral financing patterns explores whether the distinctive features of multilateral development finance reflect unique strengths of the multilateral system.

3.2.1. DAC members expect the multilateral development system to add value across a variety of areas and functions

DAC members harbour high expectations for the future role of legacy MDBs to tackle global public bads and socio-economic challenges. In the recent survey on DAC members' policies and practices vis-à-vis the multilateral development system (OECD, 2020[2]), survey respondents highlighted climate and environment, gender equality, and inclusive growth as key topics where they expect the multilateral development system to increase its contribution in the near future. Legacy MDBs, such as the World Bank Group and the main regional development banks, are expected to increase their contribution in social sectors (social protection, food security and nutrition) and economic policy (domestic resource mobilisation, and trade and financial regulation).

New MDBs, such as AIIB and NDB, are mainly expected to help close the gap in infrastructure investment. This reflects in part these two entities' self-declared focus on infrastructure financing: infrastructure projects are a standout feature of the AIIB since its inception, and the NDB's five-year strategy states that about two-thirds of all projects will be devoted to sustainable infrastructure development. In the survey results, infrastructure development is the only area where the two new banks are expected to significantly step up their contribution relative to other multilateral organisations (Figure 3.4).

DAC members anticipate a larger role for the UN in supporting peace and security, and delivering humanitarian aid. The UN is already very active in these areas, which have been at the heart of its mandate since its inception, witnessed by the early creation of the United Nations Children's Fund (UNICEF) in 1946, the United Nations High Commission for Refugees (UNHCR) in 1950, and the World Food Programme (WFP) in 1961.

Figure 3.4. DAC members expect legacy MDBs to do more to support global public goods and social sectors

In what areas (if any) would you like multilateral organisations to focus more in the future?

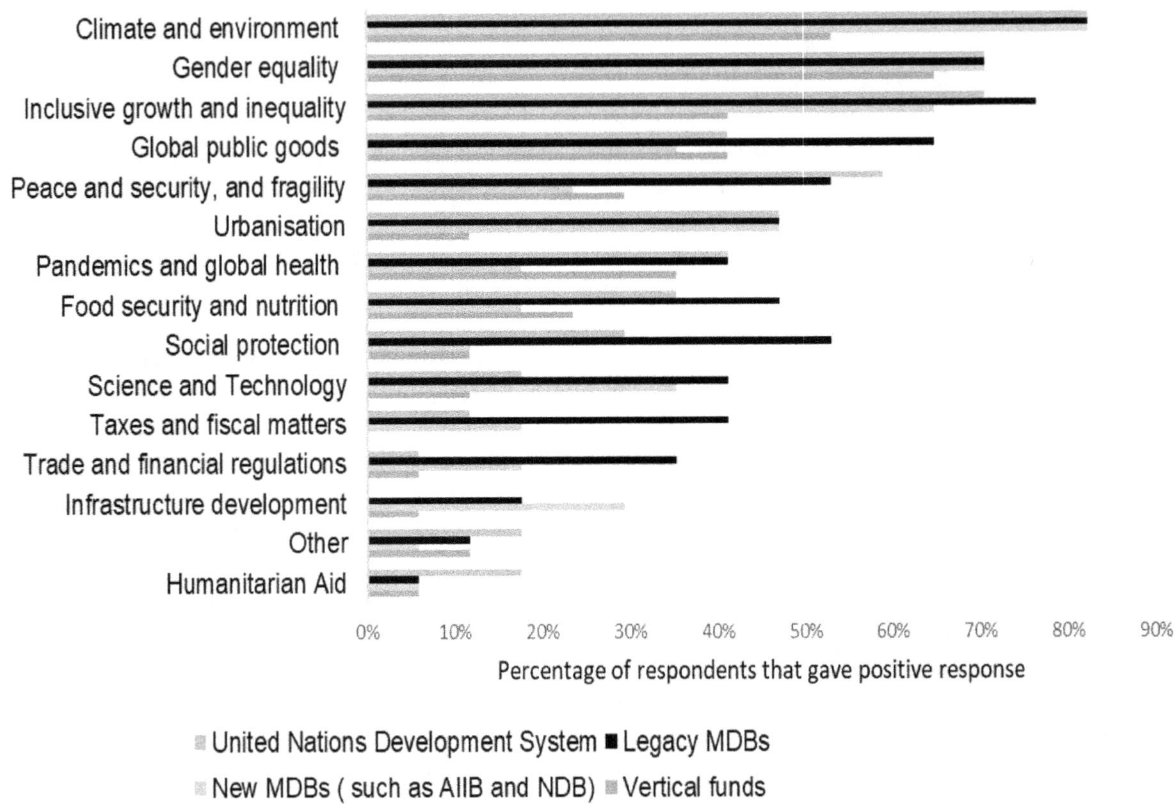

Source: (OECD, 2020[2]), "Survey on DAC providers' policies and practices vis-a-vis the multilateral development system" (unpublished).

StatLink https://doi.org/10.1787/888934177594

3.2.2. Development effectiveness is at the core of the multilateral value proposition

An effective multilateral system is indispensable for increasing the scale, pace and sustainability of development co-operation. This is especially true in the current context, as the financial constraints that will result from the economic impact of the COVID-19 pandemic call for an effective and efficient use of ODA that optimises the resources available for the 2030 Agenda. The qualities usually attributed to the multilateral development system (e.g. impartiality, coverage, scale) suggest that multilateral organisations may provide an effective channel for DAC members' ODA.

The 2018 monitoring round of the Global Partnership for Effective Development Co-operation indicated that the multilateral system performed better in most areas of development effectiveness than bilateral channels (Figure 3.5**).** Overall, multilateral development partners appear to show greater alignment with partner countries' priorities, results indicators, statistics, and monitoring and evaluation systems than bilateral partners, although results vary among the different types of multilateral organisations and across indicators. They also tend to engage governments and national development actors in the development of their country strategies to a greater extent than bilateral partners. In addition, multilateral partners are more likely than bilateral partners to make forward expenditure and implementation plans available to partner countries. Nevertheless, multilateral partners appear less likely than bilateral partners to disburse their funding according to their original schedules and, since 2011, they have made less progress than bilateral partners in using partner countries' public financial management (PFM) systems.

Figure 3.5. Multilateral partners out-perform bilateral partners on most effectiveness indicators

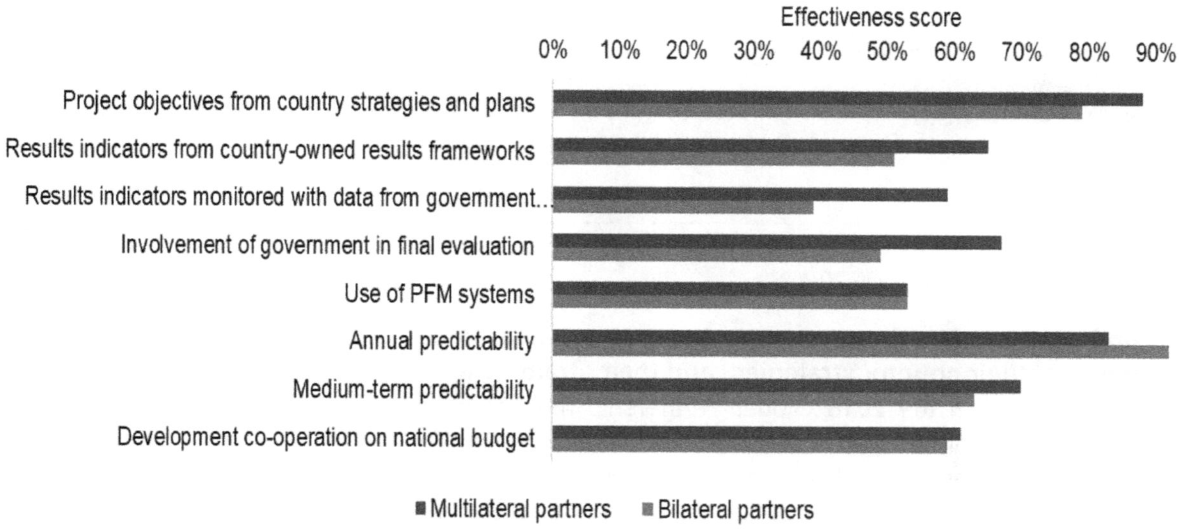

Note: Detailed information on the calculation of effectiveness scores can be found at https://www.effectivecooperation.org/system/files/2020-09/Technical%20Companion%20-%20Final%20online.pdf.
Source: Analysis from Global Partnership for Effective Development Co-operation (GPEDC) based on raw data collated in (GPEDC, 2018[4]), 2018 Global Partnership Monitoring Round, https://www.effectivecooperation.org/content/gpedc-monitoring-excel-database.

StatLink https://doi.org/10.1787/888934177613

Box 3.1. Tracking the implementation of effectiveness commitments in multilateral development co-operation

The Global Partnership for Effective Development Co-operation (GPEDC) is a multi-stakeholder platform set up to increase the effectiveness of development efforts by all actors in delivering results that are long-lasting and contribute to the achievement of the SDGs. The Global Partnership provides practical guidance and shares knowledge to improve development impact. It supports countries' implementation of five internationally agreed effectiveness principles: ownership by partner countries, a focus on results, inclusive partnerships, transparency and mutual accountability. The Global Partnership's flagship instrument is its biennial monitoring exercise, which since 2013 has tracked progress towards the effectiveness principles, and is a recognised source of data and evidence on upholding effectiveness commitments.

In the 2018 GPEDC monitoring round, 86 partner countries reported on development co-operation funding received from 69 multilateral development partners, including 16 multilateral development banks, 28 UN agencies, 13 vertical funds and initiatives, the European Institutions and 11 other international organisations. Partner countries reported on qualitative characteristics of more than 1 600 multilateral projects and programmes approved in 2017 with a total multi-year budget of USD 40.3

billion. They also reported on USD 29.7 billion in development co-operation funding disbursed as grants and loans by multilateral partners, including USD 23.6 billion disbursed directly to the public sector.

As part of the 2020-2022 Global Partnership Work Programme,[1] the monitoring exercise will be to develop a new monitoring proposal for endorsement at the Third High-Level Meeting of the Global Partnership, scheduled to take place in 2022. This revision will capture effective partnering to deliver on the SDGs across different co-operation approaches and modalities, including through the multilateral development system.

Note: [1]The 2020-2022 Global Partnership Work Programme can be accessed at https://www.effectivecooperation.org/content/2020-2022-global-partnership-work-programme.
Source: Analysis from Global Partnership for Effective Development Co-operation (GPEDC) based on raw data collated in (GPEDC, 2018[4]), 2018 Global Partnership Monitoring Round, https://www.effectivecooperation.org/content/gpedc-monitoring-excel-database.

Alignment with country priorities

Multilateral partners tend to engage government and national development actors in the development of their country strategies, and their strategic level alignment is better than bilateral partners. Results from the 2018 Global Partnership monitoring round show that overall, multilateral partners are more likely to have country-specific strategies in place to guide their development co-operation (84% of cases) than bilateral partners (69% of cases) (OECD/UNDP, 2019[3]). Furthermore, in developing their country strategies, multilateral partners tend to consult more with country governments, civil society organisations and the private sector. Multilateral partners are also more inclined than bilateral ones to fully align their strategies with partner countries' priorities.

Multilateral partners align their projects with partner countries' results indicators, statistics, and monitoring and evaluation systems to a greater extent than bilateral partners. In 2018, the alignment[2] of multilateral development projects with partner countries' objectives, results indicators, statistics and monitoring systems, as well as the involvement of country governments in project evaluations, remained at 2016 levels. Despite the lack of progress over this two-year period, multilateral partners still performed significantly better than bilateral partners (Figure 3.6), whose alignment scores appeared to have declined since 2016. In particular, multilateral bodies perform better in using data and statistics from the partner government to track progress towards results, and in involving the government in the final evaluation of projects. In fact, GPEDC data analysis shows that closer alignment of providers' country strategies with partner countries' results frameworks often translates into alignment at the project level (OECD/UNDP, 2019[3]).

Multilaterals vary in their degree of alignment. Vertical funds and UN agencies tend to perform better on average across the various elements of alignment. The Islamic Development Bank (IsDB) and the World Health Organisation (WHO) are two of the best performers on average across all elements related to alignment (with scores above 90%). In the case of the WHO, this performance seems to be driven by the strong emphasis on aligning country-level interventions with national development strategies and country results frameworks. The WHO develops a Country Cooperation Strategy (CCS) in each country where it operates. These CCSs ensure the alignment of the WHO's support with national health plans and strategies, and integrate monitoring and evaluation tools to assess the agency's performance in each country.

Figure 3.6. Comparison of project-level alignment of multilateral and bilateral partners

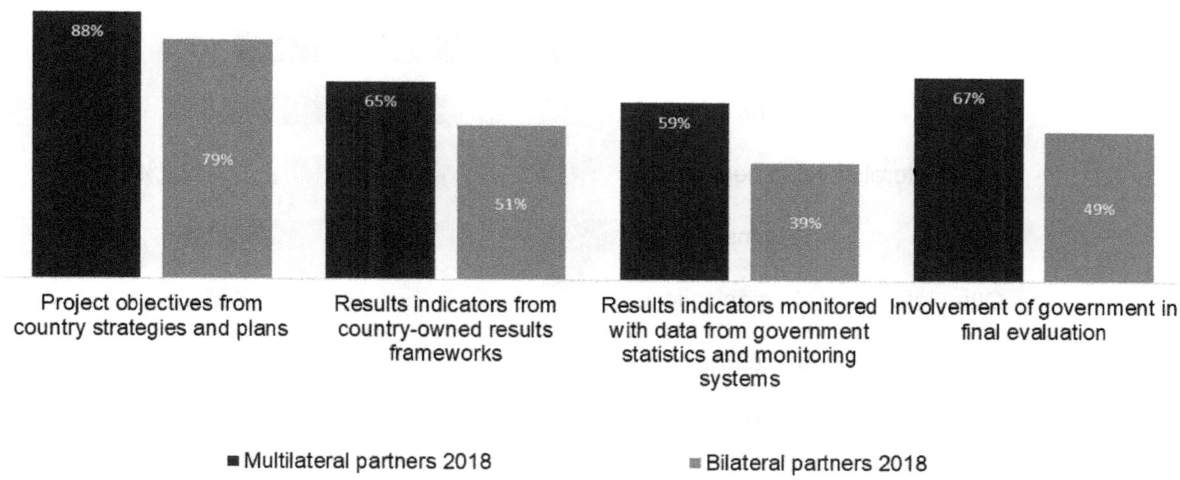

Source: Analysis from Global Partnership for Effective Development Co-operation (GPEDC) based on raw data collated in (GPEDC, 2018[4]), 2018 Global Partnership Monitoring Round, https://www.effectivecooperation.org/content/gpedc-monitoring-excel-database.

StatLink https://doi.org/10.1787/888934177632

Use of country systems

Multilateral development banks lead in the use of country PFM systems. The proportion of development co-operation disbursed to the public sector that uses countries' own public financial management (PFM) and public procurement systems has not improved since 2011 for multilateral partners[3] overall (53%). While there has been an increase in the use of countries' procurement systems, this gain has been offset by a decrease in the use of budget execution procedures, financial reporting and auditing systems. The overall use of country PFM systems by multilaterals in 2018 is similar to that of bilateral partners (Figure 3.7), although the latter group has improved since 2011. This is especially the case for DAC members, which have substantially increased their use of country PFM systems (from 44% to 55% between 2011 and 2018). Despite a decline since 2011, MDBs present the highest use of PFM systems among multilateral partners, which seems to largely reflect their country-based engagement model. EU institutions, which are the next-best performers after the MDBs, have improved their use of PFM systems since 2011 (from 48% in 2011 to 53% in 2018). On the other hand, the use of PFM systems continues to be particularly low for UN agencies (18%).

Figure 3.7. Proportion of development co-operation disbursed using partner countries' PFM systems

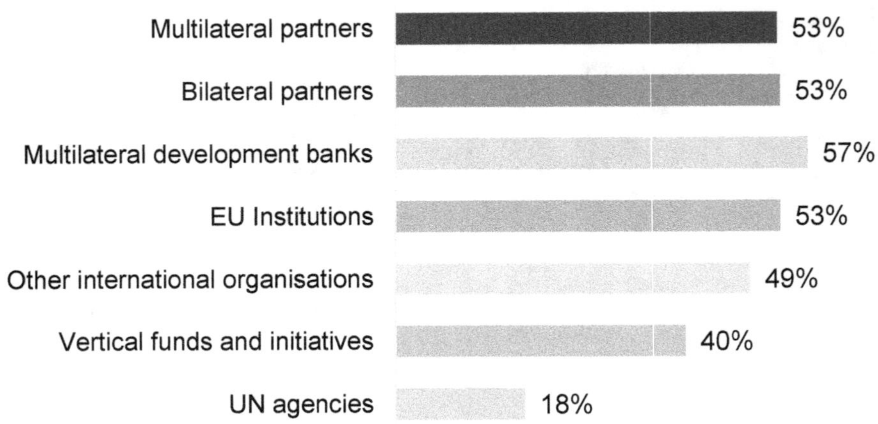

Source: Analysis from Global Partnership for Effective Development Co-operation (GPEDC) based on raw data collated in (GPEDC, 2018[4]), 2018 Global Partnership Monitoring Round, https://www.effectivecooperation.org/content/gpedc-monitoring-excel-database.

StatLink https://doi.org/10.1787/888934177651

Predictability of development co-operation

Multilateral partners' funding is less predictable than bilateral partners' funding. The share of development co-operation disbursed on time has slightly increased for multilateral partners since 2016, but it remains lower than its 2011 level (from 81% to 83% between 2016 and 2018; 85% in 2011). Bilateral partners' annual predictability remains much higher on average (92%). Both under and over-disbursements in the total amount of funding to the public sector can affect the government's ability to implement its development efforts as planned. In 2018, 17 multilateral partners reported disbursing a total of USD 1 billion less than the amount they had originally planned. On the other hand, 28 multilateral partners reported having disbursed more funding (a total of USD 3.7 billion) than the amount originally scheduled.

Finance from vertical funds and multilateral development banks is more predictable than from UN agencies and EU institutions. Performance in this area seems to vary significantly across the different categories of multilateral organisations. The proportion of financing disbursed in the year it was planned is 86% for both MDBs and vertical funds, but 83% for UN agencies and 71% in the case of EU institutions (Figure 3.8).

Figure 3.8. Multilateral organisations' funding is less predictable than bilateral partners

Proportion of development co-operation disbursed in the year it was planned

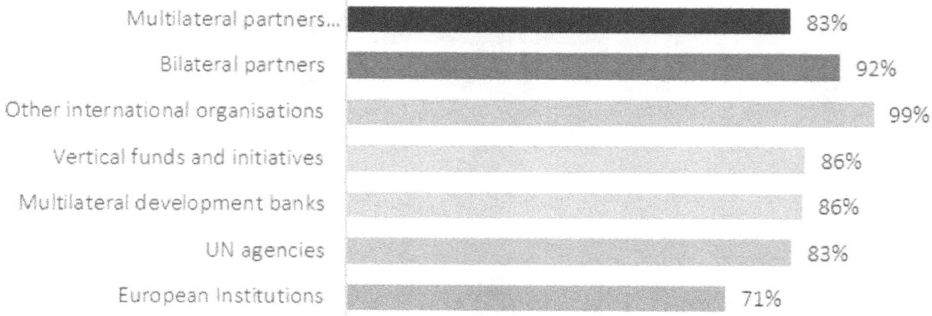

Source: Analysis from Global Partnership for Effective Development Co-operation (GPEDC) based on raw data collated in (GPEDC, 2018[4]), 2018 Global Partnership Monitoring Round, https://www.effectivecooperation.org/content/gpedc-monitoring-excel-database.

StatLink https://doi.org/10.1787/888934177670

On the other hand, forward visibility of development co-operation is greater for multilateral development partners. On average between 2016 and 2018, partner country governments reported they had received forward expenditure plans from multilateral partners covering 70% of estimated development co-operation funding (75% in 2016), compared to 63% from bilateral partners. This could be explained by the greater share of funding disbursed by multilateral partners than bilateral partners to the public sector, as well as multilaterals' greater tendency to design country strategies, which often contain forward expenditure plans.

Multilateral partners' provision of forward expenditure and implementation plans to their partner countries has decreased since 2016, reflecting an overall trend. Between 2016 and 2018, the share of multilateral development co-operation covered by forward expenditure plans decreased from 75% to 70%. Although MDBs also experienced a decline in this indicator, they continue to perform better than other categories of multilateral organisations. The Asian Development Bank (ADB; see Box 3.2) and the World Bank Group (WBG), in particular, make forward expenditure plans available to partner countries that cover more than 80% of their estimated development co-operation funding – well above the global average (Figure 3.9).

The share of multilateral development co-operation recorded on partner countries' national budgets also declined between 2016 and 2018. Despite dropping from 67% to 61%, multilateral partners continue to perform better than bilateral partners on this particular indicator.

Figure 3.9. MDBs and the EU seem to consistently provide forward plans to partner countries

Proportion of development co-operation for which forward plans are made available to partner countries

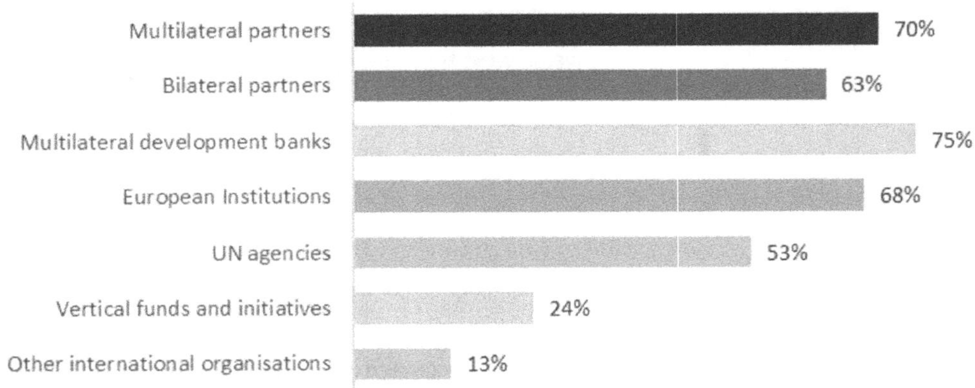

Source: Analysis from Global Partnership for Effective Development Co-operation (GPEDC) based on raw data collated in (GPEDC, 2018[4]), 2018 Global Partnership Monitoring Round, https://www.effectivecooperation.org/content/gpedc-monitoring-excel-database.

StatLink https://doi.org/10.1787/888934177689

Box 3.2. Good practice in the use of PFM systems and forward expenditure plans: the case of the Asian Development Bank

Because of their operating model, which is closely aligned with country strategies and relies on partner countries' public sector to channel their funds, multilateral development banks tend to outperform other development partners on their use of country systems. Among the MDBs, the Asian Development Bank (ADB) appears as the top performer, administering 92% of its funds through country systems. The ADB also provides its partners with forward expenditure plans covering a larger share of its estimated development co-operation funding (89%, compared to an average of 70% for all multilateral partners).

These results partly reflect the ADB's effort to build strong relations with country governments: in fact, the ADB designs country strategies guiding its development co-operation in all countries where most of its funding is channelled through the public sector. GPEDC data analysis found that the existence of country strategies determines the use of country systems and the greater availability of forward expenditure plans. Furthermore, the ADB also relies greatly on loans to deliver its funding, which GPEDC data analysis also found are more frequently administered using country systems.

Source: Analysis from Global Partnership for Effective Development Co-operation (GPEDC) based on raw data collated in (GPEDC, 2018[4]), 2018 Global Partnership Monitoring Round, https://www.effectivecooperation.org/content/gpedc-monitoring-excel-database.

Transparency

Multilateral development partners perform well in global assessments of transparency. The Global Partnership assessment of transparency in development co-operation is based on development partners' reporting to three global information systems and standards: the OECD Creditor Reporting System (CRS), the OECD DAC Forward Spending Survey (FSS) and the International Aid Transparency Initiative (IATI).[4]

In the 2018 monitoring round, half of the multilateral development partners achieved excellent ratings in the assessment of information reported to the OECD CRS (compared to less than one-third in 2016). The UN agencies are the top performers among the multilaterals, with 57% rated as excellent in the CRS transparency rating. Similarly, multilateral development partners also perform well, and demonstrate progress, in the FSS and the IATI assessments, with a greater proportion of multilaterals achieving a rating of excellent compared to 2016. Among the multilateral organisations reported on in all three assessments, the Asian Development Bank (ADB) obtains excellent scores in all three assessments; the African Development Fund (ADF), UNICEF and EU institutions obtained "excellent" ratings in two out of the three assessments, and a "good" rating in the third.[5]

3.2.3. The financing patterns of multilateral organisations confirm they complement and add value to the work of other development partners

Multilateral organisations' financing patterns illustrate some of their comparative advantages, both relative to bilateral partners and to each other. This section analyses the performance of multilateral organisations in relation to five features thought to distinguish multilateral approaches from bilateral ones. These five features are selected based on a review of the literature on multilateral development finance, as well as the data available in the OECD Creditor Reporting System: (i) economies of scale; (ii) degree of specialisation; (iii) ability to pursue multisector and cross-country approaches; (iv) use of government channels; and (v) support in difficult environments, such as fragile contexts.

The analysis shows that MDBs can generate significant economies of scale and work closely with recipient governments (Figure 3.10**).** Multilateral development banks have relatively large country portfolios compared to other development partners, allowing them to benefit from significant economies of scale. Moreover, they appear to work closely with recipient governments and to rely on country systems, as reflected in the relatively frequent use of recipient government channels (see the section above). While MDBs have diversified portfolios with large sectoral and geographical coverage, they seem to engage less in multisector and multi-country activities than other multilateral actors.

The entities forming the UN Development System (UNDS) devote a large share of their resources to supporting fragile contexts and display a high degree of specialisation. The UN focus on fragile contexts is in line with the original mandate of the organisation, centred on the advancement of peace and security. The UNDS includes a large number of highly specialised agencies, resulting in a large pool of expertise. These advantages, however, seem to come with a number of trade-offs. For example, the large variety of UN specialised agencies translates into lower economies of scale due to their smaller average portfolio size. And while the implementing capacity of UN agencies is an advantage when working in challenging environments, such as fragile contexts, it also means that the UN relies significantly less on recipient government channels than other multilateral entities.

Vertical funds are also highly specialised, but commit a high proportion of their funding to multisector and multi-country approaches. As their name suggests, global vertical funds are created to address a specific development challenge, which explains why their financing outflows tend to be concentrated in particular sectors. Nevertheless, this does not prevent them from engaging in multisector approaches. In fact, vertical funds must invest across sectors or work with other stakeholders in order to ensure the viability and sustainability of their approach.

As a regional body, the EU is uniquely positioned to promote integrated and cross-country solutions to tackling development challenges. The EU also features a relatively high share of multisector projects and often disburses development-related funding through recipient government channels.

Figure 3.10. Multilateral organisations offer diverse and complementary comparative advantages

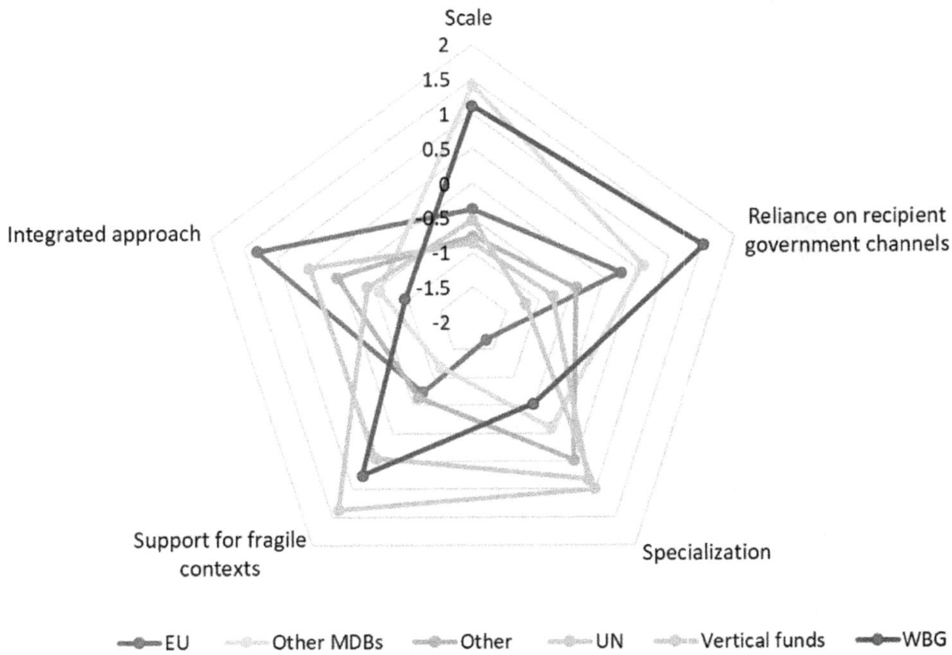

Note: The scores for the different indicators are calculated based on the average size of country portfolios and on the share of specific types of projects in the overall outflows of multilateral organisations. More details are included in the sections below.
Source: Authors' calculations based on (OECD, 2020[1]), "Creditor Reporting System", https://stats.oecd.org/Index.aspx?DataSetCode=crs1.

StatLink https://doi.org/10.1787/888934177708

The fragmentation of the multilateral development system does not seem to have eroded its scale advantages

Since multilateral organisations pool resources from different members, the general expectation is that they have greater economies of scale than bilateral providers. Figure 3.11 shows that the average portfolio size of multilateral organisations is indeed larger than that of bilateral providers.[6] The difference in portfolio size between these two groups has even increased in recent years, suggesting that the proliferation of multilateral actors has not eroded its scale advantages.

This trend is predominantly driven by the MDBs. Other types of organisation, such as UN entities and vertical funds, tend to have smaller portfolios on average than bilateral providers. However, some vertical funds may be able to achieve efficiency gains through economies of scale when they channel their resources through MDBs or UN agencies or use the latter as implementing entities to deliver programmes in individual countries.

Figure 3.11. Multilateral organisations tend to have larger country portfolios than bilateral partners

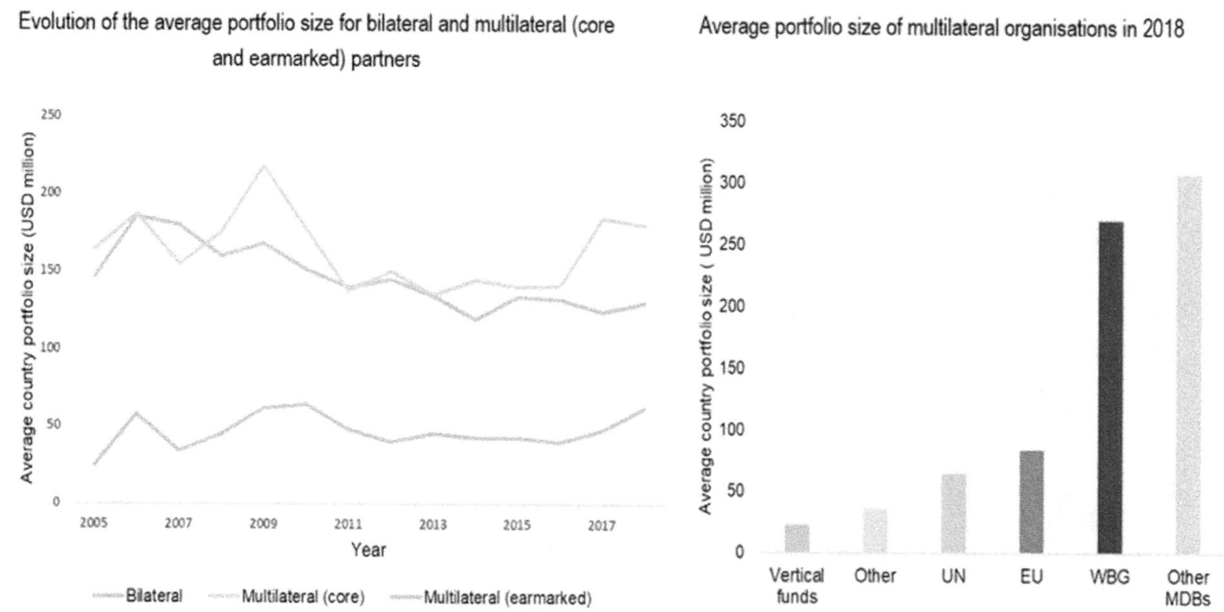

Source: Authors' calculations based on (OECD, 2020[1]), "Creditor Reporting System", https://stats.oecd.org/Index.aspx?DataSetCode=crs1.

StatLink https://doi.org/10.1787/888934177727

Multilaterals choose between specialisation and diversification

Multilateral organisations are uniquely positioned to develop and provide highly specialised support. Unlike their bilateral counterparts, many multilateral organisations are created with a specific mandate that requires them to develop and share specialised knowledge and expertise. While specialisation can be defined in multiple ways, this analysis focuses on the sectoral specialisation of development partners, which is calculated using the purpose codes in the OECD Creditor Reporting System.

On average, multilateral organisations tend to have a stronger sectoral specialisation than bilateral development partners.[7] Figure 3.12 shows the degrees of specialisation, measured as the highest share of a specific sector in the overall portfolio of a multilateral or bilateral provider. Multilateral organisations feature a higher level of specialisation in the activities funded from their core resources than in those funded from earmarked contributions, which seem to branch out into a more diverse set of sectors. This may reflect donors' tendency to use earmarking to steer multilaterals into areas that are outside their traditional focus, sometimes to bring to their attention otherwise under-prioritised areas.

Figure 3.12. Multilateral organisations are more specialised than bilateral providers

Share of the largest recipient sector in the portfolio of development partners

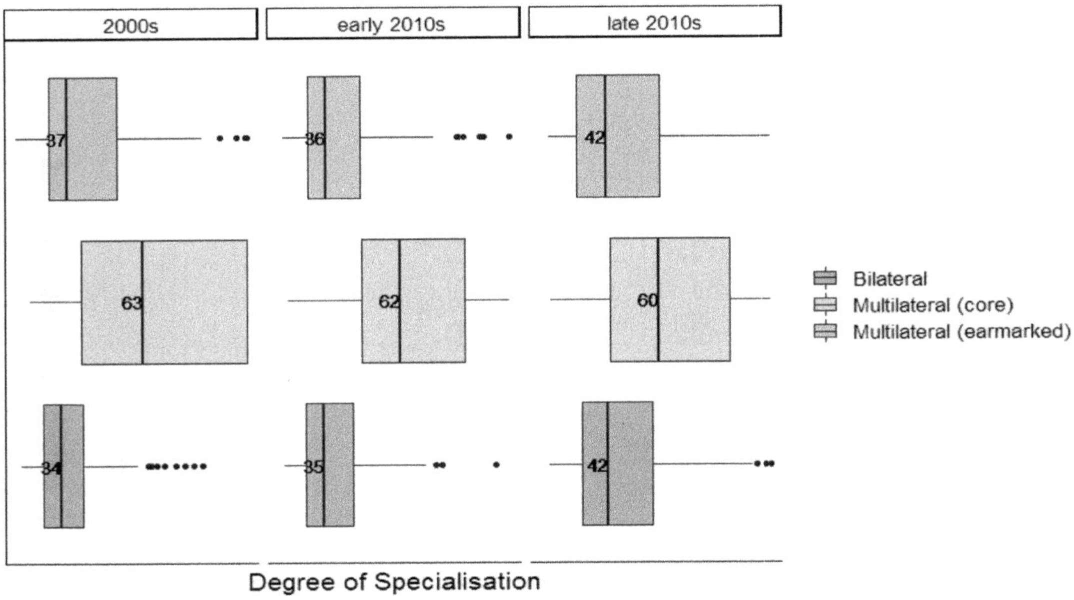

Source: Authors' calculations based on (OECD, 2020[11]), "Creditor Reporting System", https://stats.oecd.org/Index.aspx?DataSetCode=crs1.

StatLink https://doi.org/10.1787/888934177746

In general, organisations with larger portfolios tend to display more sectoral diversity. This trend is mainly driven by MDBs, whose operations usually span a large array of sectors despite their traditional focus on infrastructure development.[8] Among the MDBs, the World Bank Group presents the most diversified portfolio.

Conversely, smaller organisations tend to have stronger regional or sectoral specialisation. As a consequence, organisations that are more prone to benefit from economies of scale are less likely to be highly specialised in a particular thematic or geographic area. This suggests the existence of trade-offs between the various comparative advantages of multilateral organisations. It should be noted, however, that a lower degree of specialisation does not mean that those organisations lack expertise in the areas they are operating in. Larger organisations often have staff and departments that are highly specialised in one area. Instead, the concept of specialisation used in this analysis refers to the orientation of the organisation as a whole.

It is also noteworthy that no organisation has both high regional and high sectoral specialisation. Vertical funds, such as the Global Fund and Gavi; and UN bodies serving humanitarian and social purposes, such as WHO, UNFPA, UNAID, and UNHCR; are highly specialised in certain sectors (Figure 3.13). MDBs with a regional or sub-regional focus, such as the Arab Bank for Economic Development in Africa (BADEA), the Council of Europe Development Bank (CEB), and the Development Bank of Latin America (CAF); as well as some specialised UN entities, such as the UNRWA and the UN Economic Commission for Europe (UNECE); are among the organisations with the highest geographical specialisation.

Figure 3.13. Multilateral organisations are varied in their regional and sectoral specialisation

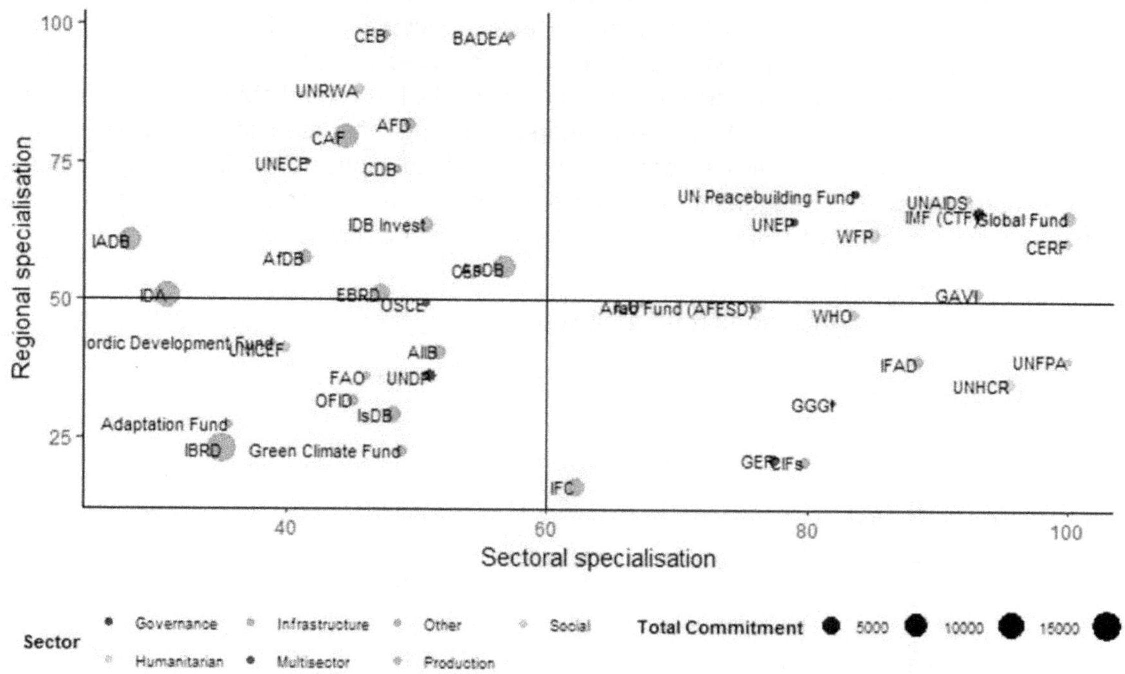

Source: Authors' calculations based on (OECD, 2020[1]), "Creditor Reporting System", https://stats.oecd.org/Index.aspx?DataSetCode=crs1.

StatLink https://doi.org/10.1787/888934177765

Specialisation patterns seem fairly stable over time, but organisations may adjust their sectoral focus to meet evolving client needs and demands. When tracing changes in these patterns over time, we observe that most organisations show continuity in the area and degree of specialisation. However, where a change is observed, it tends to be to sectoral rather than regional specialisation. This appears evident for organisations with a predefined regional focus in their mandates, such as the regional and sub-regional development banks. However, the analysis reveals that this is also true for organisations with no particular geographic mandate, such as the WHO and International Fund for Agricultural Development (IFAD). This implies that multilateral organisations retain a strong commitment to their partner countries, possibly shifting technical expertise to adapt to partner countries' evolving needs. For example, the sectoral focus of the European Bank for Reconstruction and Development (EBRD) appears to have shifted significantly between the periods 2001-2010 and 2010-2018 as its financing of infrastructure-related projects, which used to be the largest recipient sector of the organisation, has progressively given way to investments in productive sectors.

Multisector and cross-country approaches are rare

The multilateral development system, with its wide-ranging expertise and global membership, seems well placed to spearhead the integrated approaches called for by the 2030 Agenda. The SDGs emphasise the multidimensionality of sustainable development, as well as the interlinkages existing between the various development areas, such as the eradication of poverty, the promotion of economic and social development, or the protection of the planet (Durand and Scott, 2016[5]). Moreover, by emphasizing the global nature of many development challenges, the 2030 Agenda also highlighted the need to work across borders, combining local, national, regional and global approaches to face development challenges such as climate change, refugee crises and pandemics.

Surprisingly, multilateral organisations devote a smaller share of their funds than bilateral providers to multisectoral projects.[9] The analysis shows that multisector projects account for a minor share of the overall portfolio of multilateral organisations, fluctuating between about 1% and 7% (Figure 3.14). While a surge in multisector outflows was observed in 2015 – the year the SDGs were adopted – the share has quickly subsided back to very low levels. It is remarkable, though, that the share of multisector projects is considerably higher in earmarked funding: after reaching a peak level of 12% in 2015, the share of multisector activities declined but remained higher than for purely bilateral and multilateral approaches. This suggests that bilateral development partners may use earmarked contributions to steer multilateral organisations towards multisector approaches.

Figure 3.14. Multilateral organisations fund multisector activities less than bilateral providers

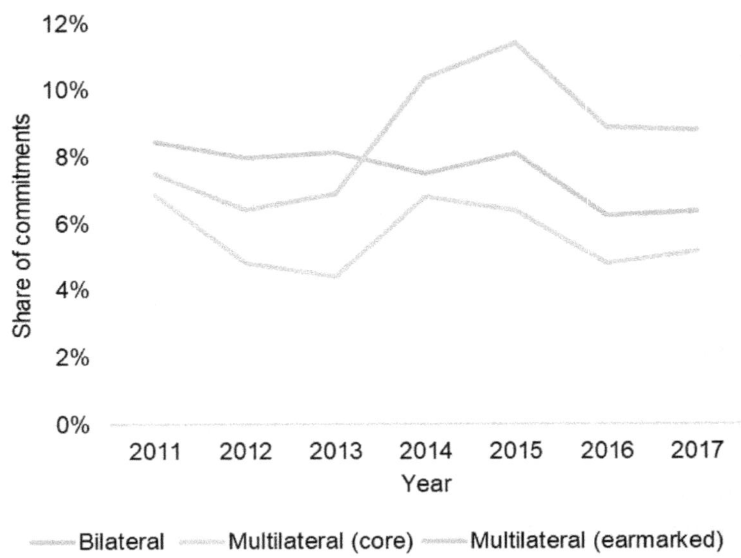

Source: Authors' calculations based on (OECD, 2020[1]), "Creditor Reporting System", https://stats.oecd.org/Index.aspx?DataSetCode=crs1.

StatLink https://doi.org/10.1787/888934177784

A similar pattern is observed for cross-country or regional activities. Multilateral outflows from multilateral organisations' core resources are the least likely to target multiple countries (around 3% in 2018). Bilateral providers commit a higher share of their funds to cross-country or regional projects than multilateral organisations (around 8%). On the other hand, a large share of the contributions earmarked through the multilateral development system (around 16%) seems to be directed at cross-country or regional activities (Figure 3.15).

Figure 3.15. Multilateral organisations commit less of their funds to cross-regional initiatives

Share of cross-country or regional projects in bilateral, multilateral and multi-bi aid

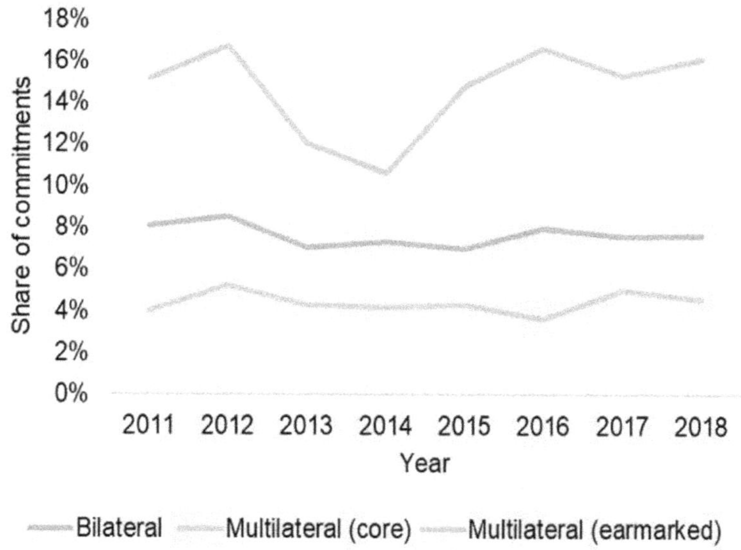

Source: Authors' calculations based on (OECD, 2020[1]), "Creditor Reporting System", https://stats.oecd.org/Index.aspx?DataSetCode=crs1.

StatLink https://doi.org/10.1787/888934177803

Counter-intuitively, there seems to be no trade-off between sectoral specialisation and the capacity to engage in multisector approaches. Organisations with a relatively diversified portfolio, such as the MDBs, do not commit a higher share of their funds to multisector activities. This suggests that different departments in those organisations may operate as silos. On the other hand, vertical funds, while highly specialised, present the largest shares of funds committed to multisector purposes. The Global Environment Facility (GEF) is a notable example: in 2016, it committed 83% of its portfolio to multisector projects.

In a similar vein, the regional specialisation of multilateral organisations does not seem to determine the use of cross-country or regional approaches. MDBs and UN entities tend to have a low share of cross-country or regional activities.[10] The Nordic Development Fund (NDF) is a notable outlier: in 2017, the NDF committed 98% of its portfolios to cross-country or regional activities. The WHO also features a relatively high share of cross-country or regional projects compared to the other major multilateral organisations (between 27% and 31% over the 2016-2018 period).

The low uptake of cross-country or regional initiatives reflects a dichotomy within the global development agenda. While the global policy framework provided by the SDGs calls for integrated approaches, and underscores the interlinked and cross-border nature of 21st century development challenges, the delivery of development solutions still hinges on partner country governments. As a consequence, despite their global mandates, most multilateral organisations retain a country-based engagement model. The analysis suggests that these traditional structures and operating models may hamper multilateral organisations' ability to provide global and regional public goods.

Partner governments are the main channels used by multilateral development finance

A large share of multilateral development finance is channelled through recipient governments. The results of the GPEDC monitoring exercise presented in Section 3.2.2 suggested that multilateral organisations tend to make greater use of partner countries' PFM and procurement systems than bilateral partners and to be better aligned with their development priorities. Analysis based on data from the OECD Creditor Reporting System seems to confirm this observation: it shows that multilateral development finance is more often channelled through recipient governments than is bilateral aid, which tends to rely more on alternative delivery channels, such as NGOs (Figure 3.16).

Figure 3.16. A large share of multilateral resources is passed through recipient governments

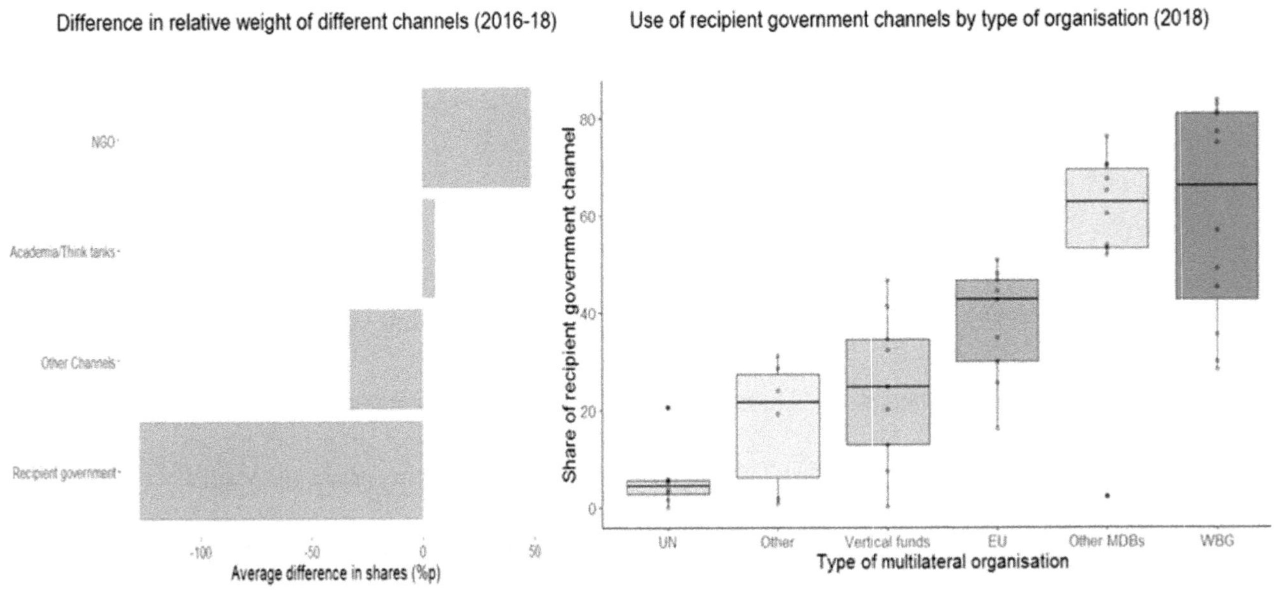

Note: The period of analysis is 2016-2018. The bars in the left-hand graph indicate the difference between the share of a specific channel in the total portfolios of all bilateral providers and that of all multilateral organisations.
Source: Authors' calculations based on (OECD, 2020[1]), "Creditor Reporting System", https://stats.oecd.org/Index.aspx?DataSetCode=crs1.

StatLink https://doi.org/10.1787/888934177822

Recipient governments are a particularly prominent channel for multilateral development banks. This can be explained by the MDBs' business model and their focus on infrastructure finance, which is often provided to partner countries in the form of loans. In comparison, the UNDS very rarely relies on recipient government channels for implementation. This is partly explained by the high proportion of UN activities carried out in fragile contexts and other difficult environments, where the low capacity and weak institutions of partner country governments can render the use of country systems impractical.

Support to fragile contexts

An abundant literature suggests that the multilateral development system brings substantial comparative advantages in dealing with fragile contexts. The OECD (2009[6]), for example, highlighted three key strengths of multilateral organisations that allow them to perform in this area. First, their systematic involvement in fragile contexts enables them to generate first-hand, comparative expertise. Most bilateral donors, in contrast, focus their aid on a smaller subset of countries and lack specialised expertise in multiple fragile contexts. Second, multilateral organisations have international staff who can bring skills in co-operation with a variety of cross-cultural state forms and institutional arrangements. Third, multilateral organisations have the convening power and legitimacy to pull different stakeholders together under a common strategy. This is in contrast with most bilateral development partners, which may have a harder time convincing partner countries and other stakeholders of their legitimacy and impartiality to carry out such a role.[11]

Multilateral organisations tend to devote a greater share of resources to fragile contexts than bilateral partners. Remarkably, the share of outflows benefitting fragile contexts is broadly similar between earmarked and core resources (Figure 3.17). However, there are considerable differences across the different categories of multilateral organisations. The UNDS leads, devoting more than half of its funding to fragile contexts. Regional MDBs commit the lowest share of their funding to fragile contexts, although their share is still higher than that of bilateral partners. Considering that this group had the highest share of funding channelled through recipient governments, this shows that there may be a trade-off between the support to fragile contexts and the reliance on country systems. The higher share of support to fragile contexts by the UNDS may also reflect the different needs of fragile countries (e.g. humanitarian aid or peace building activities, rather than longer-term development interventions in social, productive or infrastructure-related sectors). This finding may also reveal the particular distribution of roles within the multilateral development system in the humanitarian-peace-development nexus.

Figure 3.17. UN entities are the largest multilateral channel of aid to fragile contexts

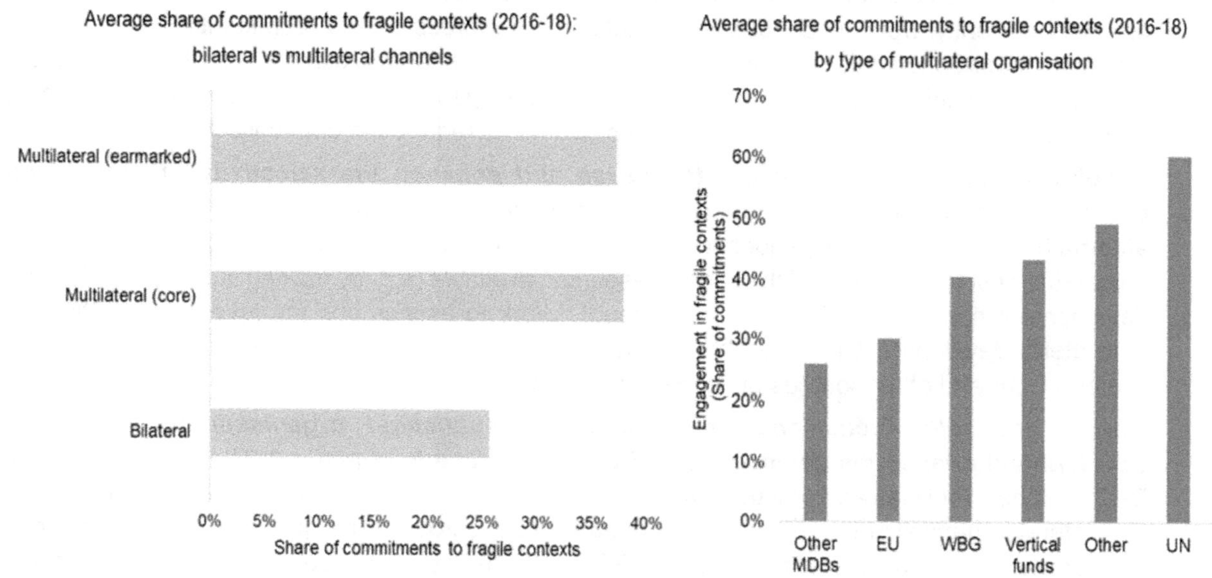

Source: Authors' calculations based on (OECD, 2020[1]), "Creditor Reporting System", https://stats.oecd.org/Index.aspx?DataSetCode=crs1.

StatLink https://doi.org/10.1787/888934177841

3.3. Conclusions and policy recommendations

The magnitude of the development challenges facing the world on the threshold of the "decade of action"[12] requires a multilateral development system operating at its full potential. Now is a crucial time for multilateral organisations to assert their value added relative to other channels of development co-operation, and for multilateral stakeholders to push for the reforms required to make the multilateral development system fit for purpose. In addition to the reform areas outlined in Chapter 1, the following actions by multilateral stakeholders could help ensure that the multilateral development system is well-positioned to confront upcoming challenges:

- ***Draw lessons from the multilateral response to the COVID-19 crisis.*** Assessing the effectiveness of multilateral organisations' immediate response to the COVID-19 crisis should be a priority for multilateral stakeholders. This would reveal whether multilateral organisations are equipped to confront challenges of this type of magnitude (in particular challenges requiring collaboration and co-ordination across a wide range of sectors), and could also help identify specific areas for improvement. Progress on this front would require a concerted effort from multilateral organisations to disclose details of their COVID-related activities in a comparable format.

- ***Develop statistical methodologies and tools to shed light on the financial leverage and mobilisation capacity of multilateral organisations.*** The capacity to use its financial resources as leverage to mobilise other sources of finance is considered as a key comparative advantage of the multilateral development system. However, evidence on this aspect of multilateral development finance is difficult to come by due to the lack of detailed data and information in the public domain. One concrete example is the amount mobilised by multilateral organisations from the private sector, which remains a major blind spot of multilateral development finance: the data are shared by multilateral organisations on a strictly confidential basis and can only be presented at the aggregate level. A more granular and better understanding of the financial leverage and mobilisation capacity of the multilateral development system could help identify specific measures to increase the scale of its impact and enhance trust in the system. An MDB – OECD DAC working group is currently working on possible solutions to address MDBs' confidentiality constraints regarding mobilisation data reporting and disclosure. A potential next step for the OECD DAC could be to conduct an initial mapping and quantification of data gaps in multilateral development finance, which would help to prioritise and plan the improvements required in data collection.
- ***Develop an analytical framework to assess and enhance the selectivity of multilateral organisations' operations.*** In a context of constrained resources, as is likely to emerge in the aftermath of the COVID-19 pandemic, better prioritisation of multilateral activities will be key to ensure the best possible use of the scarce resources available (e.g. by making sure that multilateral development finance targets the most in need). Work to assess and improve the selectivity of multilateral development finance should rely on a careful analysis of its complementarity with bilateral ODA and other sources of development finance.
- ***Review the role, focus and contribution of multilateral organisations to specific development challenges deemed a priority for the "decade of action".*** The recent survey on DAC members' policies and practices vis-à-vis the multilateral development system confirmed that multilateral organisations are expected to add value across a range of development areas considered key to progress towards the SDGs in the next decade. An assessment of the contributions of multilateral organisations to some of these key development challenges could help to ensure an adequate focus, prioritisation and alignment of their operations with the expectations of multilateral stakeholders. It could also help explore whether multilateral organisations are sufficiently leveraging potential synergies and opportunities for collaboration, and could help to identify the specific reforms and ways of working required to maximise the contribution of multilateral organisations to the 2030 Agenda. Specific topics to explore could include multilateral organisations' contribution to: (i) the immediate response to the COVID-19 pandemic, (ii) the fight against climate change; and (iii) a green, resilient and inclusive COVID-19 recovery.

References

Durand, M. and S. Scott (2016), "Measuring multidimensional well-being and sustainable development", in *Debate the Issues: New Approaches to Economic Challenges*, OECD Publishing, Paris, https://dx.doi.org/10.1787/9789264264687-6-en. [5]

GPEDC (2018), *2018 Global Partnership Monitoring Round*, https://www.effectivecooperation.org/content/gpedc-monitoring-excel-database. [4]

OECD (2020), *Creditor Reporting System (database)*, OECD, Paris, https://stats.oecd.org/Index.aspx?DataSetCode=crs1. [1]

OECD (2020), *Survey on DAC providers' policies and practices vis-a-vis the multilateral development system*, Unpublished. OECD, Paris. [2]

OECD (2009), "Concepts and dilemmas of State building in fragile situations: From fragility to resilience", *OECD Journal on Development,*, Vol. 9/3, https://doi.org/10.1787/journal_dev-v9-art27-en. [6]

OECD/UNDP (2019), *Making Development Co-operation More Effective: 2019 Progress Report*, OECD Publishing, Paris, https://dx.doi.org/10.1787/26f2638f-en. [3]

Notes

[1] The fact that the Development Bank of Latin America (CAF) started reporting to the Creditor Reporting System in 2017 and the Islamic Development Bank (IsDB) Invest started reporting from 2016 onwards, may also explain part of that growth.

[2] The Global Partnership monitoring assessment of project-level alignment looks at whether: 1) project objectives are drawn from country development plans and strategies; 2) project targets and indicators are drawn from the Country-owned Results Frameworks (CRFs); 3) government data and statistics are used to monitor project results; and 4) the government is involved in project evaluation. For bilateral partners, the average of the first three elements of alignment – when all are available – provides the official data to report on the extent to which development partners respect partner countries' policy space and leadership in setting their own development path (SDG Target 17.15).

[3] In this section, multilateral partners refer to all non-bilateral partners that have participated in the 2018 Global Monitoring Round. These include multilateral development banks, vertical funds, UN entities and other multilateral organisations as well as EU institutions. However, the exact list differs from the multilateral organisations reporting to the Creditor Reporting System and that are captured in the quantitative analyses in other sections of the report.

[4] The results for transparency (Indicator 4) of the 2016 and 2018 monitoring rounds capture the latest assessments available at the time of reporting for each of the respective rounds. CRS data for the 2018 round refer to assessment on reporting to the CRS in 2017; CRS data for the 2016 round refer to assessment on reporting to the CRS in 2014. FSS data for the 2018 round refer to the 2018 survey; FSS data for the 2016 round refer to the 2015 survey. IATI data for the 2018 round refer to scores extracted from the online platform in December 2018; IATI data for the 2016 round refer to scores extracted in May 2016.

[5] The Global Partnership does not carry out direct comparisons of transparency between bilateral and multilateral partners since their reporting requirements are different and categories for the transparency indicator also differ in some cases. For example, multilateral organisations do not report on tying status, or on both DAC tables and the CRS. Most of them only have one type of aid "project-type interventions" since most of the other categories do not apply to multilateral reporters.

[6] This analysis uses the average size of an organisation's country portfolio to assess its potential to achieve economies of scale. However, it should be noted that portfolio size is not sufficient in itself to determine the actual economies of scale achieved by an organisation. To achieve economies of scale, development partners need to leverage the size of their portfolio in a way that generates efficiency gains.

[7] The definition of specialisation used in this analysis does not imply that organisations with a more specialised portfolio have more technical expertise, or that they provide higher quality and value in their area of speciality compared to organisations that are more diversified. Rather, the degree of specialisation is indicative of the specificity of an organisation's mandate and operational portfolio.

[8] Infrastructure still represents around a third of the overall portfolio of the multilateral development banks.

[9] It should be noted that differences in reporting practices between bilateral and multilateral organisations partly explain the differences in the weight of multisector activities. Multilateral organisations often use automatic mappings between their units or strategic objectives and CRS purpose codes to categorise their financing outflows, while many bilateral donors categorise their outflows on an individual project basis.

[10] In the case of the World Bank Group, this trend could evolve significantly in coming years since the IDA has increased the size of its regional window by more than 50% in its latest replenishment (IDA19).

[11] There are, however, multiple examples of lead donors successfully playing that role on specific occasions (e.g. the role played by Australia, alongside other regional partners, in Timor Leste and Solomon Islands).

[12] At the SDGs Summit in September 2019, the UN Secretary-General Antonio Guterres made a global call for a decade of action to deliver the SDGs by 2030, and world leaders renewed their commitment to the 2030 Agenda.

Annex A. Glossary

2030 Agenda 2030 or the 2030 Agenda for Sustainable Development: The 2030 Agenda for Sustainable Development is centred on the 17 Sustainable Development Goals (SDGs) agreed in September 2015. It is also conceived as a broad agenda that includes the AAAA as a framework for implementation and the Paris Agreement on Climate Change, and that builds on a history of multilateral agreements such as the Universal Declaration of Human Rights.

Addis Ababa Action Agenda (AAAA): Negotiated at the Third Financing for Development Conference in Addis Ababa, Ethiopia, in July 2015, the AAAA sets out a financing strategy for implementing the global sustainable development agenda adopted in September 2015. It includes more than 100 measures covering all sources of finance and includes co-operation on a range of issues include technology, science, innovation, trade and capacity building.

Core contributions/multilateral ODA: Core contributions to multilateral organisations are resources transferred to multilateral organisations and that the governing boards of these organisations have the unqualified right to allocate as they see fit within the limits prescribed by the organisation's mandate.

Earmarked/non-core/multi-bi contributions: Earmarked contributions are resources channelled through multilateral organisations over which the donor retains some degree of control on decisions regarding disposal of the funds. Such flows may be earmarked for a specific country, project, region, sector or theme, and they technically qualify as bilateral ODA.

Multilateral organisations: This report covers the over 200 multilateral organisations with governmental membership that carry out development activities. The OECD maintains the list of ODA-eligible organisations (OECD, 2020[1]), which is publicly available at: https://www.oecd.org/dac/financing-sustainable-development/development-finance-standards/annex2.htm.

Multilateral outflows: Financial flows from multilateral organisations to partner countries or global/regional development issues.

ODA funding to the multilateral system: This term refers to all funds channelled to and through multilateral organisations. It encompasses core contributions to multilateral organisations (multilateral ODA) and earmarked resources channelled through multilateral organisations (also known as non-core resources or multi-bi funding).

Project-type earmarking: Project-type earmarked contributions are resources strictly earmarked for a specific use, at the project level, leaving no, or limited flexibility to the recipient organisation on their allocation. These resources include contributions to project-type interventions (aid type C01 in the DAC CRS list of codes), as well as contributions in terms of donor country personnel (aid type D01) and other technical assistance (aid type D02).

Programmatic earmarking: Programmatically earmarked contributions are resources that are earmarked with a greater degree of flexibility. These resources include contributions to specific-purpose programmes and funds managed by implementing partners (aid type B03 in the DAC CRS list of codes), as well as contributions to basket funds/pooled funding (aid type B04).

Annex B. Country factsheets: DAC providers' use of the multilateral development system

Figure A B.1. AUSTRALIA, use of the multilateral system

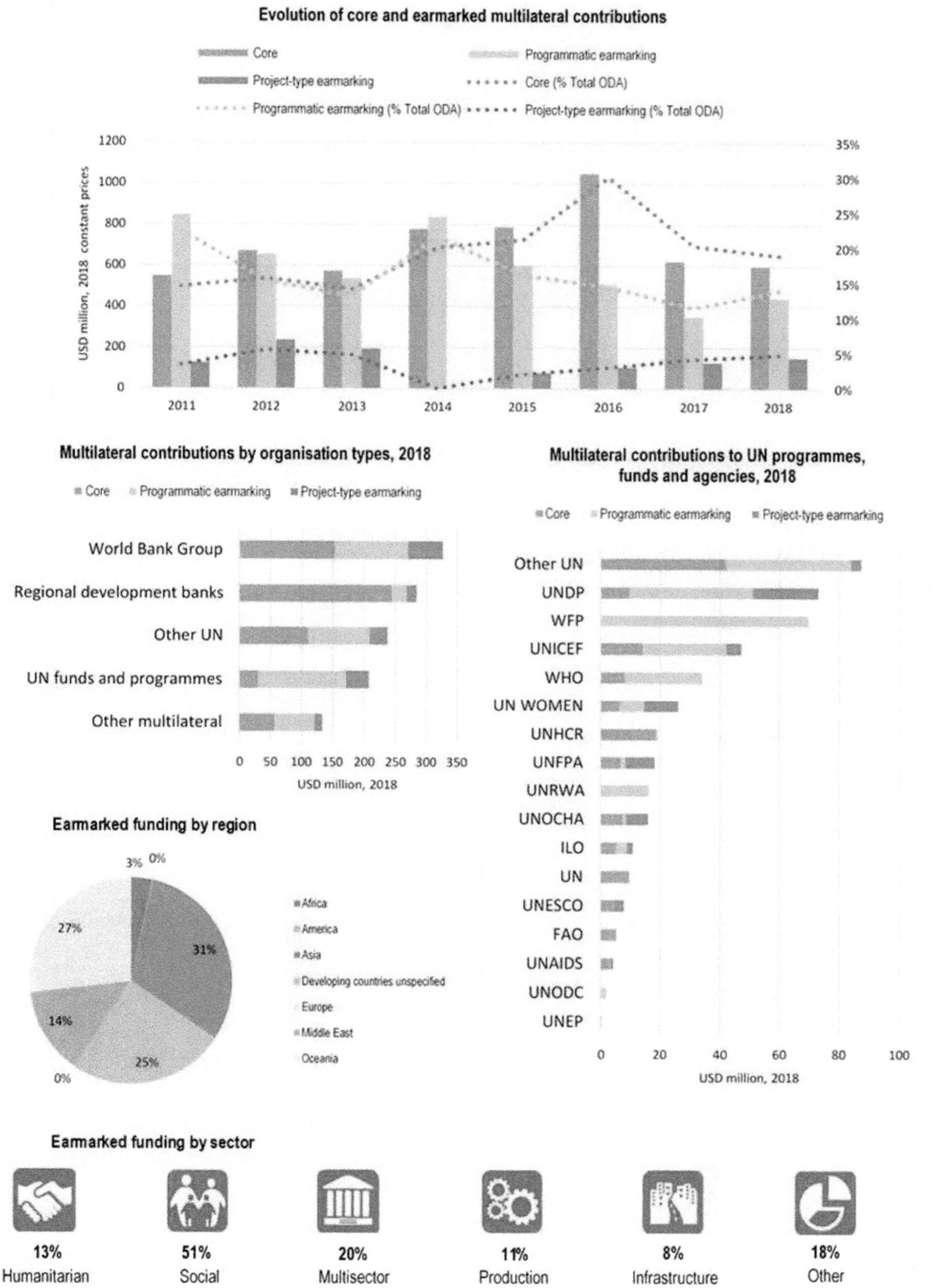

Source: Authors' calculations based on (OECD, 2020[2]), "Creditor Reporting System", https://stats.oecd.org/Index.aspx?DataSetCode=crs1.

StatLink https://doi.org/10.1787/888934177860

Figure A B.2. AUSTRIA, use of the multilateral system

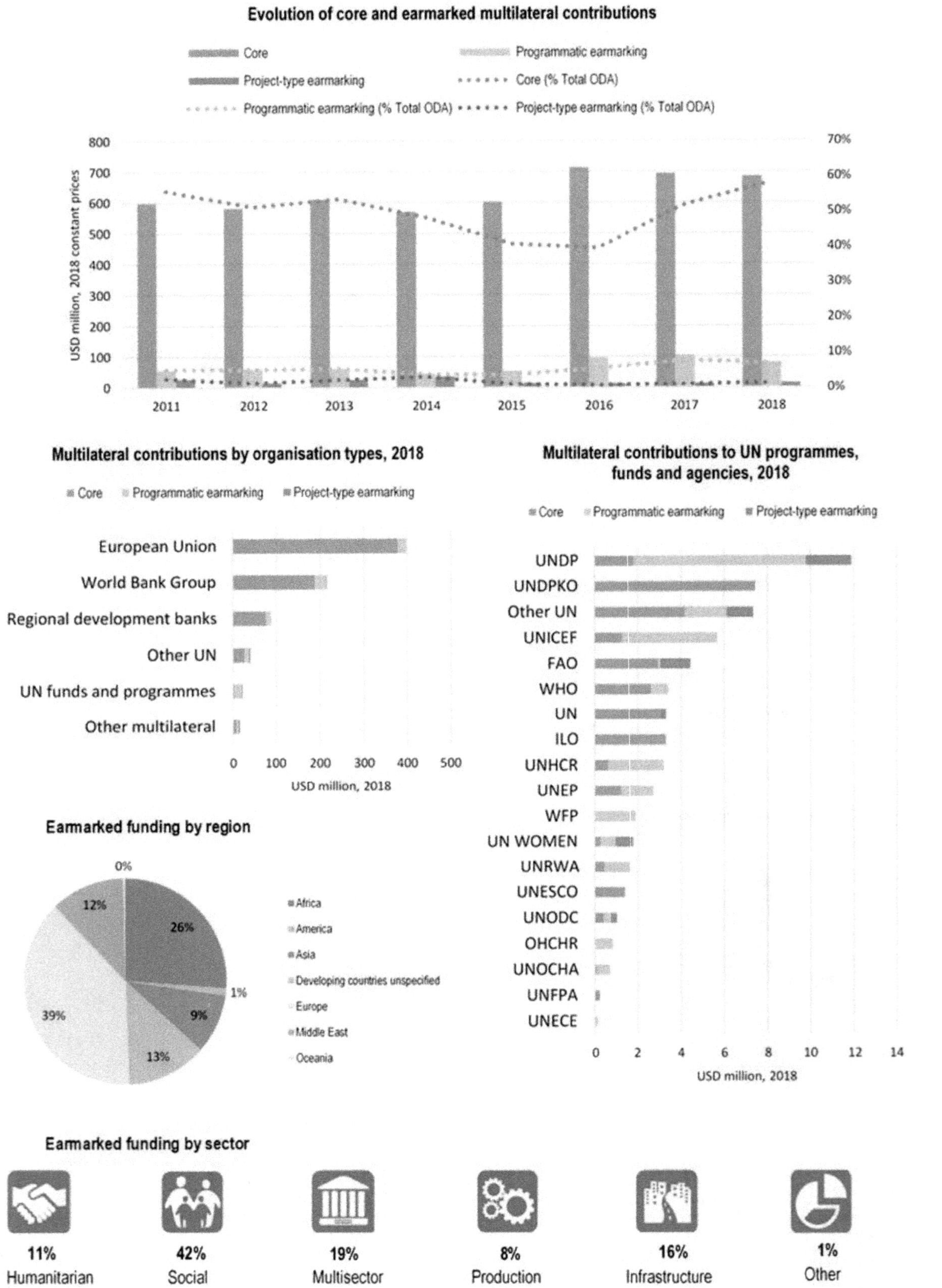

Source: Authors' calculations based on (OECD, 2020[2]), "Creditor Reporting System", https://stats.oecd.org/Index.aspx?DataSetCode=crs1.

StatLink https://doi.org/10.1787/888934177879

Figure A B.3. BELGIUM, use of the multilateral system

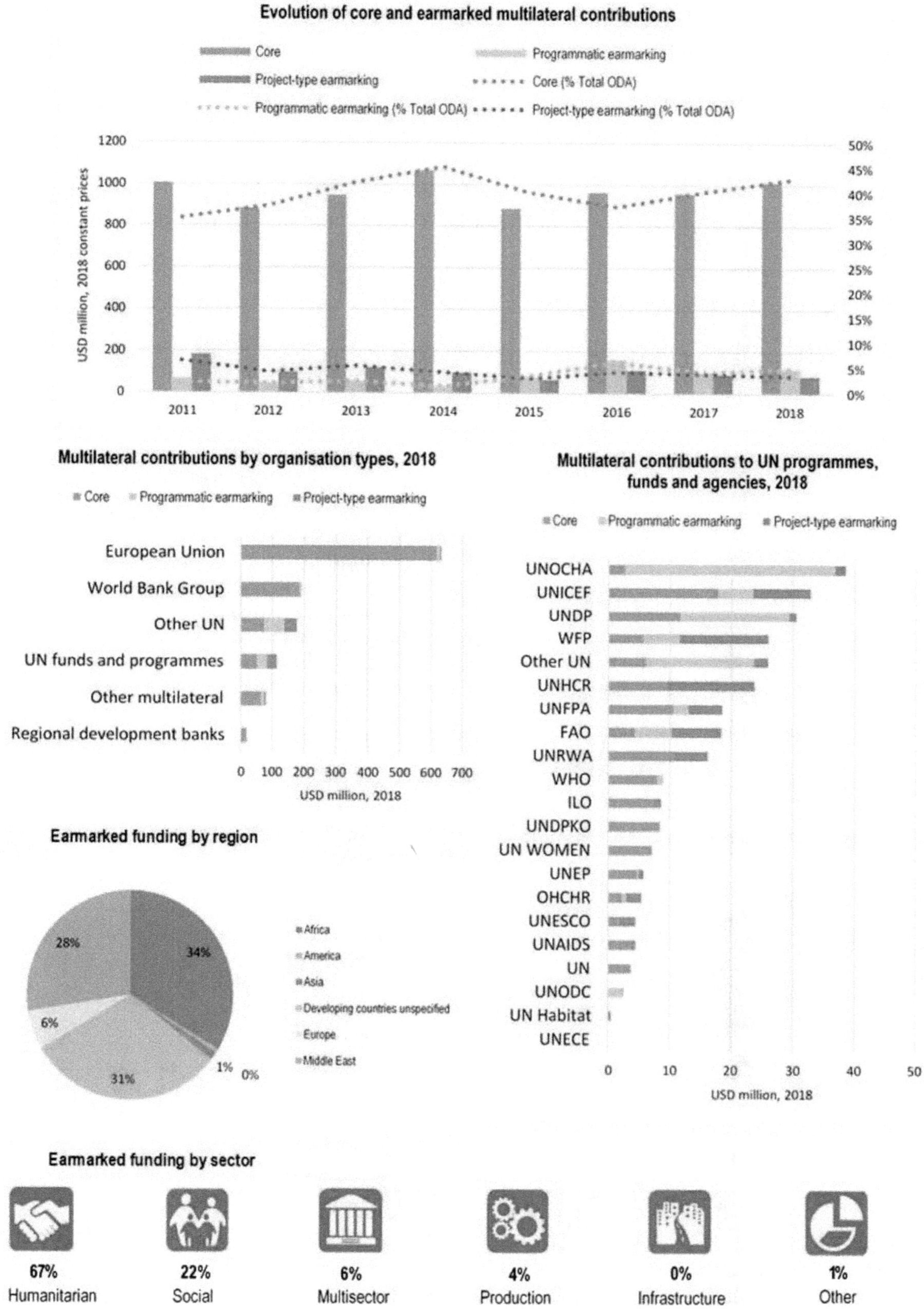

Source: Authors' calculations based on (OECD, 2020[2]), "Creditor Reporting System", https://stats.oecd.org/Index.aspx?DataSetCode=crs1.

StatLink https://doi.org/10.1787/888934177898

Figure A B.4. CANADA, use of the multilateral system

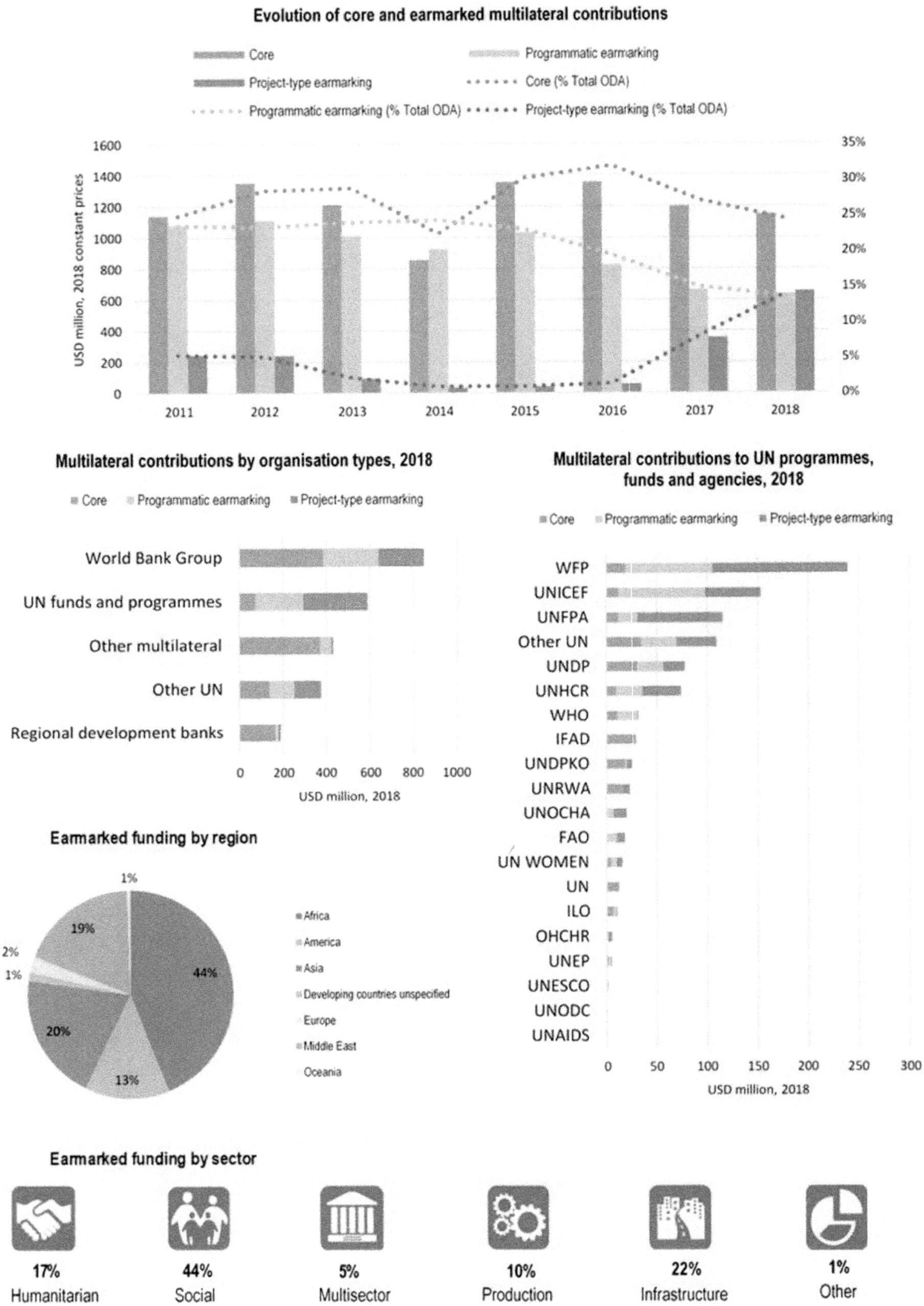

Source: Authors' calculations based on (OECD, 2020[2]), "Creditor Reporting System", https://stats.oecd.org/Index.aspx?DataSetCode=crs1.

StatLink https://doi.org/10.1787/888934177917

Figure A B.5. CZECH REPUBLIC, use of the multilateral system

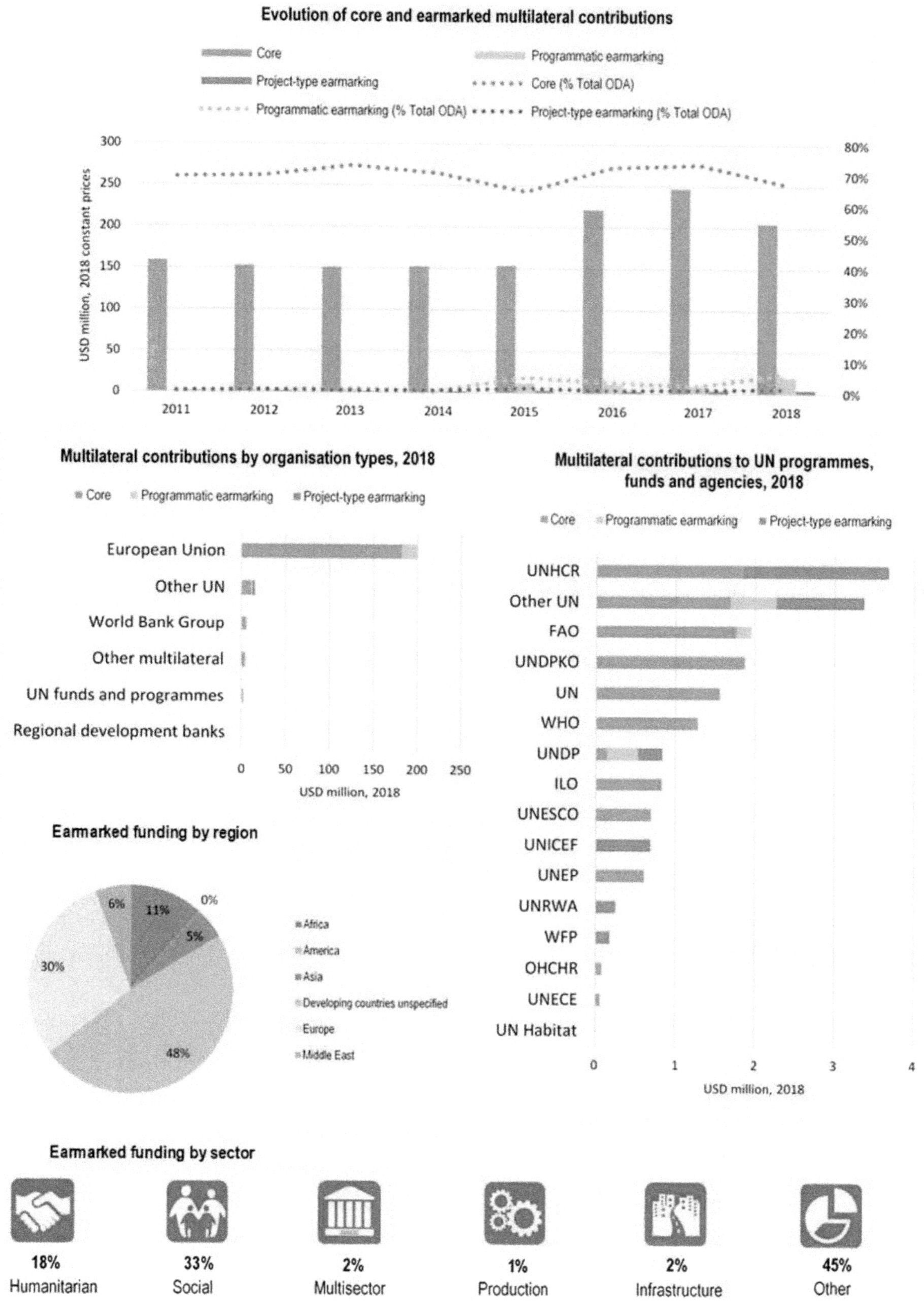

Source: Authors' calculations based on (OECD, 2020[2]), "Creditor Reporting System", https://stats.oecd.org/Index.aspx?DataSetCode=crs1.

StatLink https://doi.org/10.1787/888934177936

Figure A B.6. DENMARK, use of the multilateral system

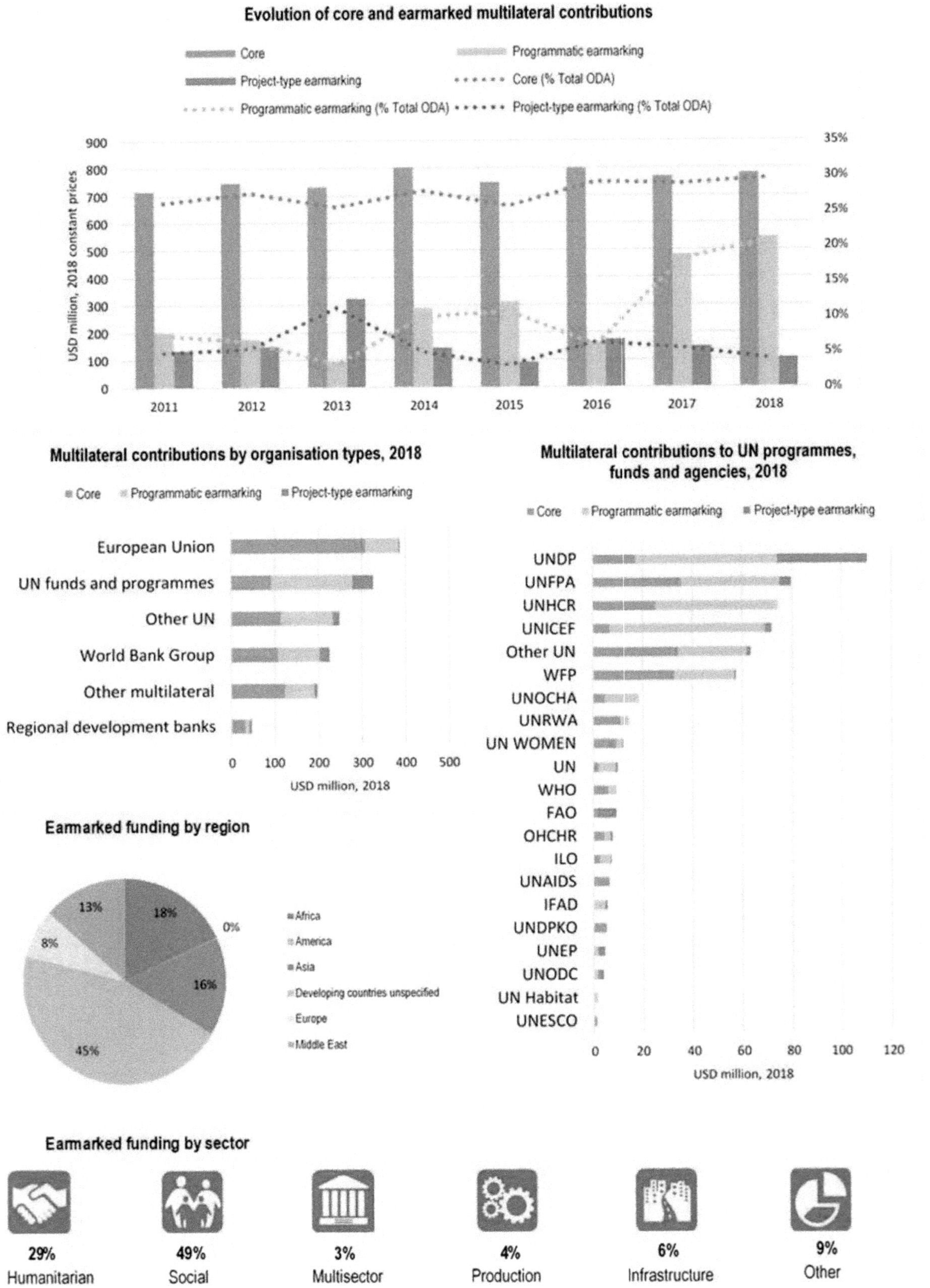

Source: Authors' calculations based on (OECD, 2020[2]), "Creditor Reporting System", https://stats.oecd.org/Index.aspx?DataSetCode=crs1.

StatLink https://doi.org/10.1787/888934177955

Figure A B.7. EU INSTITUTIONS, use of the multilateral system

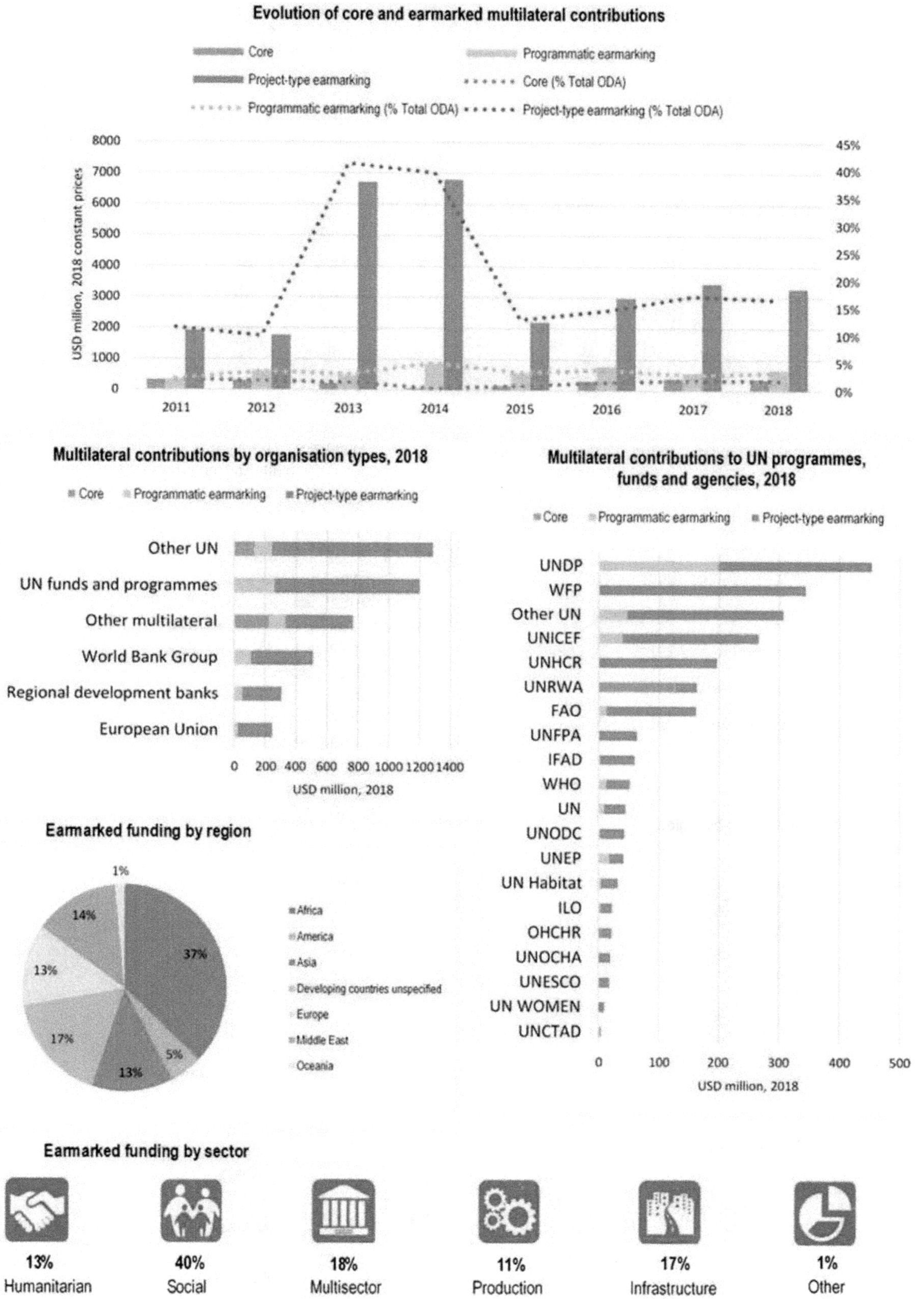

Source: Authors' calculations based on (OECD, 2020[2]), "Creditor Reporting System", https://stats.oecd.org/Index.aspx?DataSetCode=crs1.

StatLink https://doi.org/10.1787/888934177974

Figure A B.8. FINLAND, use of the multilateral system

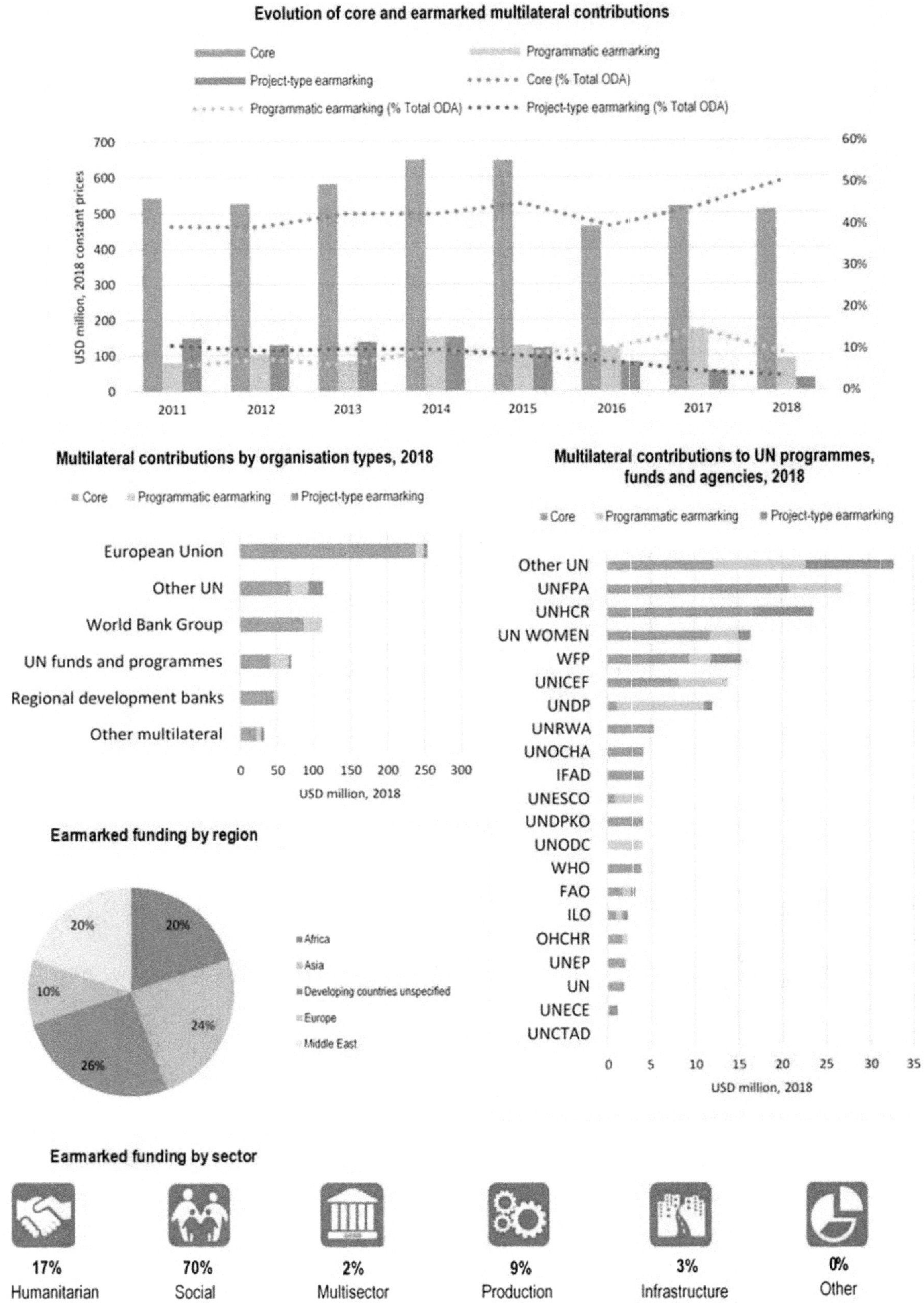

Source: Authors' calculations based on (OECD, 2020[2]), "Creditor Reporting System", https://stats.oecd.org/Index.aspx?DataSetCode=crs1.

StatLink https://doi.org/10.1787/888934177993

Figure A B.9. FRANCE, use of the multilateral system

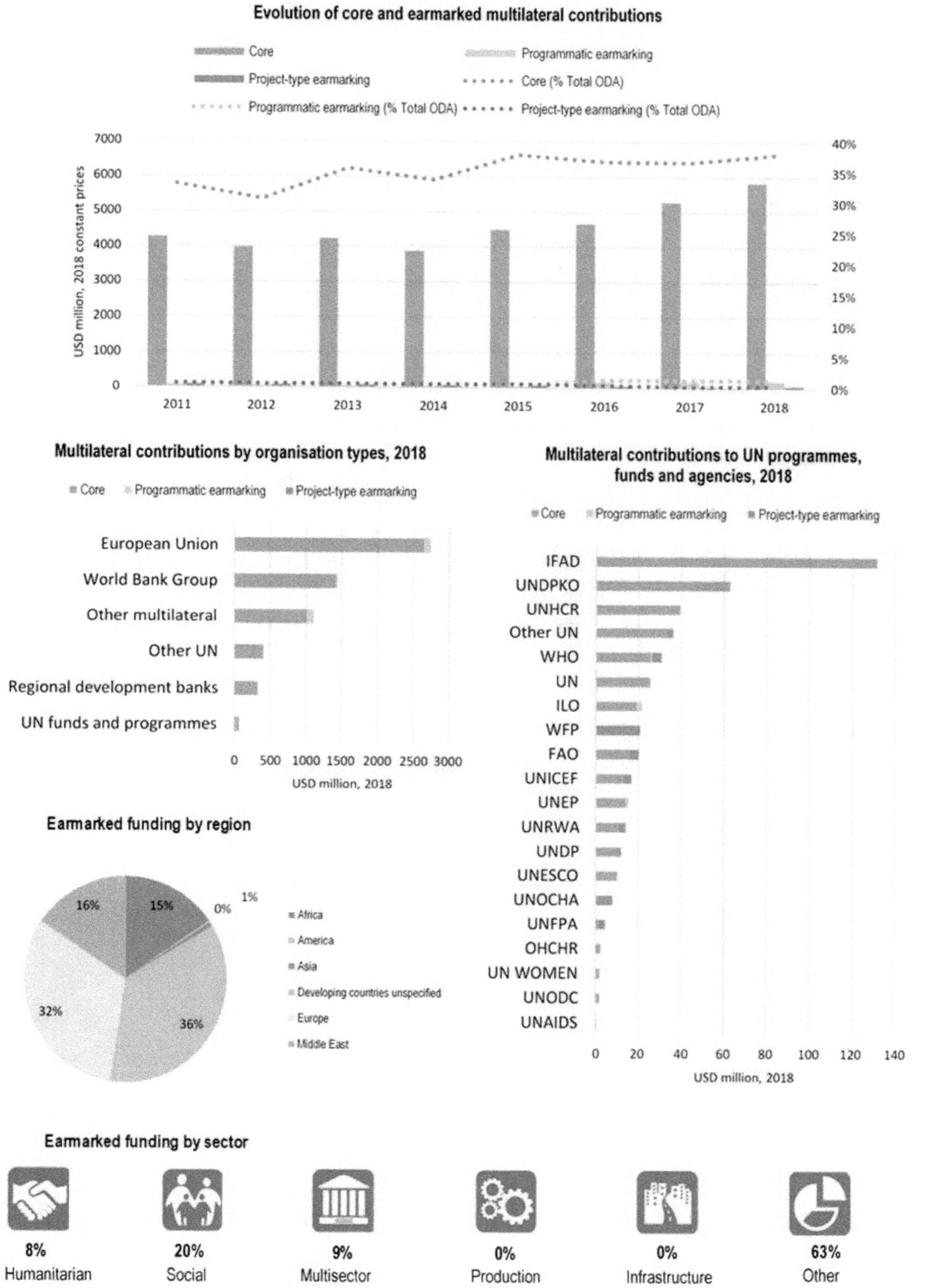

Source: Authors' calculations based on (OECD, 2020[2]), "Creditor Reporting System", https://stats.oecd.org/Index.aspx?DataSetCode=crs1.

StatLink https://doi.org/10.1787/888934178012

Figure A B.10. GERMANY, use of the multilateral system

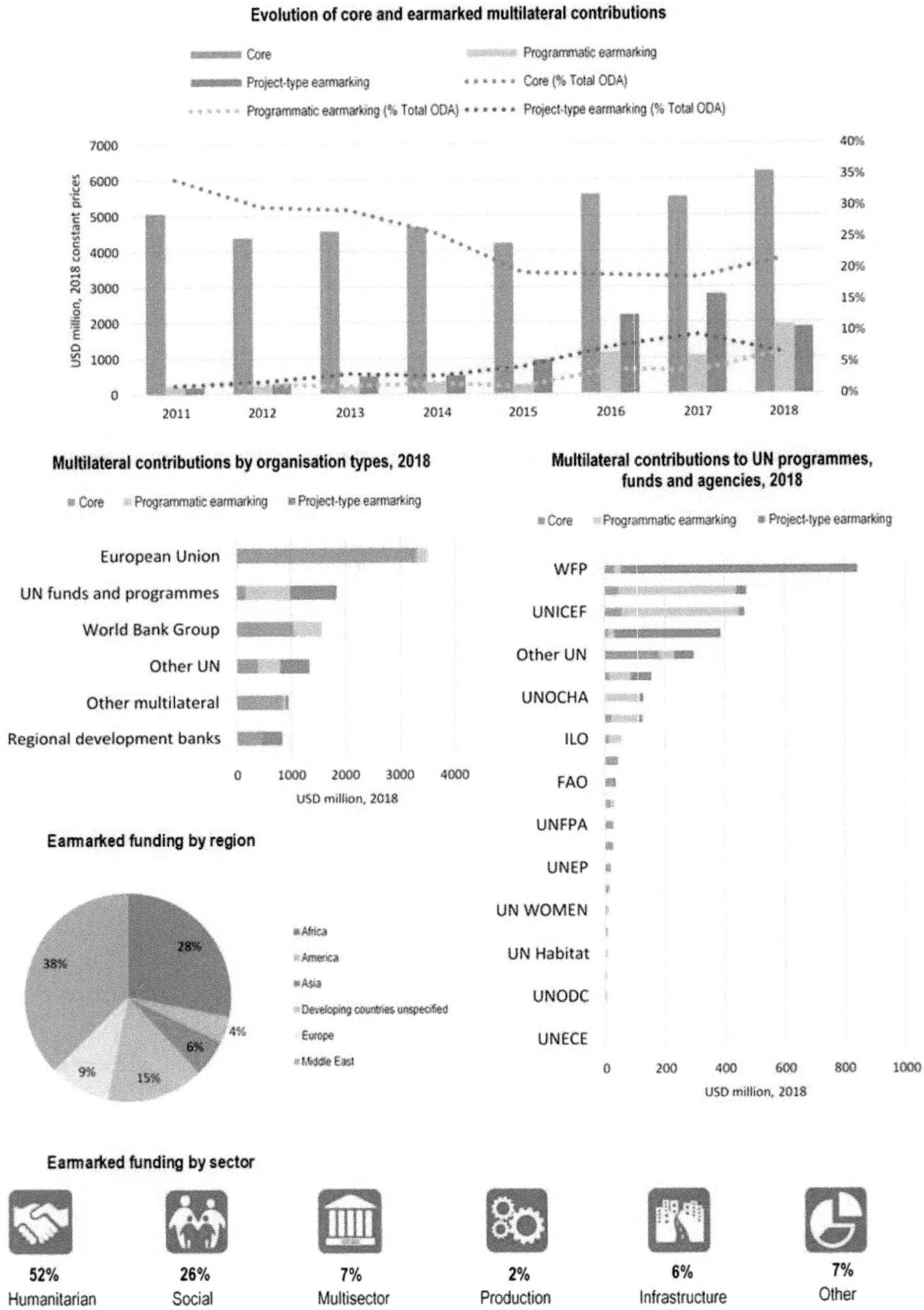

Source: Authors' calculations based on (OECD, 2020[2]), "Creditor Reporting System", https://stats.oecd.org/Index.aspx?DataSetCode=crs1.

StatLink https://doi.org/10.1787/888934178031

Figure A B.11. GREECE, use of the multilateral system

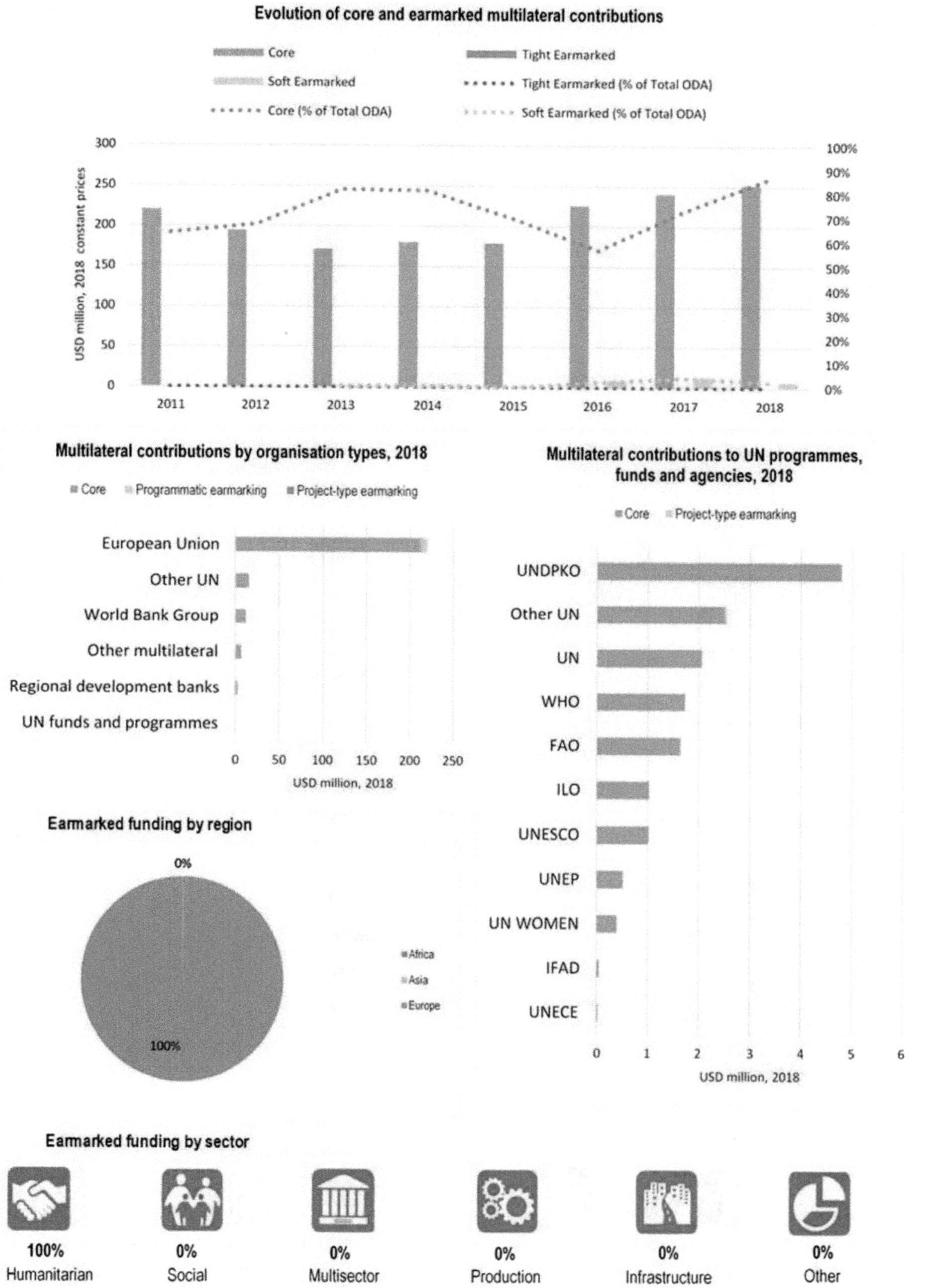

Source: Authors' calculations based on (OECD, 2020[2]), "Creditor Reporting System", https://stats.oecd.org/Index.aspx?DataSetCode=crs1.

StatLink https://doi.org/10.1787/888934178050

Figure A B.12. HUNGARY, use of the multilateral system

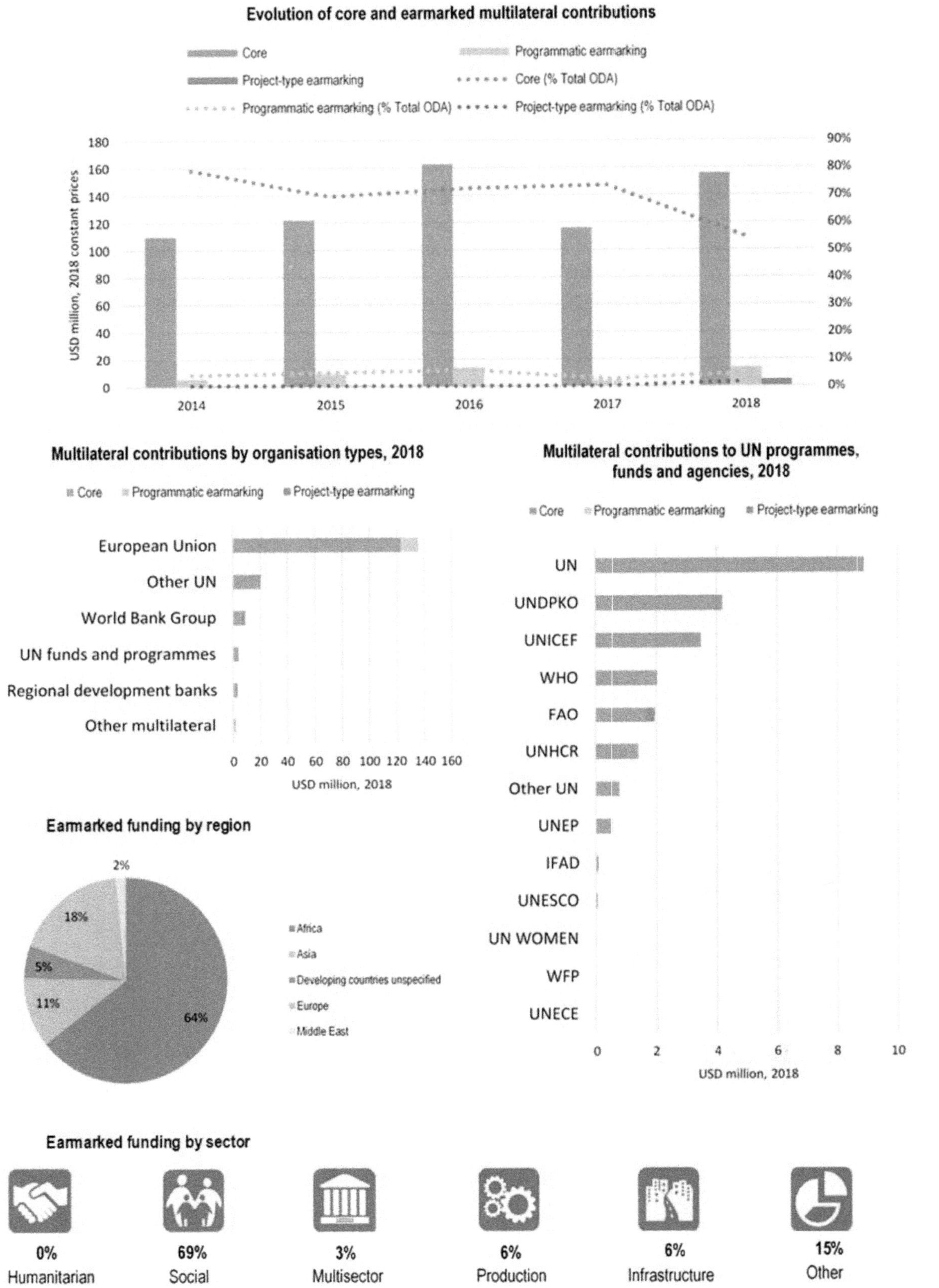

Source: Authors' calculations based on (OECD, 2020[2]), "Creditor Reporting System", https://stats.oecd.org/Index.aspx?DataSetCode=crs1.

StatLink https://doi.org/10.1787/888934178069

Figure A B.13. ICELAND, use of the multilateral system

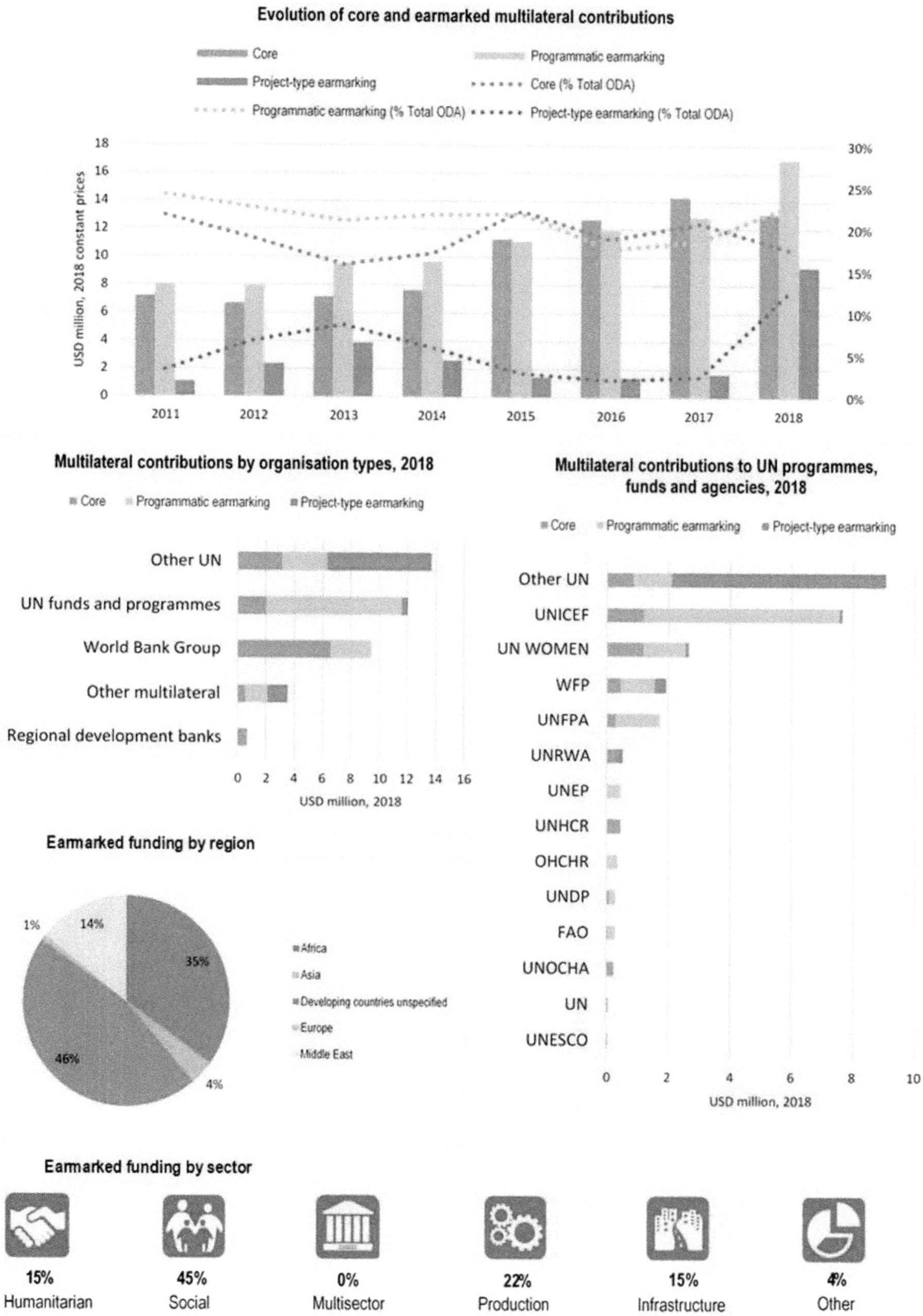

Source: Authors' calculations based on (OECD, 2020[2]), "Creditor Reporting System", https://stats.oecd.org/Index.aspx?DataSetCode=crs1.

StatLink https://doi.org/10.1787/888934178088

Figure A B.14. IRELAND, use of the multilateral system

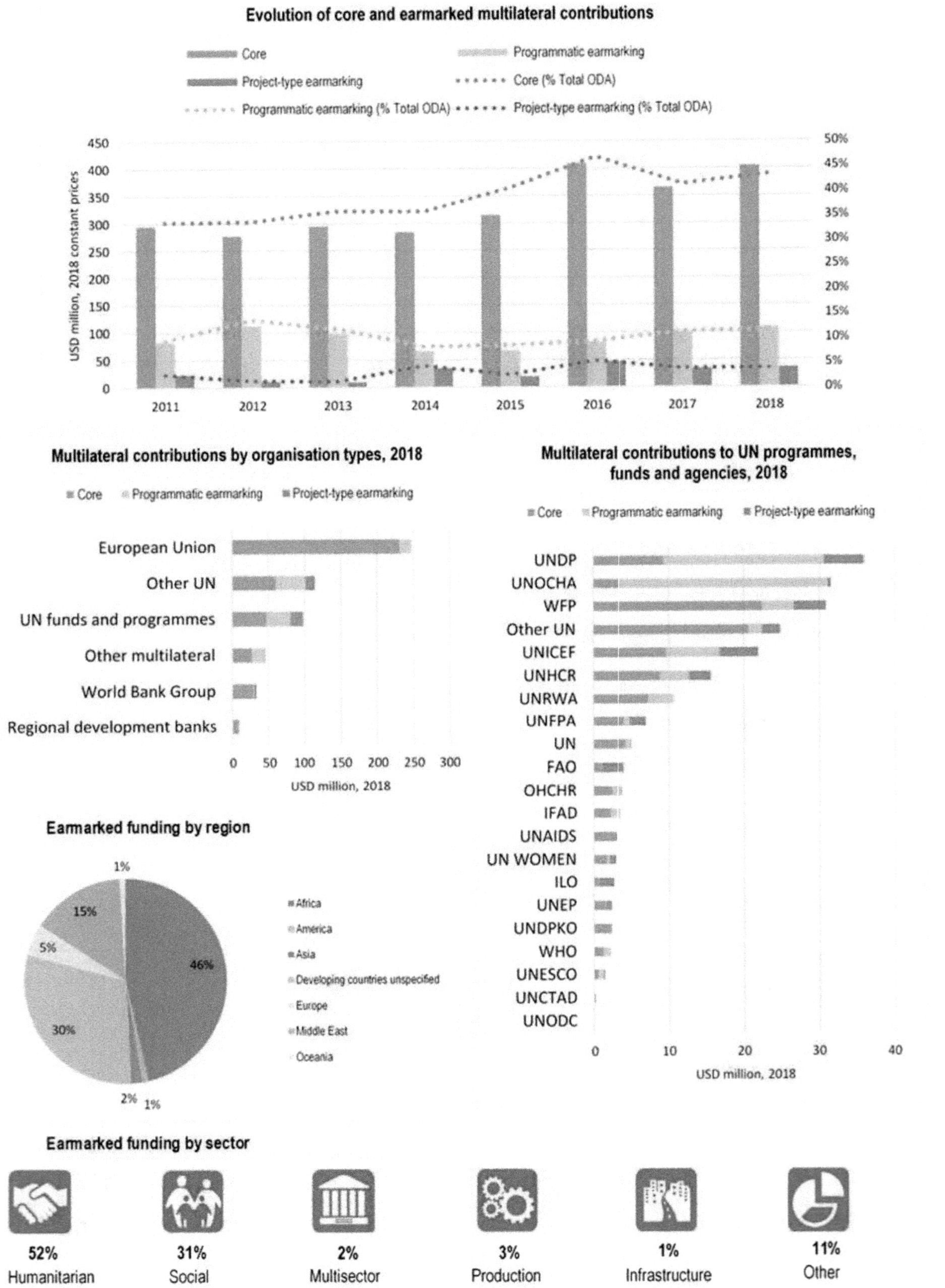

Source: Authors' calculations based on (OECD, 2020[2]), "Creditor Reporting System", https://stats.oecd.org/Index.aspx?DataSetCode=crs1.

StatLink https://doi.org/10.1787/888934178107

Figure A B.15. ITALY, use of the multilateral system

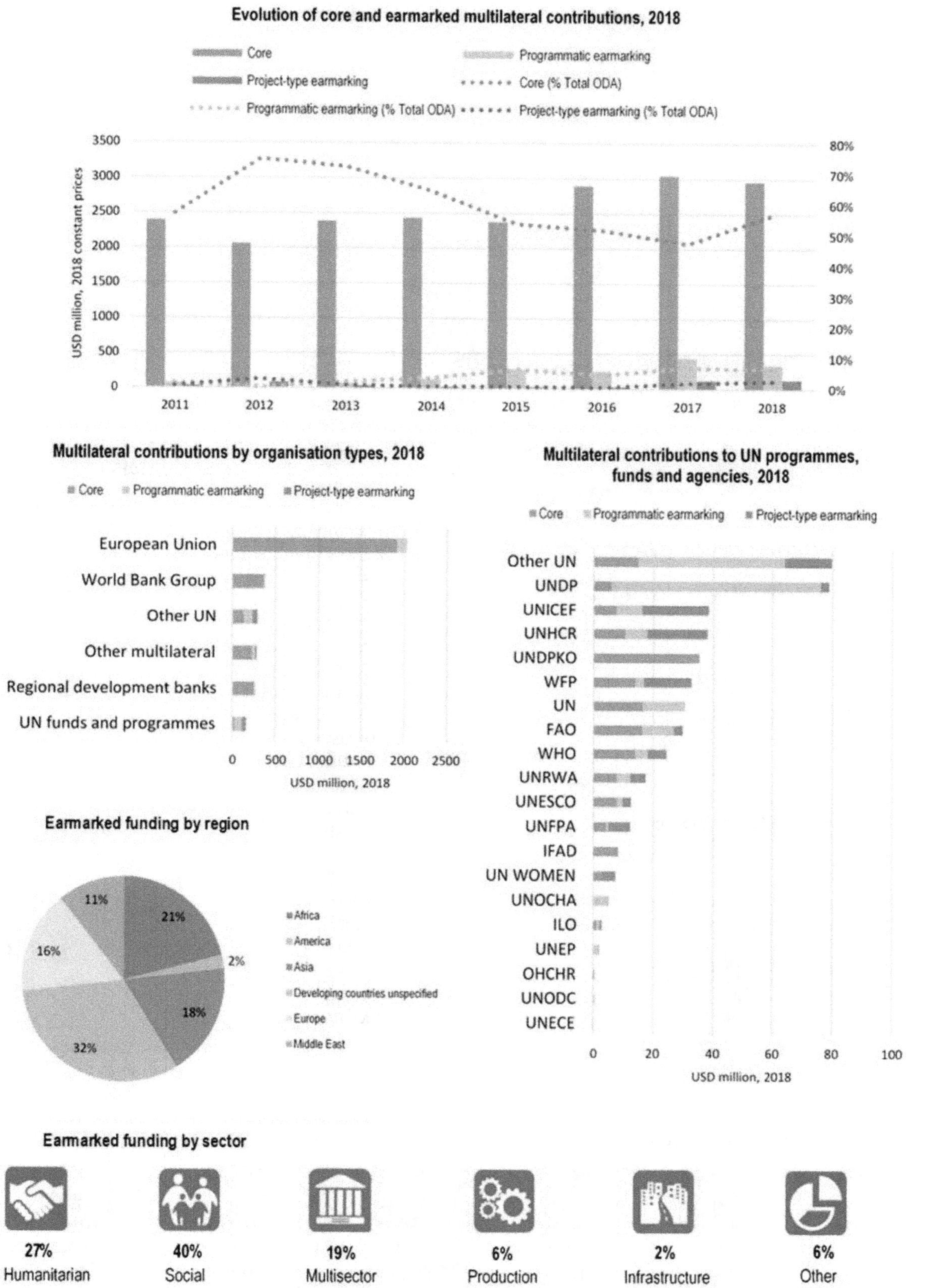

Source: Authors' calculations based on (OECD, 2020[2]), "Creditor Reporting System", https://stats.oecd.org/Index.aspx?DataSetCode=crs1..

StatLink https://doi.org/10.1787/888934178126

Figure A B.16. JAPAN, use of the multilateral system

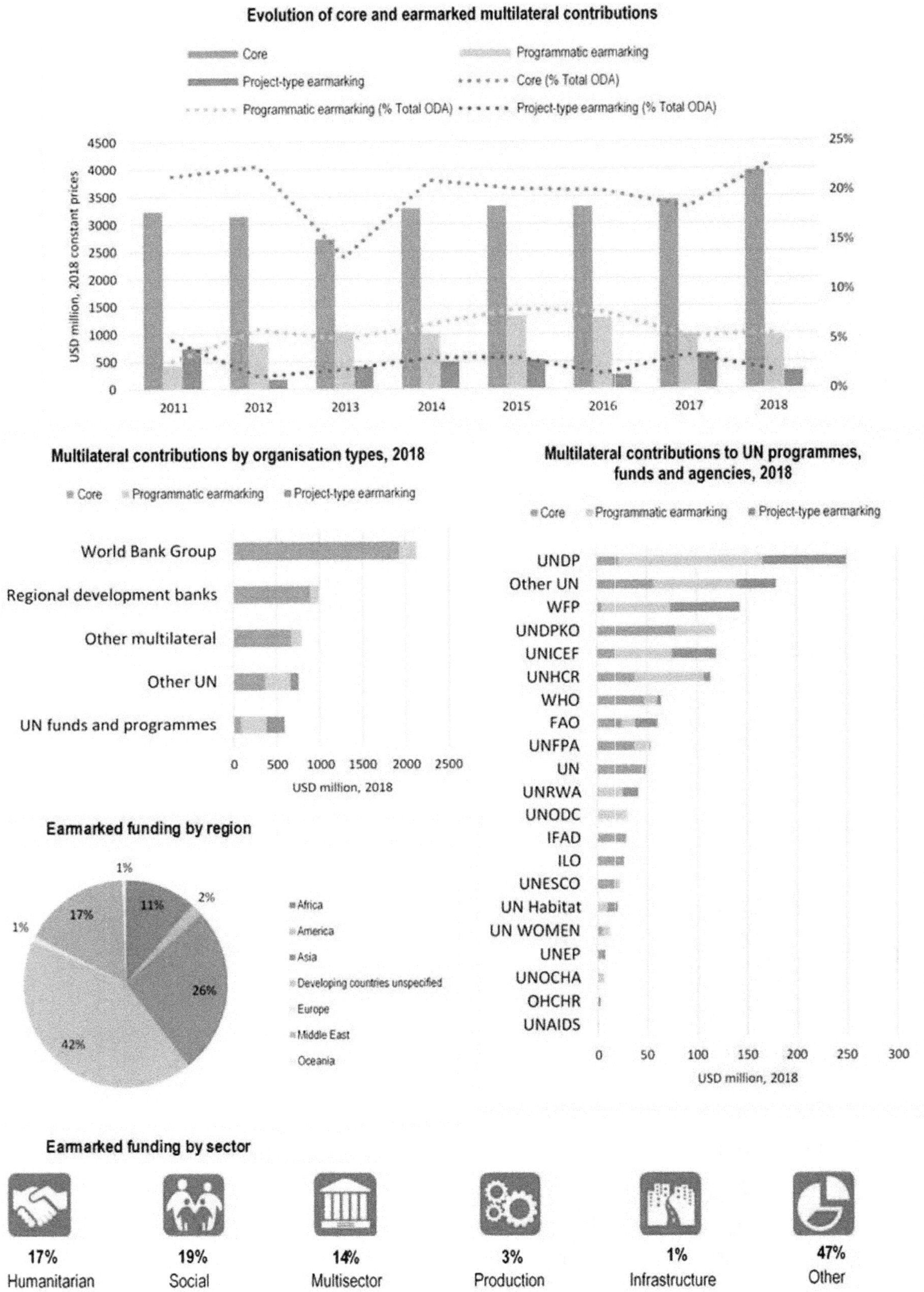

Source: Authors' calculations based on (OECD, 2020[2]), "Creditor Reporting System", https://stats.oecd.org/Index.aspx?DataSetCode=crs1.

StatLink https://doi.org/10.1787/888934178145

Figure A B.17. KOREA, use of the multilateral system

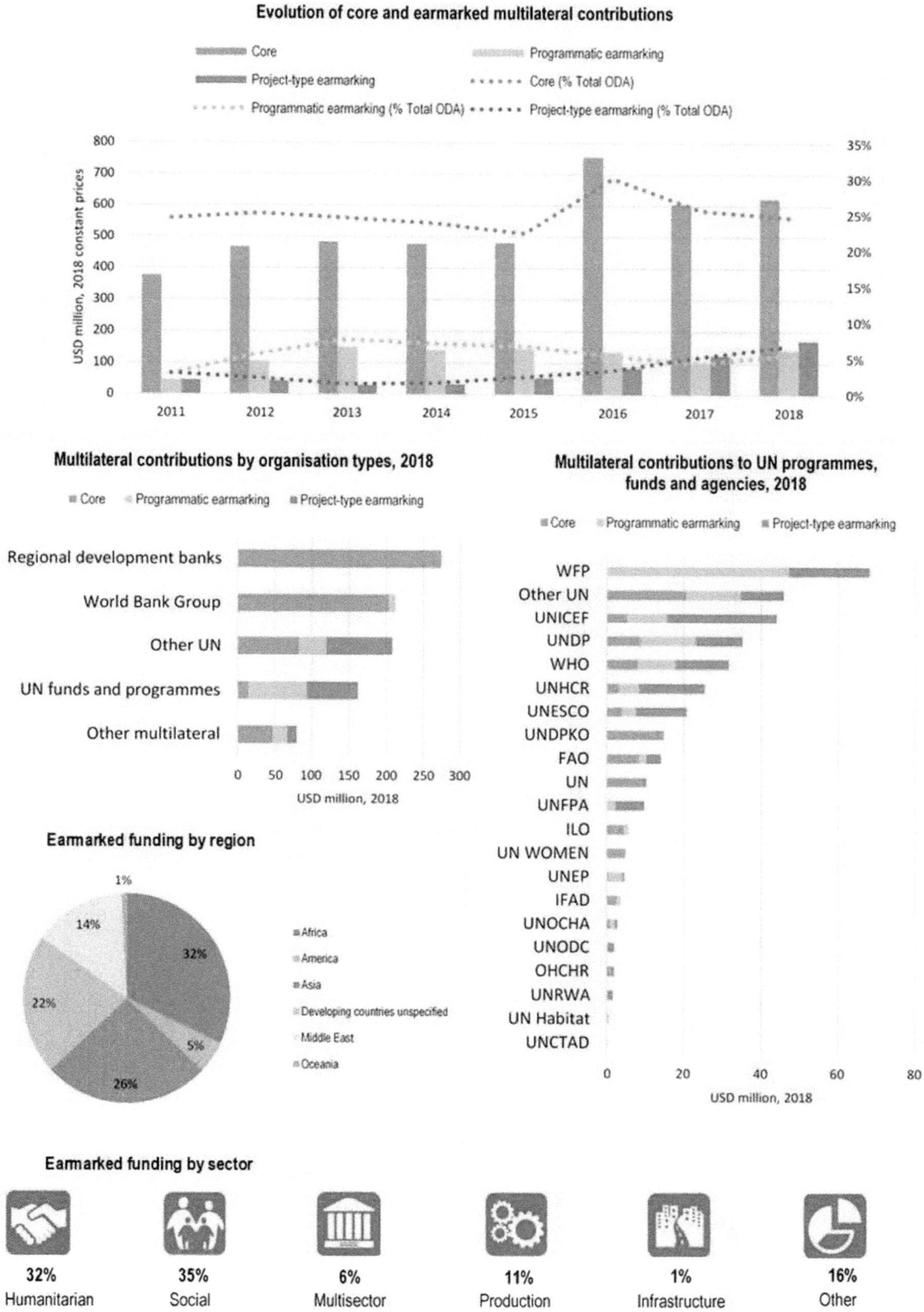

Source: Authors' calculations based on (OECD, 2020[2]), "Creditor Reporting System", https://stats.oecd.org/Index.aspx?DataSetCode=crs1.

StatLink https://doi.org/10.1787/888934178164

Figure A B.18. LUXEMBOURG, use of the multilateral system

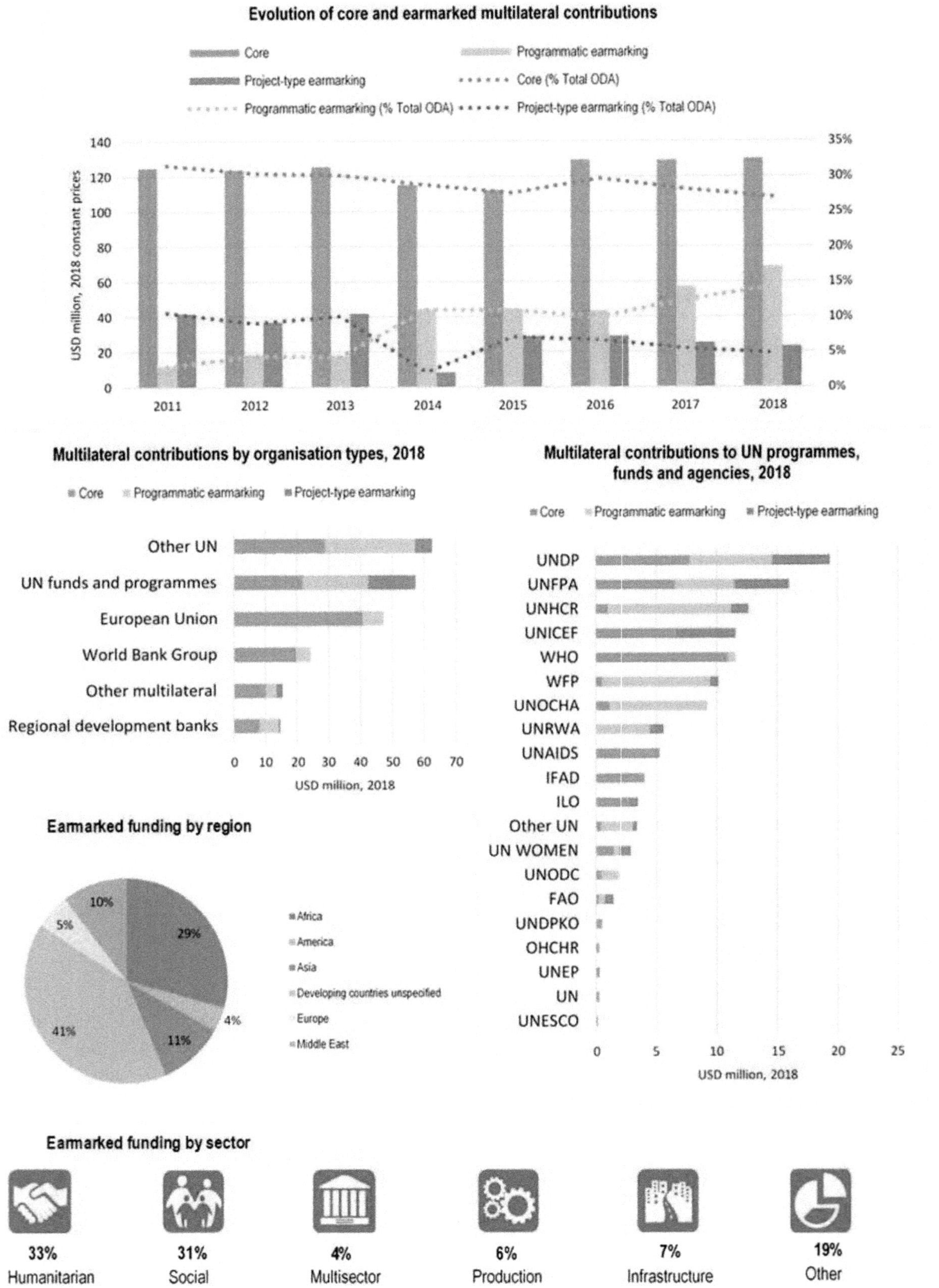

Source: Authors' calculations based on (OECD, 2020[2]), "Creditor Reporting System", https://stats.oecd.org/Index.aspx?DataSetCode=crs1.

StatLink https://doi.org/10.1787/888934178183

Figure A B.19. NETHERLANDS, use of the multilateral system

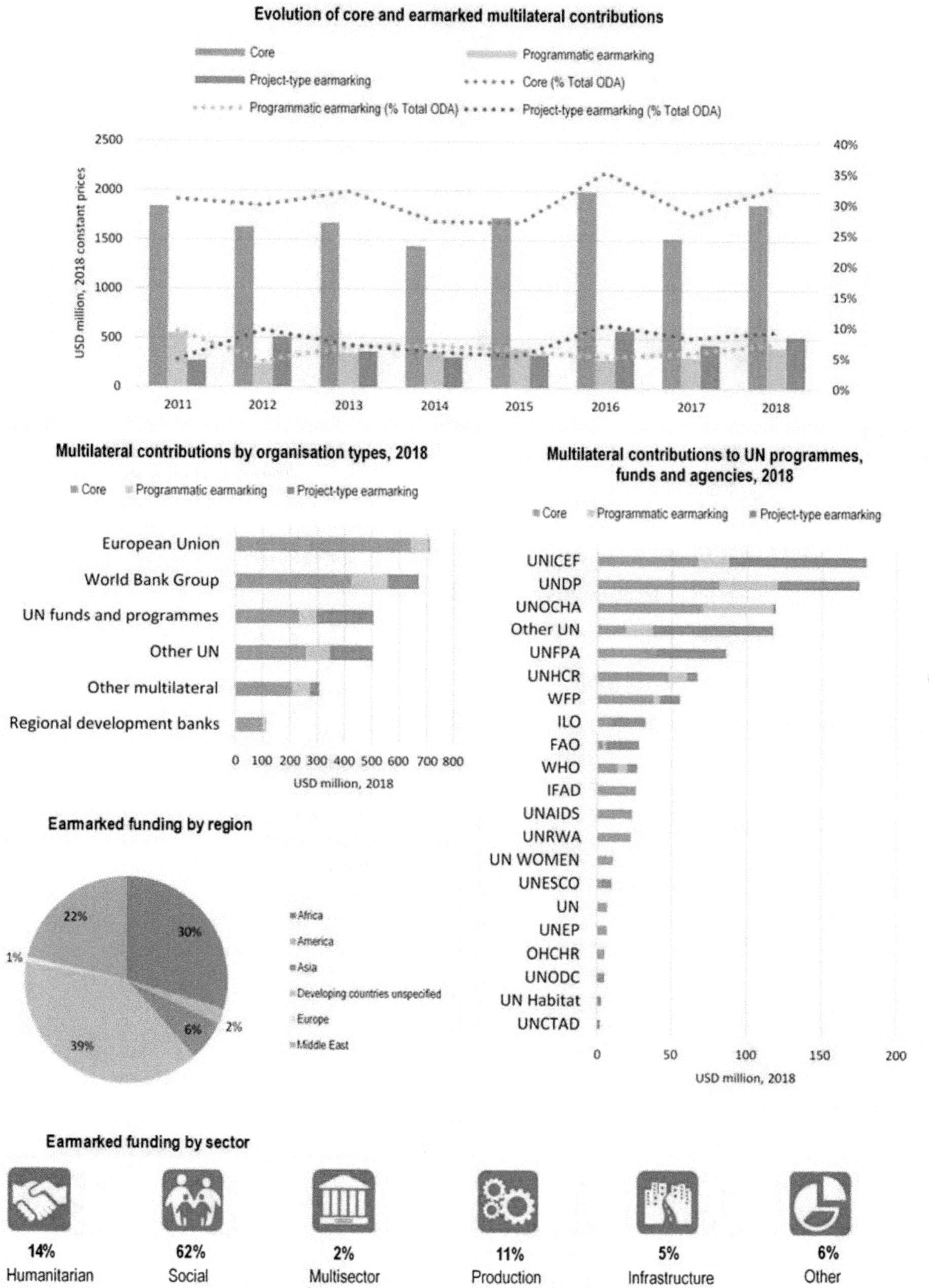

Source: Authors' calculations based on (OECD, 2020[2]), "Creditor Reporting System", https://stats.oecd.org/Index.aspx?DataSetCode=crs1.

StatLink https://doi.org/10.1787/888934178202

Figure A B.20. NEW ZEALAND, use of the multilateral system

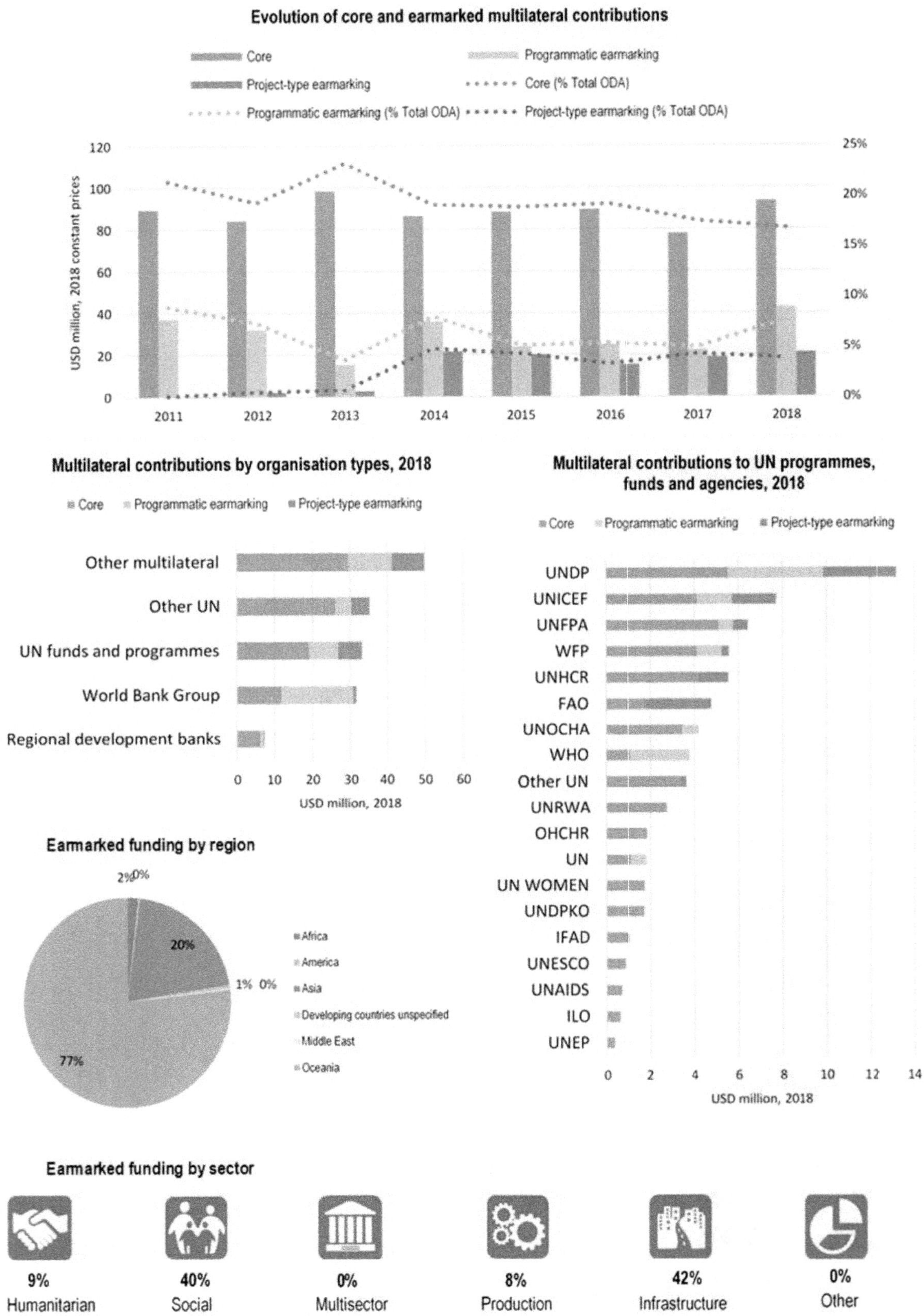

Source: Authors' calculations based on (OECD, 2020[2]), "Creditor Reporting System", https://stats.oecd.org/Index.aspx?DataSetCode=crs1.

StatLink https://doi.org/10.1787/888934178221

Figure A B.21. NORWAY, use of the multilateral system

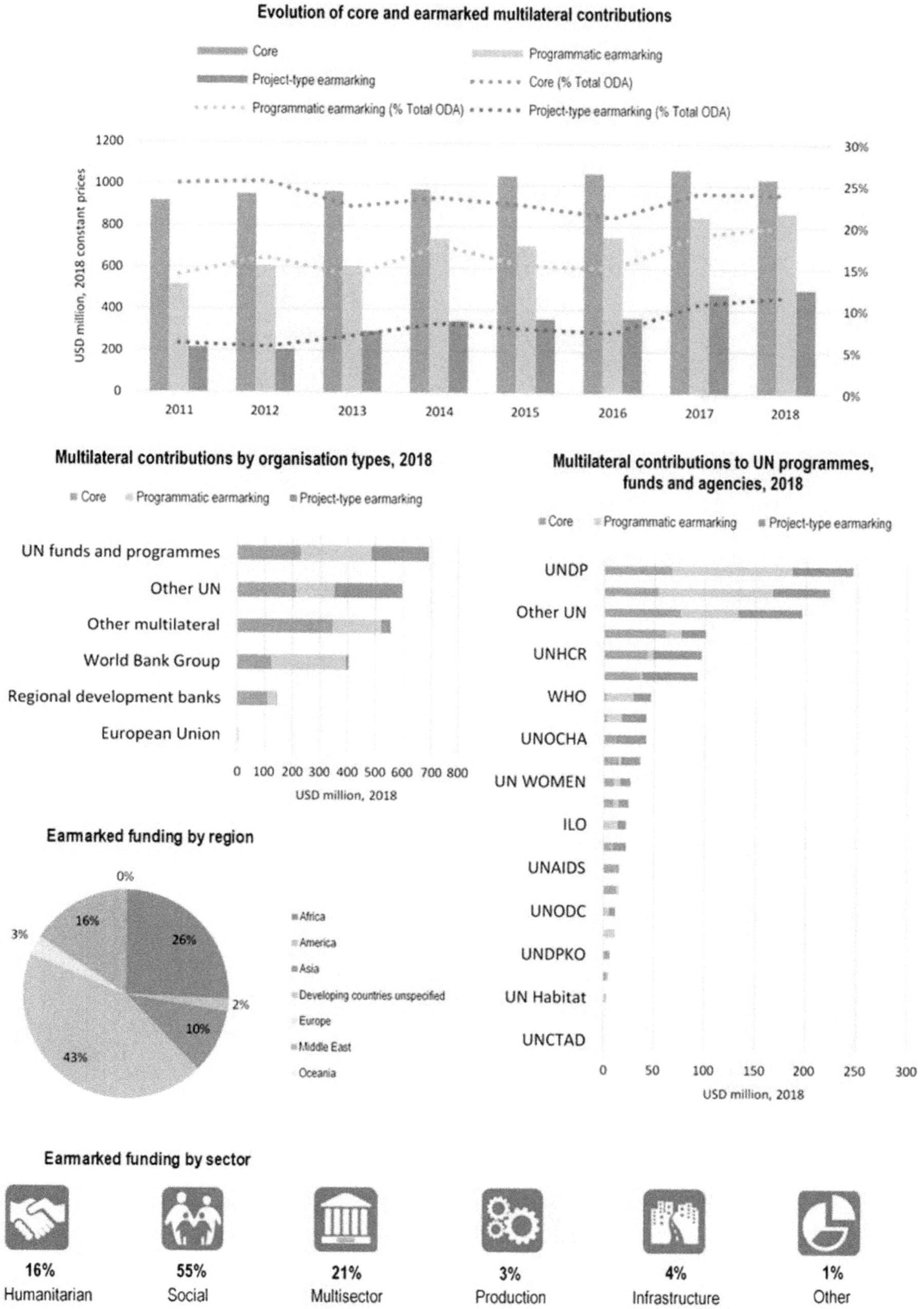

Source: Authors' calculations based on (OECD, 2020[2]), "Creditor Reporting System", https://stats.oecd.org/Index.aspx?DataSetCode=crs1.

StatLink https://doi.org/10.1787/888934178240

Figure A B.22. POLAND, use of the multilateral system

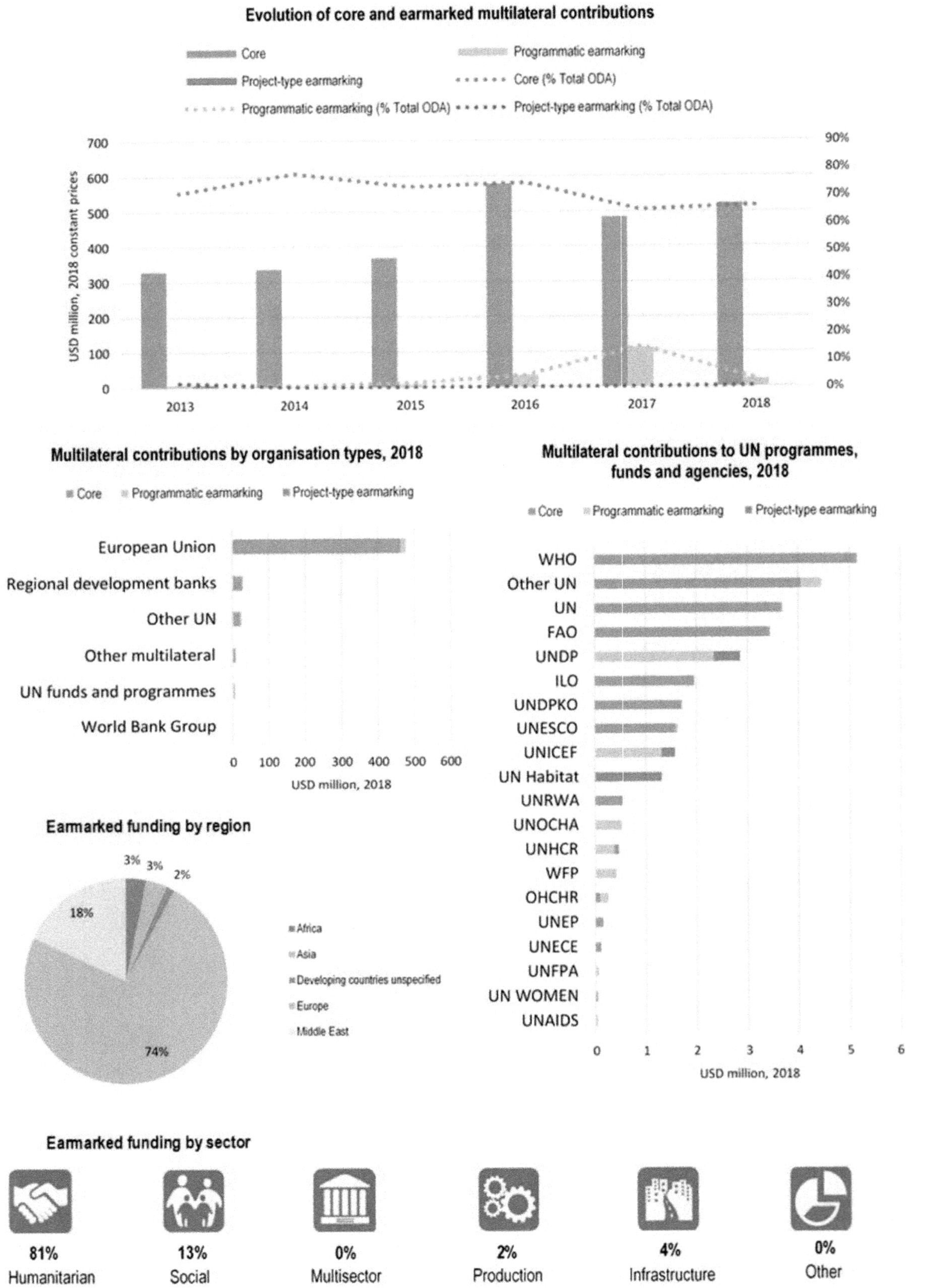

Source: Authors' calculations based on (OECD, 2020[2]), "Creditor Reporting System", https://stats.oecd.org/Index.aspx?DataSetCode=crs1.

StatLink https://doi.org/10.1787/888934178259

Figure A B.23. PORTUGAL, use of the multilateral system

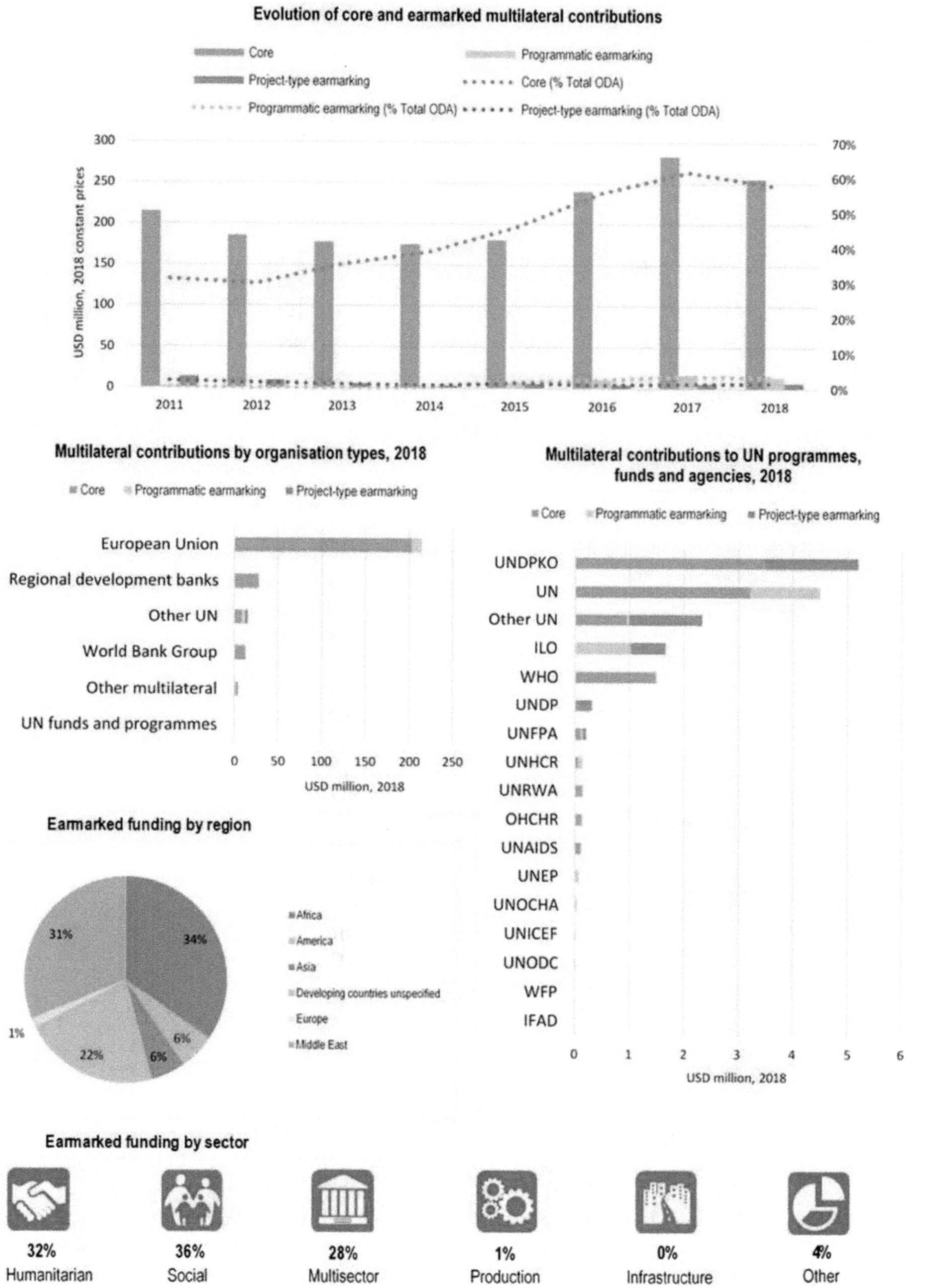

Source: Authors' calculations based on (OECD, 2020[2]), "Creditor Reporting System", https://stats.oecd.org/Index.aspx?DataSetCode=crs1.

StatLink https://doi.org/10.1787/888934178278

Figure A B.24. SLOVAK REPUBLIC, use of the multilateral system

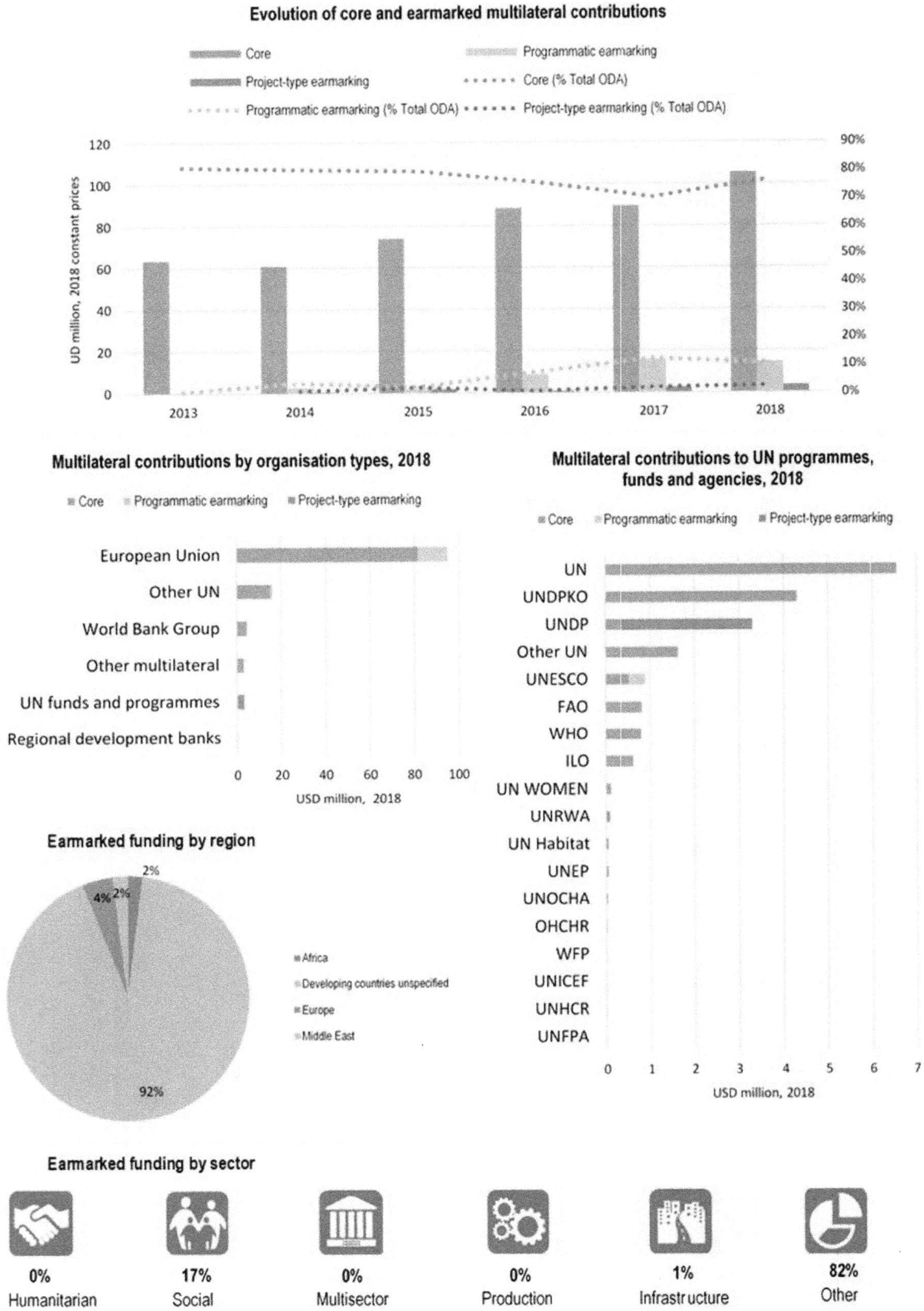

Source: Authors' calculations based on (OECD, 2020[2]), "Creditor Reporting System", https://stats.oecd.org/Index.aspx?DataSetCode=crs1.

StatLink https://doi.org/10.1787/888934178297

Figure A B.25. SLOVENIA, use of the multilateral system

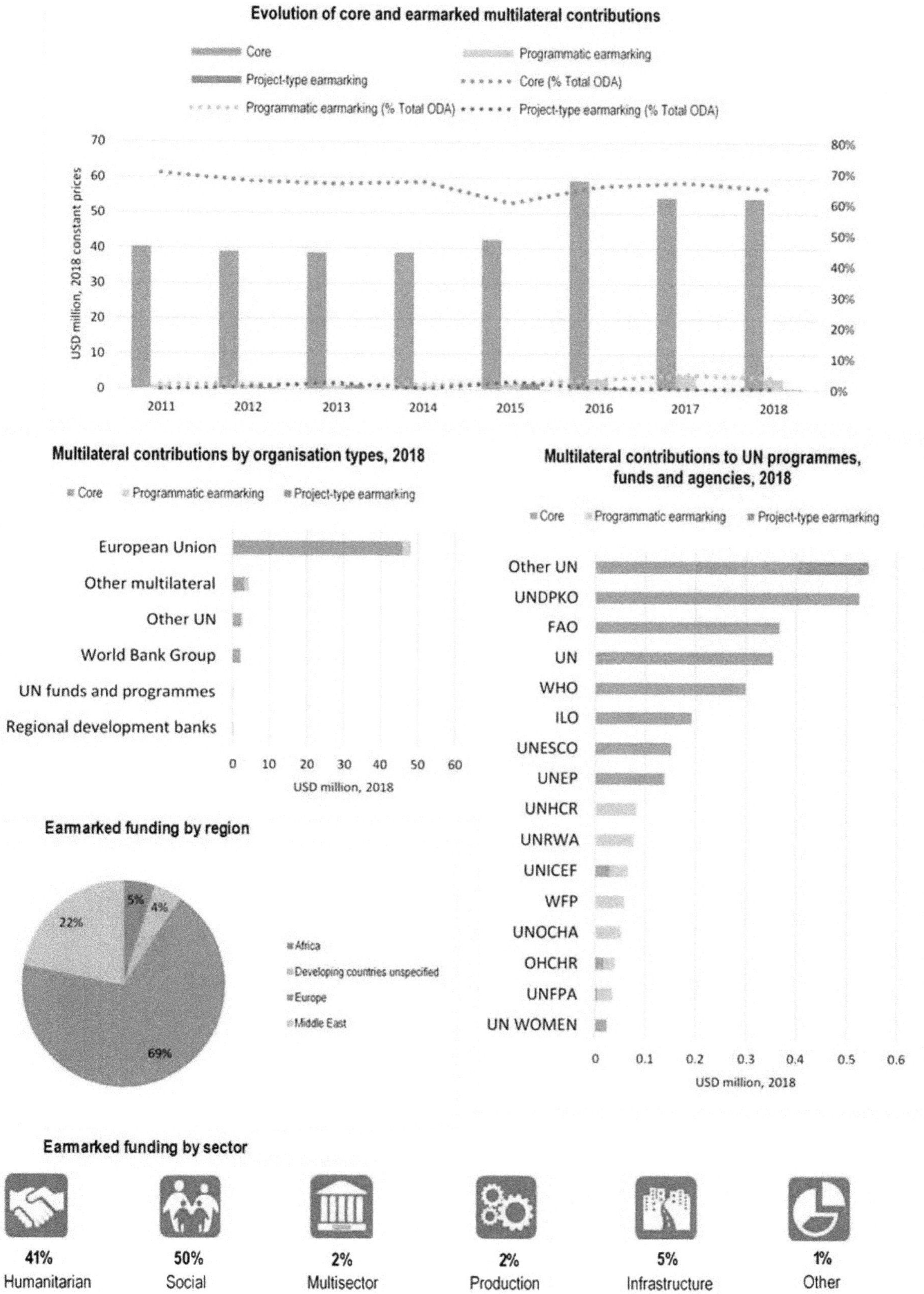

Source: Authors' calculations based on (OECD, 2020[2]), "Creditor Reporting System", https://stats.oecd.org/Index.aspx?DataSetCode=crs1.

StatLink https://doi.org/10.1787/888934178316

Figure A B.26. SPAIN, use of the multilateral system

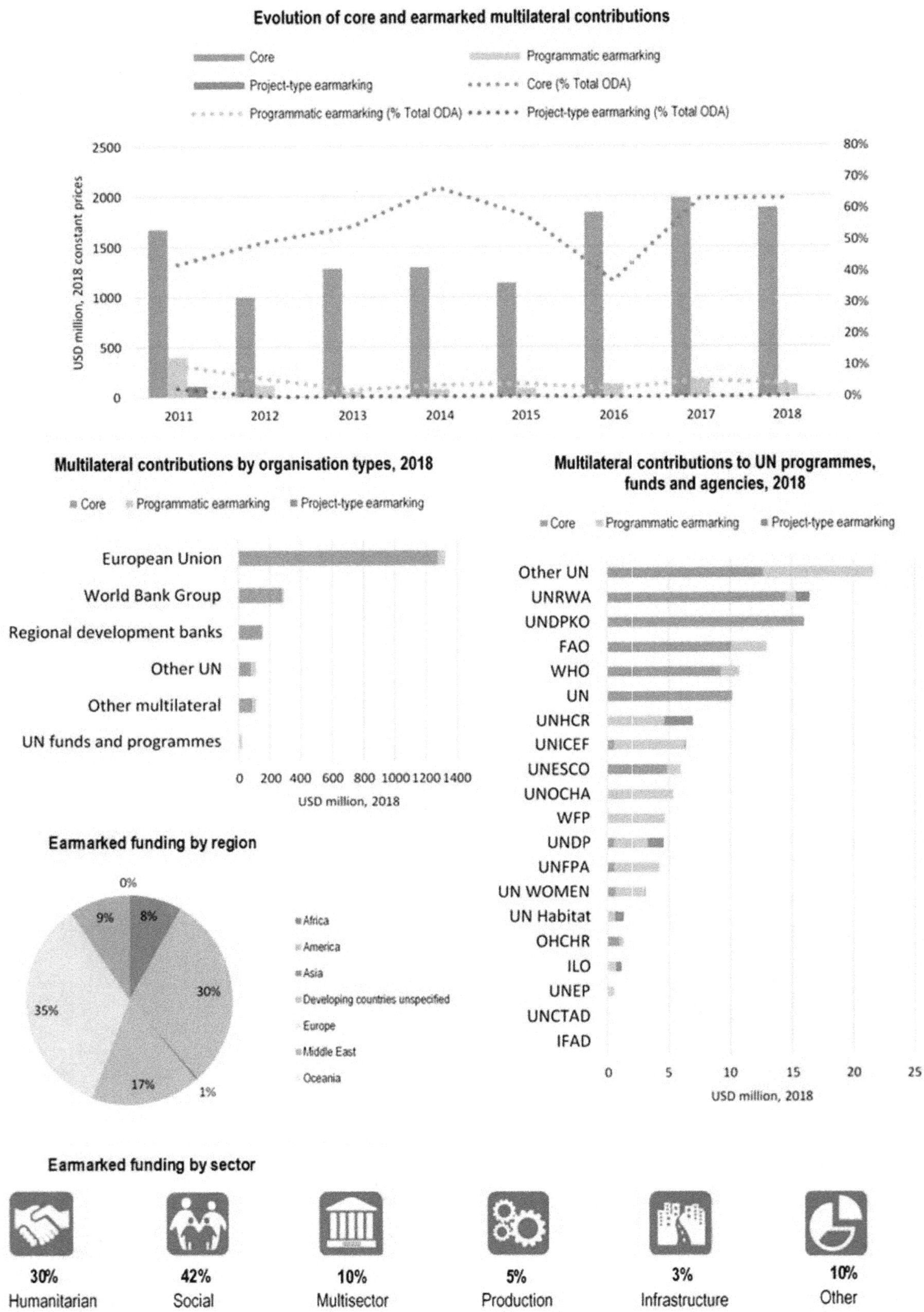

Source: Authors' calculations based on (OECD, 2020[2]), "Creditor Reporting System", https://stats.oecd.org/Index.aspx?DataSetCode=crs1.

StatLink https://doi.org/10.1787/888934178335

Figure A B.27. SWEDEN, use of the multilateral system

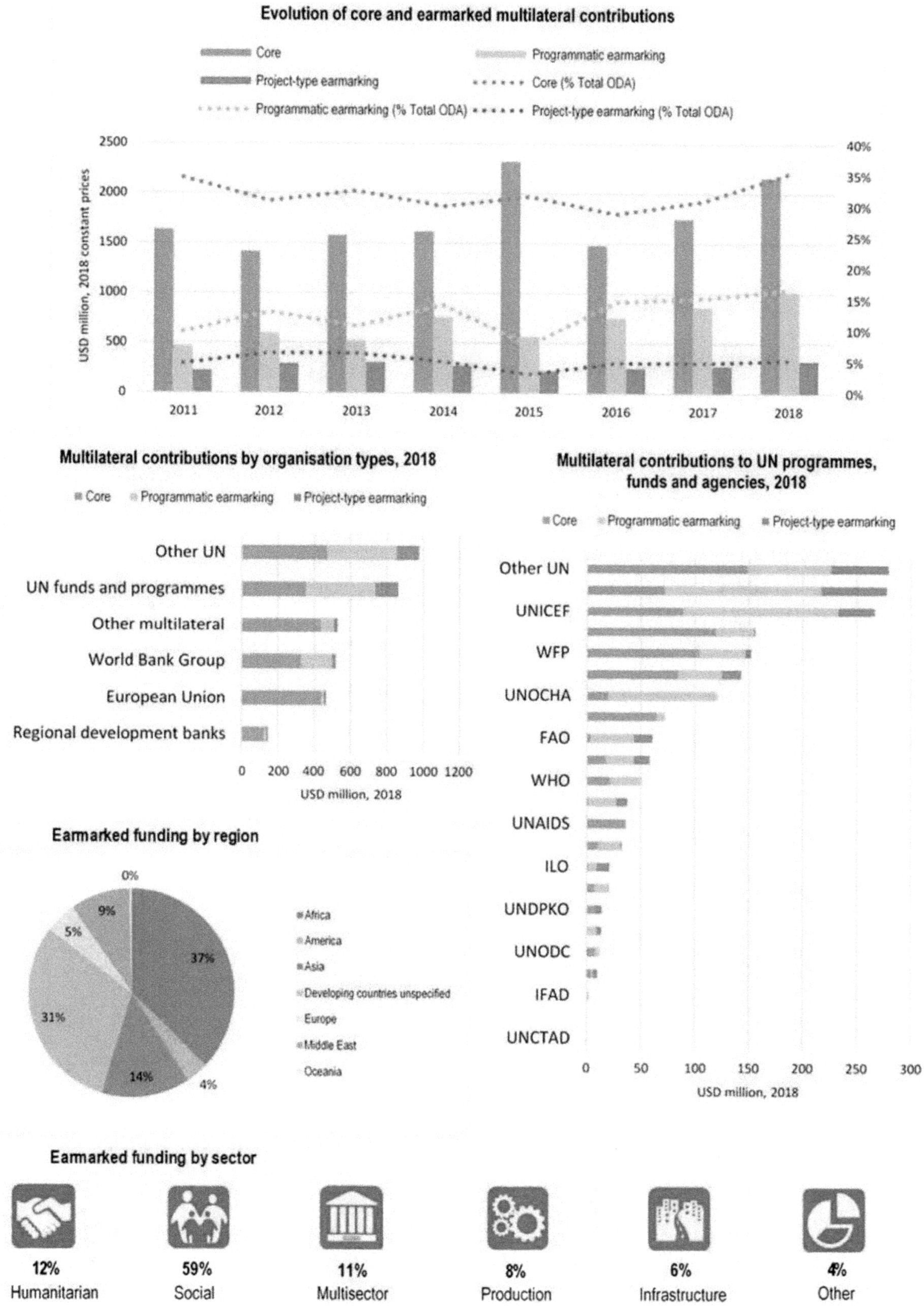

Source: Authors' calculations based on (OECD, 2020[2]), "Creditor Reporting System", https://stats.oecd.org/Index.aspx?DataSetCode=crs1.

StatLink https://doi.org/10.1787/888934178354

Figure A B.28. SWITZERLAND, use of the multilateral system

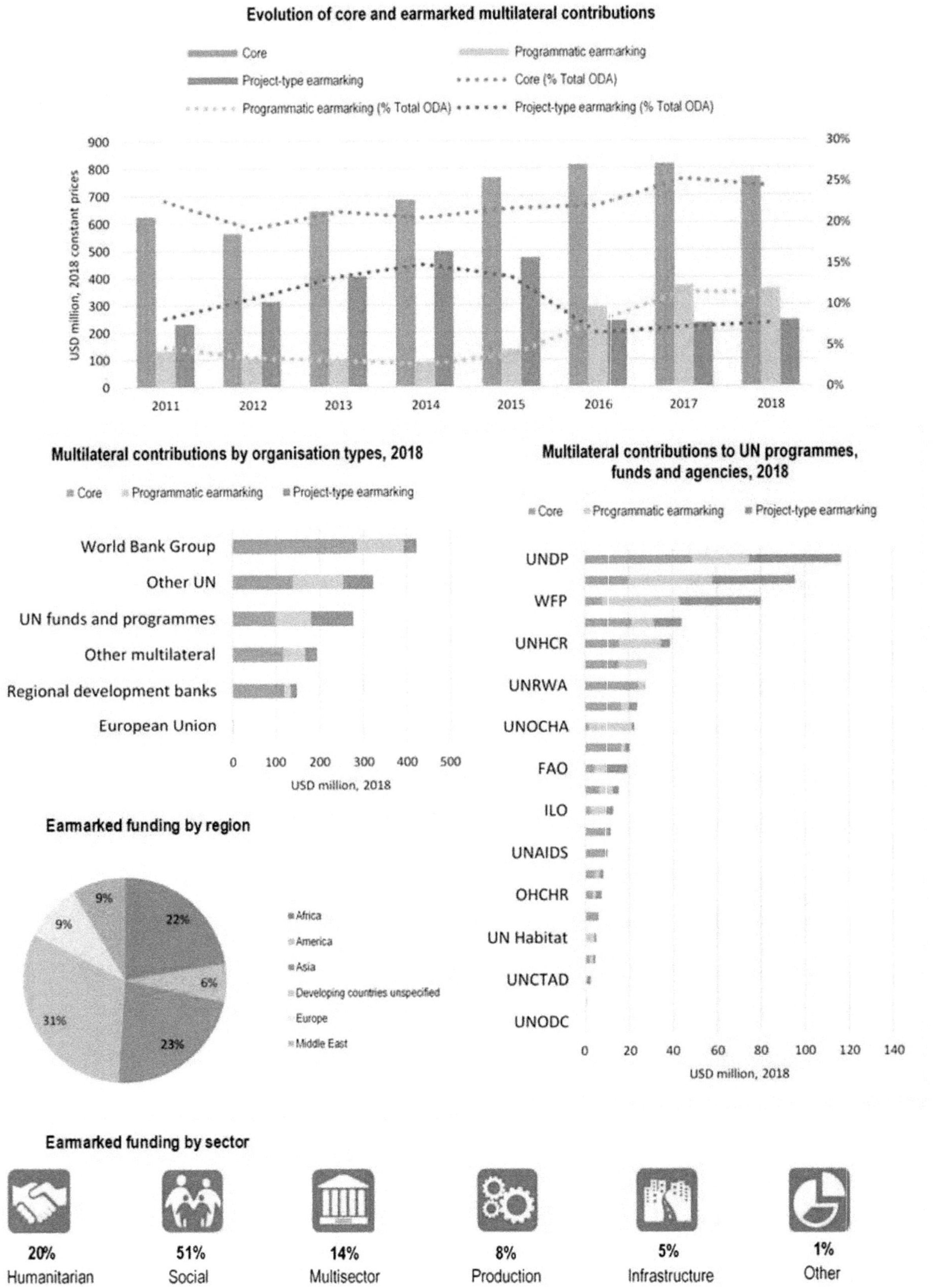

Source: Authors' calculations based on (OECD, 2020[2]), "Creditor Reporting System", https://stats.oecd.org/Index.aspx?DataSetCode=crs1.

StatLink https://doi.org/10.1787/888934178373

Figure A B.29. UNITED KINGDOM, use of the multilateral system

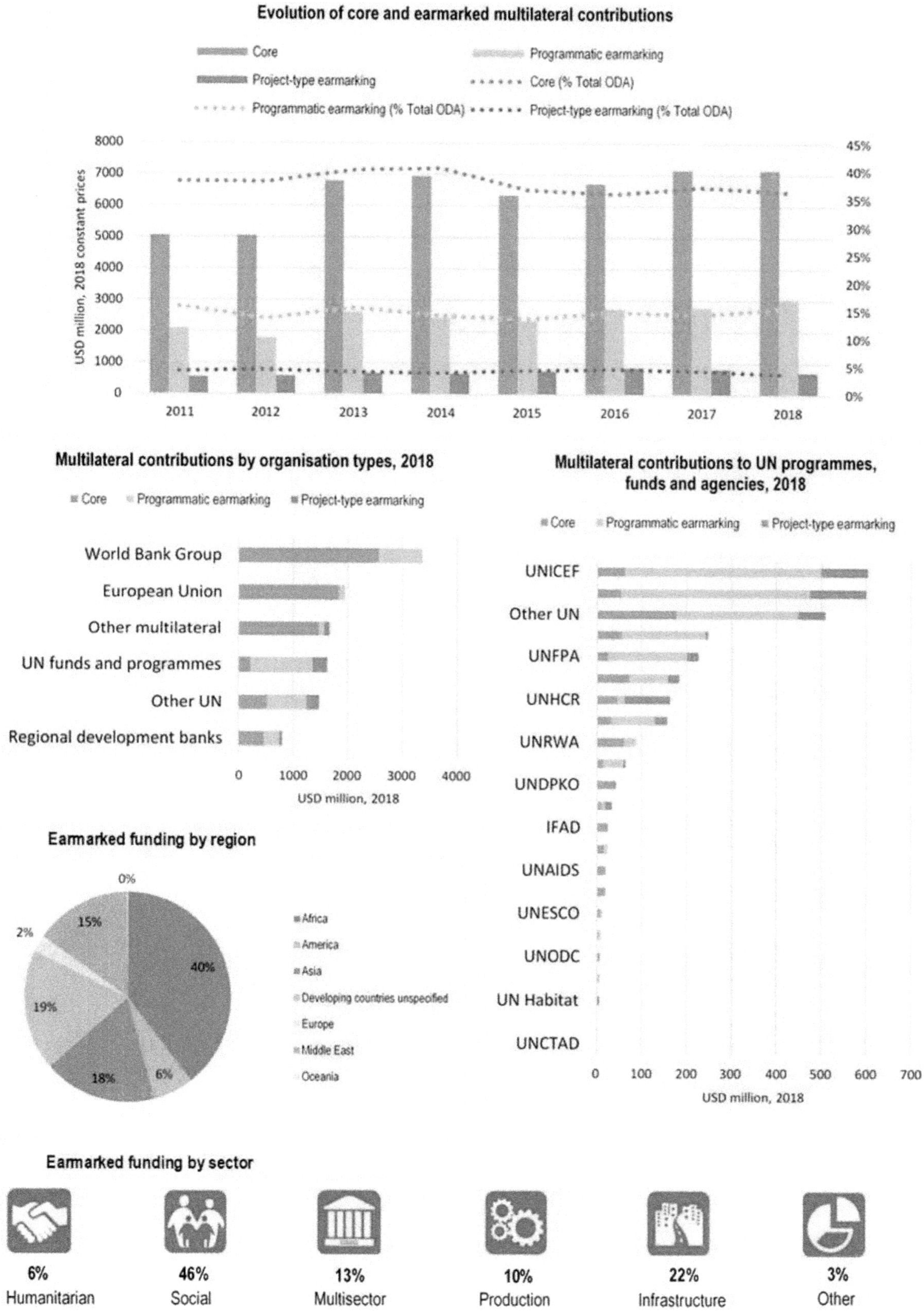

Source: Authors' calculations based on (OECD, 2020[2]), "Creditor Reporting System", https://stats.oecd.org/Index.aspx?DataSetCode=crs1.

StatLink https://doi.org/10.1787/888934178392

Figure A B.30. UNITED STATES, use of the multilateral system

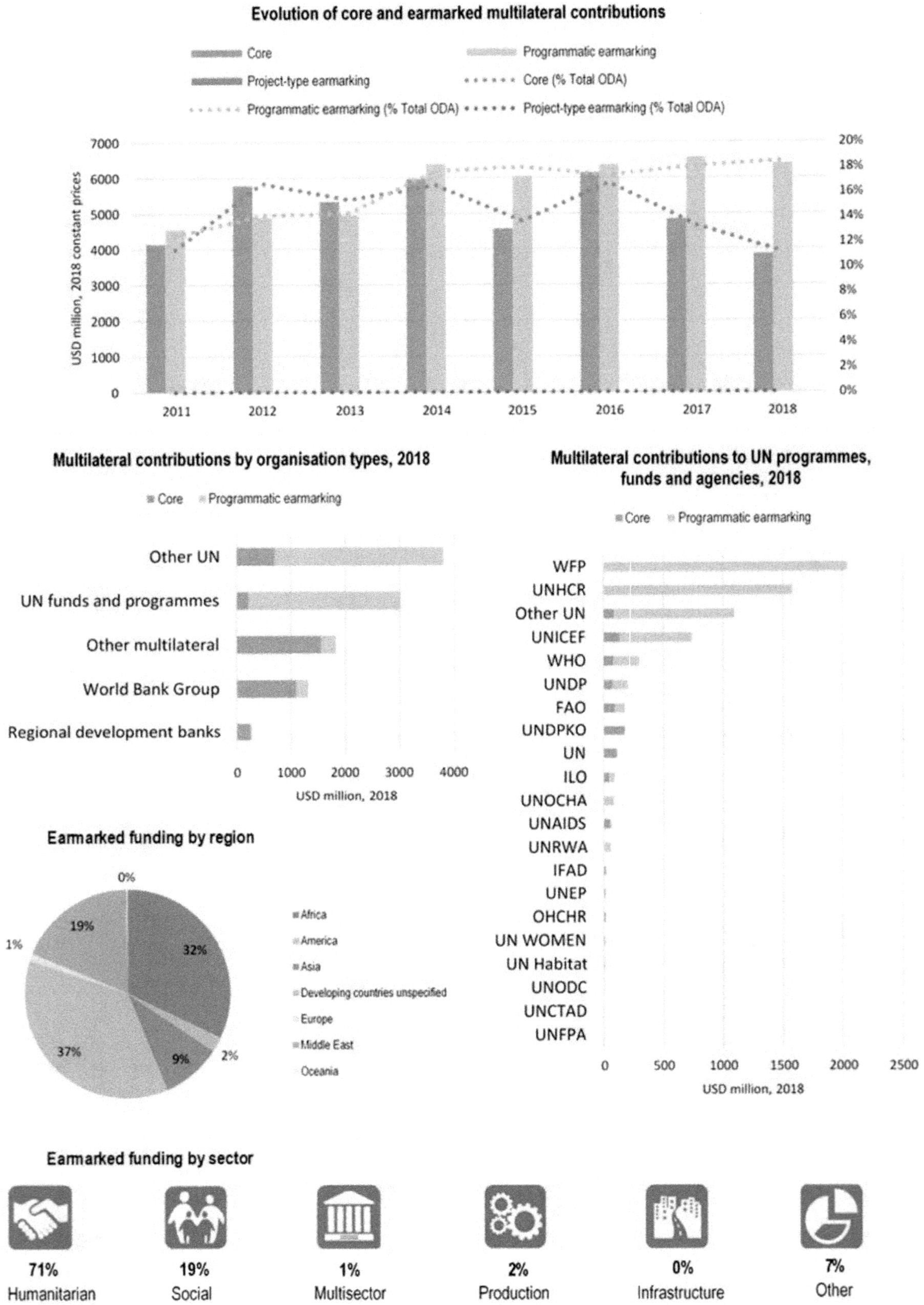

Source: Authors' calculations based on (OECD, 2020[2]), "Creditor Reporting System", https://stats.oecd.org/Index.aspx?DataSetCode=crs1.

StatLink https://doi.org/10.1787/888934178411

References

OECD (2020), *Annex 2 - List of ODA-eligible international organisations*, https://www.oecd.org/dac/financing-sustainable-development/development-finance-standards/annex2.htm. [1]

OECD (2020), *Creditor Reporting System (database)*, OECD, Paris, https://stats.oecd.org/Index.aspx?DataSetCode=crs1. [2]

www.ingramcontent.com/pod-product-compliance
Lightning Source LLC
Chambersburg PA
CBHW061219240926
51846CB00006B/1274
9789264897656